Susan Windley-Daoust

Theology of the Body, Extended

The Spiritual Signs of Birth, Impairment, and Dying

D0139768

Lectio Publishing, LLC

Hobe Sound, FL
Cincinnati, OH

www.lectiopublishing.com

Jeff Thanks
for the
Support —
peace + all
Blessings to
you + your
family —

Susan
Windley-
Daoust

Portions of chapter 4, The Gift of the Dying Body, have been previously published by the author in *Homiletic and Pastoral Review* as "The Sign Of The Dying Body: How the Theology of the Body helps us to die in love," Nov 2013.

The digital image of the painting "Isaiah in the Temple" is used with the kind permission of the artist, Edward Knippers. His online portfolio may be found at www.edwardknippers.com.

The Our Lady of Vladimir icon—the 12th century Russian version of The Virgin of Tenderness—is part of the public domain.

Cover design by Linda Wolf
Edited by Susan Goldberg

ISBN 978-0-9898397-5-4
Library of Congress Control Number: 2014936442

Published by Lectio Publishing, LLC

Hobe Sound, Florida 33455
www.lectiopublishing.com

Printed and bound in the United States of America

"The eye is the lamp of the body.
So, if your eye is healthy, your whole body will be full of light;
but if your eye is unhealthy, your whole body will be full of darkness.
If then the light in you is darkness, how great is the darkness!"

Matthew 6:22-23

Contents

Preface

There are not many theologies in today's age that spawn popular movements replete with flourishing institutes, national conferences, free standing certificate programs, abundant new religious education materials for Catholics of all ages and states of life, and coverage on mainstream media news magazine shows.[1] There are not many contemporary theological texts that have people sitting in the pews drop everything to become evangelists and enthusiasts in their hometowns, saying "I read this; it changed my life."[2] There are not many papal audiences cited as a "kind of theological time bomb set to go off with dramatic consequences, sometime in the third millennium of the Church."[3] Yet John Paul II's 1979–1984 audiences, popularly called "The Theology of the Body," have brought forth just this: something of a theological phenom for our time.

This is not to say everyone has been as enamored of this theology: it has had critics as vociferous as its evangelists. Those most critical of this theology argue that the audiences say nothing new, are ambiguous, or are fatally idealistic.[4] Some feminists have found the presentations offensive, one to the point of inspiring an entire book of political poetry against the theology.[5] Others appreciate the audiences but have questioned how the texts have been presented to popular audiences: do they lose their nuance, even misrepresent the material?[6] I know when I have shared with people my topic of research for this book, the reactions have ranged from overwhelmingly positive to somewhat appalled, and not a lot in between. It gives one pause, to put it mildly.

All of this passion, and for what? For a theology that argues that:

- the human being, man and woman, was created as a sign pointing to union with God;

- the ensouled human body serves as a "pre-given language of self-giving and fruitfulness," a revelation of the pattern of love in which God created and sustains the universe;

- marriage is the primordial sacrament of God's love and is a way of participation in the endlessly lavish love of God;

- a call to celibacy is a call to sacrifice the earthly sign of joining for union with God, becoming another sign that points us to God's sustaining gift of Godself;

- one of the first results of living in a fallen world is that these primordial relationships of God to person and persons to each other cracked, and our original sight twisted.

All this passion is for a theology that calls us to see, through the help of the Redeemer, the ensouled body via the lens of "the law of the gift."

When a set of texts collects these intense reactions, it is immediately clear: the writer has touched something very hot. Heat tells us something is burning, and it draws our attention. But a focus on the *smoke*— that is, the reactions—can divert us from seeing the fullness of what John Paul II called the Theology of the Body to be. I was introduced to Theology of the Body language by my undergraduate students, some of whom were very excited by it and wanted to learn more. It was not something I had studied. I was only basically aware of it through the popular movement, and I had tended to side with those who were skeptical about its enduring value. In short, I was diverted by the *smoke*. But to be in conversation with these students, I read the text of audiences, and was humbled, then touched, by the beauty of its theological vision and its organic cultural critique. The insights were both timeless and timely. I was also struck that the popular presentations of the Theology of the Body have focused almost entirely on the second half of the audiences—on moral theology, on sexuality and marriage. Academics, pro and con, have focused there as well. Although good work has been done there, the gift of the first half of the audiences—on *what it means to be human*—has been barely touched.[7] My students sensed that there was more to this literature, and I agree with them. Even John Paul agreed with that: he expected theologians to expand the insights beyond the treatment of marriage and sexuality.[8] If "[t]he body, in fact, and only the body, is capable of making visible what is invisible: the spiritual and the divine" and "It has been created to transfer into the visible reality of the world the mystery hidden from eternity in God, and thus to be a sign of it"[9]—if this is true, then it is appropriate and important to extend the Theology of the Body to other primal human experiences. How does the Theology of the Body inform a theology of childbirth? A theology of human impairment? A theology of dying? Are these bodily events, so central to human experience, spiritual signs? Are they signs created to point to God?

I dare to say that this work, scandalously, has been left undone. It is a dare because many would say that while the Theology of the Body hasn't focused on these bodily events, other theologians have. In fact, childbirth, impairment, and dying each touch on some of the most debated ethical issues of our day: the legal and moral status of women and their children waiting to be born, the intersection of medical protocol and patient choice, the struggle of the disabled to access a fuller life in society, and every "death with dignity" argument that exists out there. But John Paul II made his moral arguments for a right sexuality and marriage in the *second* half of the audiences, *after* the exploration of what it means to be human. If the ensouled body is capable of making visible what is invisible, through sign, then the primal events of childbirth, impairment, and death function as signs. Has anyone asked what these events make visible? Has anyone asked what we may be refusing to see in our fallen state? Can seeing rightly help us act? That is, does the "pre-given language of self-giving and fruitfulness" found in childbirth, impairment, and dying not only give us spiritual perception, but give us insight into how we should live?

The Theology of the Body is about *seeing*, or perception, if you prefer. It is "hot" because it touches a way of seeing that unveils the real, and nothing is more life-changing than a long, loving look at the real. I hope that this "fresh sight" evoked by the Theology of the Body—perceiving a pattern of love and self-gift within the created world, sharpened through a phenomenological[10] (and then contemplative) attitude—will naturally extend the insights of John Paul's work. Perhaps then we can more easily see God in all things, beginning with the experientially formative events of childbirth, impairment, and dying. As is obvious in his own audiences, there is the challenge of recovering these experiences from *in the beginning* (i.e., before the Fall) and attempting to perceive within our current reality the created, God-given sign despite the tarnishing of the Fall. Yet God's plan for humanity is redeemed in Christ, and with his revelation, we are given the grace to see. I am convinced that the greatest gift within the Theology of the Body literature is one that has been, in large part, missed: John Paul II gave us a *lens* in seeing the meaning of human beings rightly, a humanity created by, directed for, and pointing to the God who lavishly loves us all. The Theology of the Body is anchored in perceiving in truth, and the first chapter will spend some time discussing what that means in his audiences and the affiliated literature. The second, third, and fourth chapters present an extension of John Paul's method and insights, using that lens of the Theology of the Body to see rightly the lived experiences of childbirth, impairment, and dying.

There are many people I need to thank in the course of this project. First, I am extremely grateful to the Louisville Institute for funding this project through their sabbatical grant for researchers. Without their support, it is unlikely this project would have seen the light of day. My university, Saint Mary's University of Minnesota, also supported me in extending sabbatical leave for completing this project, and my theology department colleagues (Sr. Judith Schaefer, OP; Greg Sobolewski; Ken Stenstrup; Rose Beal; and Laurie Ziliak) bent over backwards to make the sabbatical truly "time away" from university responsibilities. There have been many readers who graciously read rough drafts of sections of the book and gave me helpful feedback (in alphabetical order): Rose Beal, Fr. Andrew Beerman, Suzanne Belongia, Corrine Carvalho, Christine Falk Dalessio, Dcn. Scott Dodge, Rev. David Hatton, Donna Kamann, Terry Nichols, Tom Reynolds, Kevin Rickert, Jeffrey Tranzillo, Jennifer Vanderlaan, Amos Yong, and Meg Waldron. I am especially in debt to Jeff Tranzillo, who read the entirety of the original draft with a fine-tooth comb, great care, and brilliant insight.

Conversations with Donna Kamaan, CNP, director of Franciscan Mayo Palliative Care and Fr. (now Bishop) Andrew Cozzens, former director of the CPE program at Saint Paul Seminary, were very helpful, especially for the last chapter on dying. I also appreciated a good e-mail conversation with Heidi Hess Sexton on the potential sign of adoption. Janet Smith kindly shared with me an unpublished paper on the Theology of the Body she delivered to a 2011 USCCB conference on Young Theologians and the New Evangelization. Susan Goldberg helped enormously through her remarkable copyediting skills, and the people at Lectio Publishing (Brennan Hill, Eric Wolf, and Linda Wolf) have been in all ways encouraging and helpful. I am certain the text is improved by their insights, but any flaws remain my own.

I also want to thank the staff at Fitzgerald Library at Saint Mary's University of Minnesota, especially Rachel Thomas and Carol Dahl-Elhindi, for their help in sharing their knowledge of the brave new media behind resource collection and their hard work in securing multiple interlibrary loans.

And, of course, I thank my family for listening to this project evolve over a couple of years. My husband Jerry in particular has been a huge supporter of this project and generously listened to "the latest research" over lunch dates, shared car rides, and "the-kids-are-finally-asleep-let's-talk" sessions. Thank you.

This book is dedicated to my spiritual directors over the years: they know who they are. I thank each one of you for honing in me the ability to see clearly, and learn to behold. I thank you for your support in becoming trained in spiritual direction myself. This text is deeply, if indirectly, influenced from our discussions on discerning the Holy Spirit in everyday life. My gratitude is endless.

One of the most poignant exchanges in the Gospels is when Jesus asks the blind man Bartimaeus what he wants—not assuming anything—and the man pleads, "Lord, I want to see." May we all desire to perceive as God desires us to see, and may we dare to make our deepest desires known to our wild, lavish God of generosity and love.

Susan Windley-Daoust
November 7, 2013

ENDNOTES

1. Examples of these phenomena in order: The Pontifical John Paul II Institute for Studies on Marriage and Family at the Catholic University of America http://www.johnpaulii.edu , The National Theology of the Body Congress http://tobcongress.com, The Theology of the Body Institute http://www.tobinstitute.org, dedicated popular and catechetical book lines at Ascension Press, the Daughters of Saint Paul, and St. Anthony Messenger Press, and a cover story on ABC's "Nightline" (May 8, 2009).
2. Two recent books that chronicle these stories are: Marcel LeJeune, *Set Free To Love: Lives Changed by the Theology of the Body* (Cincinnati, Ohio: Servant Books, 2010) and Matthew Pinto, *Freedom: Twelve Lives Transformed by the Theology of the Body* (West Chester, Penn.: Ascension Press, 2009).
3. George Weigel, *Witness to Hope: The Biography of Pope John Paul II* (first edition) (New York: HarperCollins, 1999), 343.
4. See especially Luke Timothy Johnson, "A Disembodied Theology of the Body," *Commonweal* 128, no. 2 (January 26, 2001): 11, or Charles Curran, *The Moral Theology of Pope John Paul II* (Washington, D.C.: Georgetown University Press, 2005). However, as Johnson alludes to in his article, most critical negation of the audiences is expressed through a simple lack of engagement: the audiences are simply not discussed in certain theological circles as theology.
5. The book of poetry is: Donora Hillard, *Theology of the Body* (s.l.: Gold Wake Press, 2010). She says she wrote the poetry as an angry response to John Paul II and Theology of the Body enthusiasts, after being forced to listen to a Christopher West campus presentation on the Theology of the Body: more at "Donora Hillard: The TBN Self-Interview," *The Nervous Breakdown* (blog), August 14, 2010, http://www.thenervousbreakdown.com/dhillard/2010/08/donora-hillard-the-tnb-self-interview/.
6. Some of this debate "broke through" the ivory tower of conferences to more popular Catholic presses, and an example is found here: Alex Bush, "Christopher West Debate Continues: Schindler responds to Smith and Waldstein," *Life Site News*, June 9, 2009, http://www.lifesitenews.com/news/archive//ldn/2009/jun/09060914.
7. An exception and welcome entry to broadening the focus of the Theology of the Body is found in Leah Perrault, *Theology of the Body for Every Body* (Toronto: Novalis, 2012), and theological anthropology is the focus of Christopher West's fine book *Fill These Hearts: God, Sex, and the Universal Longing* (New York: Image, 2012).
8. John Paul II, *Man and Woman He Created Them: A Theology of the Body* (Boston, MA: Pauline Books & Media, 2006), #133.1.
9. *Man and Woman*, #19:4.
10. Phenomenology is a modern school of philosophy grounded in the study of appearances. Even among phenomenologists there is debate about the term beyond that basic definition. The term as John Paul II studied and employed it is discussed starting at page 10 of the first chapter.

CHAPTER 1
"Lord, I Want To See."

Perceiving the Signs of Love

 KEY CONCEPTS

This chapter will focus on how John Paul II's unusual background yielded a theology that focuses on spiritual perception, and how that helps us recognize and respond to God's call to love. After discussing the under-recognized impact of what and how we see—in art and in prayer—I will explore some of John Paul II's unusual background in phenomenology and Carmelite spirituality, a formation that made him singularly suited in bringing spiritual perception into the forefront of theological anthropology. With background in hand, I will introduce the Theology of the Body literature: its core insights, its status as theological genre and subdiscipline, and its potential in helping us see the work of God in the visible order. Understanding this background helps forecast the promise of how the Theology of the Body may help us see the work of the Holy Spirit through three of the most profound bodily experiences—childbirth, physical impairment, and dying.

...[T]he hunger is there....Again and again, people call for an appointment "to talk to somebody"....There is urgency in their voices....Then, when they arrive, when the door is finally shut and the phone turned off, they say apologetically, "I'm not really sure why I'm here. I don't know what I want." They want God, of course, but they aren't able to say so. —Margaret Guenther, Holy Listening: The Art of Spiritual Direction

They came to Jericho. As he and his disciples and a large crowd were leaving Jericho, Bartimaeus son of Timaeus, a blind beggar, was sitting by the roadside. When he heard that it was Jesus of Nazareth, he began to shout out and say, "Jesus, Son of David, have mercy on me!" Many sternly ordered him to be quiet, but he cried out even more loudly, "Son of David, have mercy on me!" Jesus stood still and said, "Call him here." And they called the blind man, saying to him, "Take heart; get up, he is calling you." So throwing off his cloak, he sprang up and came to Jesus. Then Jesus said to him, "What do you want me to do for you?" The blind man said to him, "My teacher, let me see again." Jesus said to him, "Go; your faith has made you well." Immediately he regained his sight and followed him on the way. —Mark 10:46-52

What is your deepest desire? If the Son of David asked you, would you be able to take courage, as Bartimaeus did, and name that desire? Or are you so confused by circumstances, you say "I don't know why I'm here. I don't know what I want"?

To seriously ask oneself, *what do I want?* or *what do I desire?* may feel impossibly big. It is a question that moves us beyond the safe world of pragmatic choices and managing circumstances. It moves us into a world where we are so unfamiliar with what is before us that we may reactively respond, "I don't know what I want." Yet the mystery within this question must be lived out in the everyday: in our tangled lives of need and love, seeking shelter, food, water, wanting companionship, challenged by too many choices or a lack of good ones. There is hope, because revelation and love abide here, but it is a land where these answers are not crystal clear. But the hunger to answer this question, *what do I desire?* remains. The same hunger demands to be satisfied.

It is a question that receives answer in a set of papal audiences popularly called the Theology of the Body. In fact, sit with the question for a time, and you realize it is not just a question: it holds a call. As call, it invites response. And we are called to respond to *what we see*: in ourselves, and in others. The Theology of the Body provides an understanding of the human being that focuses on Bartimaeus's bold answer to Jesus's question, "What do you want?" He wants to see. *Spiritual sight, once found, yields a clarity of desire that enables one to more fully respond to God.*

The Impact Of What We See

> They came to Bethsaida. Some people brought a blind man to him and begged him to touch him. He took the blind man by the hand and led him out of the village; and when he had put saliva on his eyes and laid his hands on him, he asked him, "Can you see anything?" And the man looked up and said, "I can see people, but they look like trees, walking." Then Jesus laid his hands on his eyes again; and he looked intently and his sight was restored, and he saw everything clearly. Then he sent him away to his home, saying, "Do not even go into the village." (Mk 8:22-26)

We are deeply impacted by what we see. As we become an ever more visually oriented society, we understand how what we see forms us, affects us, even "rewires" our brains. For example, the unfolding impact of instant access to pornography is a disturbing social experiment playing in real time, not only making people accustomed to objectify others, but also creating addictions and diminishing people's ability to understand love and pleasure as they were created by God. On the other side of the coin, we see the power of images to change hearts and minds for virtue: contemporary theories of nonviolence underline the importance of standing up, sitting down, and being seen. Think of the young, calm African-Americans sitting down at the "whites only" counter at Woolworth's across the South, allowing themselves to be taunted, prodded, and burned with cigarette butts. Think of the impact of seeing the burning bus in the 1961 Freedom Rides in the American South. Even before recognition of "being seen" as a tool, we have the raw images that move people to compassion: children starving in a famine, an Iranian woman clutching a cell phone to record a protest—dead, and the flattened world of the Indonesian tsunami. What we see and how we interpret it is the new rhetoric of our time. We cannot always control what we see. But we fool ourselves if we think we are not profoundly impacted by it.

The passage above, from the Gospel of Mark, is admittedly unusual: a healing in two parts. According to the Gospels, Jesus healed all others who came to him at one sitting, so there seems to be a design to this two-part healing: the nameless blind man, after healing, first reports "I see people looking like trees and walking." If he had been blind since birth, this is a description that makes as much sense as any other: he sees height (trees) and movement (walking). But it is not an accurate interpretation of what is before the man. Jesus then "laid hands on his eyes a second time and he saw clearly; his sight was restored... ." The second part of the healing is a healing of interpretation. Much of the Theology of the Body is about responding rightly to God's call, and the call is evinced through the spiritual sign of the ensouled body. But we cannot see rightly without a healing of interpretation, given the dimmed sight we inherit as a consequence of the Fall. John Paul II argues forthrightly that Christian revelation, rather than being anti-corporality, actually sees the body in all its beauty as God created it. Perceiving that beauty requires a right interpretation, which he seeks through an analysis of original righteousness. But he honors the signatory value of God's creation, and the healing interpretive lens offered by Christian revelation, through the world of art.

The Help Of Artistic Perception

To know John Paul II is to know he was a man profoundly attuned to the power of what we see: he had a profound visual sense, and that was seen in his penchant for images (the Divine Mercy image), visual events (praying at the Western Wall in Jerusalem), and dramatic liturgical movement (his style of presiding at the Mass). This was not manipulative: this was a man recognizing that there is a time to pray in secret and a time to lead prayer by evocative visual cues. And he loved art. There is the well-known story of the time when the frescoes of "The Last Judgment" in the Sistine Chapel were restored. John Paul II ordered that half the painted loincloths, added after Michelangelo's death on many of the nude figures throughout that magnificent visual representation of the end of salvation history, be removed to once again show Michelangelo's original artwork. In a 1994 homily given at the Mass celebrating the restoration of the frescoes, John Paul II expounds on the icon of the human body as presented by Michelangelo:

> It seems that Michelangelo, in his own way, allowed himself to be guided by the evocative words of the Book of Genesis which, as regards the creation of the human being, Man and Woman, reveals: "The man and

his wife were both naked, yet they felt no shame" (Gn 2:35). *The Sistine Chapel* is precisely – if one may say so – *the sanctuary of the theology of the human body.* ... [I]t also expresses in a certain way, the hope of a world transfigured, the world inaugurated by the risen Christ, and even before by Christ on Mount Tabor....

...[T]he whole composition [of the Sistine Chapel] is deeply penetrated by a unique light and by a single artistic logic: *the light and the logic of faith that the Church proclaims, confessing*: "We believe in one God...." On the basis of this logic in the context of the light that comes from God, the human body also keeps its splendour and its dignity. If it is removed from this dimension, it becomes in some way an object, which depreciates very easily, since only before the eyes of God can the human body remain naked and unclothed, and keep its splendour and its beauty intact.[1]

There is more than one kind of visual depiction of the naked body. Artistic images of the body are those that reflect the presence of the Creator, and the nakedness reflects the work of God. Images of the body that are meant for sexual objectification and use are pornographic. What we see—and the comportment of the self toward that seeing—is no idle matter. We cannot see without seeing *something*.[2] And sight is rarely about procuring simple information. *Spiritual sight compels a response to God.*

Like Michelangelo, the modern-day artist Edward Knippers presents paintings of religious events that also work with the plane of the naked human body. Knippers could be called the Flannery O'Connor of painters: unabashedly Christian in a period when that goes against the artistic grain, and his thick, somewhat German Impressionist-inspired painting is very "in your face." Many of the paintings are more than life-sized, beefy, hairy, with nary a fig leaf to be seen. Critics rightly remark on the "insistent physicality" of this work.[3]

Knippers' mature work presents classic biblical scenes populated almost entirely by nudes. Jesus is nude. The disciples are nude. Those reaching out to Jesus for healing are nude. The patriarchs are nude. Those who reject Jesus are clothed. Although he paints a couple of exceptions to this rule[4], the intent is clear: nakedness is presented as a kind of openness to God. And that openness in the person of Jesus Christ is radical and unashamed. The visualized physicality—warts, wounds, and all—is the sign of spiritual transparency throughout his work. Knippers himself claims that he paints nudes because it is a way of "starkly stating we have nowhere to hide."[5] Or a more positive rendition: those turned in supplication to Christ ultimately do not need to hide and have nothing to fear. Nakedness, as an artistic move for Knippers, communicates an open response to God.

Knippers continues:

> Further, it allows me to have something of the spiritual timelessness of the Eastern Icon tradition by avoiding the cultural trappings of modern or ancient dress and, at the same time, enabling me to ground my subjects in the specifics of time and space (the glory of the Western tradition). This bridging of the two traditions is important to me because the spirituality of the Biblical events is as solid and real as the events themselves.
>
> In finding the spiritual in the interactions and choices of real people, incarnation can be shown as the symbiotic reality that it is. *In other words, the choices and actions that we make always have profound spiritual ramifications because we are human beings.* This uniquely human cause and effect is at the core of my painting, and I find that the nude allows me to cut past the shroud of ordinary expectations in order to see ourselves and our actions for what they are.[6]

If you look at Knippers' Isaiah in the Temple, you see the nudity of body and the nudity of spirit expressed through the body. Isaiah, encountering the spiritual world breaking through within the Temple, is unclothed, arms thrown in a position of charged energy and vulnerability, open to this in-breaking reality. He is allowing himself to be impaled by a visibly invisible spirit's coal of fire, pressed to his lips to purify him to speak God's word. Meanwhile, incense smoke—a symbol of prayer rising to God as well as a sign of God's presence among us[7]—floats gently in the foreground. Knippers presents a wholly fleshy Isaiah, body expressing a posture of prayer and amazement before God. The cubist-inspired ribbons of color and light are his language for the transformative spiritual realm "beyond the veil," where our eyes (in this case literally) cannot rest and see the Divine: we see fragments, pieces of a whole, and cannot quite put it together.[8]

John Paul II on Michelangelo and Edward Knippers notes two things: that what we see is important, and the posture we take to what we see is critical. The human artist can see, and help others see, *reality in the light of God*. As Knippers says: "I have maintained over the years that art is not merely self-expression but an exploration of a reality greater than the Self. I have also maintained that the artist should be concerned about the most profound parts of that reality, not just play in the shallows."[9] John Paul is, if anything, more direct: "Artists are constantly in search of the hidden meaning of things, and their torment is to succeed in expressing the world of the ineffable. How then can we fail to see what a great source of inspiration is offered by that kind of homeland of the soul that is religion?"[10] Artists, through sign and symbol, are able to help us interpret the deeper reality imbued in what we see.

But, stepping away from humanly created art, there is also the seeing of the work of the Divine Artist, God. Perception is the first move of participation in reality. To that end, I want to address a very different form of perception by which we encounter the Holy Spirit: Ignatian prayer.

The Help Of Perception In Prayer

Ignatius of Loyola, in his classic *The Spiritual Exercises*, advocates a style of prayer that others have embraced in the past but have not presented as clearly as Ignatius has as a way to deepened prayer with God. He calls it contemplation, but to avoid confusion with a more common understanding of contemplation (see John of the Cross below), I will follow many other interpreters' leads and call it imaginative prayer.

Ignatius is brief and direct in *The Spiritual Exercises*, which really serves as a handbook to those in retreat and discernment. Imaginative prayer is described below:

> I will consider how God our Lord looks upon me. >
> I offer all my will and actions to God.
> I review the Scripture for this prayer.
> I imaginatively enter the place of this Scripture.
> I ask of God what I wish and desire in this prayer.
> For each point,

I see the persons.
I hear the words.
I observe the actions.
I speak to God as my heart is moved.
I conclude with an Our Father.[11]

It is tempting—but would be a real loss—to gloss over the depth of this brief sketch. What Ignatius does in 10 short sentences is provide a conscious way to put yourself in God's presence for prayer, open yourself to God's word, and listen for God. This happens through offering your whole self at this point to the God who loves you, offering your own will and actions, prayerfully reading the assigned Scripture, and allowing yourself to be in that event. He encourages the use of active imagination (what he called "composition of place") not to create an entertaining prayer experience, but to seek, engage, and respond through all the human senses. God does not speak only through words; in fact, in prayer, God does not commonly speak to us through words. And in the set up of the prayer, you have given God permission to speak to you and pray through you. The Holy Spirit is directing this "imaginative exercise" to express Himself in a way you can understand.[12]

An example, for those not familiar with the practice: Suppose you are praying with the Gospel of Matthew's Temptation of Jesus (Mt 4:1-11) and have deliberately sat down in your "prayer chair" and offered the preparatory prayer. You read the passage, and your composition of place may spontaneously begin with heat, and dryness. (It is set in a desert, after all). You "see" swells of sand in every direction, with the wind whipping some sand into "dust devils." Entering more fully into the space, you "feel" sweat, the unsteadiness of the sand underfoot, and squint into the bright sun. Suddenly, you are aware of Jesus, realizing he has been right next to you the whole time. He is speaking to the voiced temptations, which seem to be spoken out of some sort of the living, writhing air, coming from every direction but not quite visible. You realize by the last line Jesus utters, "The Lord your God shall you worship, and Him alone shall you serve," you are saying it with him. You are trying to help him—he looks strong, but so gaunt—and the temptations are coming from everywhere. You realize Jesus is repeating the line again, and again, and through you as well. As you begin to be overwhelmed by the temptations, sinking in the sand, you keep your voice in tandem with Jesus, and now, invisible others are saying the same words: "The Lord your God shall you worship, and Him alone shall you serve." Then there is quiet, and Jesus reaches out and pulls you up, smiling, saying "They're gone." And you collapse in that offered embrace, knowing that he is the only reason the evil spirits departed. The place and prayer fades. Now: what did you "say" to God? What do you say now? You "speak to God as your heart is moved." And finally, formally conclude the prayer.[13]

Ignatius' visuality (and his employment of every other sense as well) recognizes the multiple forms of expression and communication and that the visual sense is an inordinately strong sense. It is a very bodily sense that takes full advantage of the gift of our incarnation and assumes the incarnation of God, that God can be "seen," and that we pray to a God who desires intimate relationship. Imaginative prayer "works" because he encourages people to trust God to communicate in a profoundly effective medium. The power of seeing God see you cannot be underestimated. *Spiritual sight calls to response.*

Given John Paul's attunement to the visual, he employs twin sources for his Theology of the Body discourses: a branch of philosophy called phenomenology and the Carmelite spirituality of St. John of the Cross. The somewhat unusual backstory of John Paul's intellectual and spiritual life frames the entirety of the Theology of the Body.

The Background: Phenomenological Philosophy And Carmelite Spirituality

The Role Of The "Phenomenological Attitude"

The importance of "seeing," of experiencing what appears, is the distinctive but often unnoticed cornerstone that undergirds much of John Paul II's theological reflection. Karol Wojtyla wrote presciently in a book on an early 20th century phenomenological philosopher he admired, Max Scheler:

> [The theologian] should not forego the great advantages which the phenomenological method offers his[/her] work. It impresses the stamp of experience on works of ethics and nourishes them with the life-knowledge of concrete [humanity] by allowing an investigation of moral life from the side of its appearance.[14]

The very seeing of the body, John Paul II announces, has theological importance. Something happens through the encounter we call see-ing—opening our eyes, comporting our position toward what we see, receiving sight, interpreting—which either opens our soul to God and inspires action in harmony with God's will and love, or closes our soul to God and leads to callousness and objectification. This act of seeing, although clearly bodily, is also a spiritual act: when spiritual writers say we "see with the heart," they are not failing basic biology. They use the biblical language of heart as the seat of the human wholeness, body and spirit, and know that it takes the Spirit to lend light to sight. "Speaking of the *heart* in this way means precisely that [humanity's] perceptive powers play in concert, which also requires the proper interplay of body and soul, since this is essential for the totality of the creature we call '[human].'"[15] Sight, understood in this manner, becomes a call of the present moment. And this call, all calls, beg for response.

Despite the pervasive sacramentality of Catholic practice and thought, the art of seeing is not a predominant theme within theological reflec-tion. And the man much responsible for the full flowering of sacramen-tal theology in the middle ages, Thomas Aquinas, is not a significant part of the Theology of the Body.[16] But John Paul II's philosophical dialogue partners are a constellation of 20th century philosophers—Max Scheler, Gabriel Marcel, Martin Buber, Emmanuel Levinas, and others[17]—who find themselves occupied with reflection on seeing, classified as phe-nomenologists (philosophers who focus on the study of appearances) and personalists (philosophers from a European philosophical school who focus on the primacy of the human person in relationship to God, Truth, and others).[18]

Phenomenology, as a stream of philosophical thought, is famously diffi-cult to nail down. Scheler himself, the subject of John Paul's philosophy dissertation,[19] hesitated when asked to write an article defining phenomenological method for a philosophical journal:

> [I] claim only to report my own viewpoint. There is no phenomenological "school" …there is only a circle of researchers, inspired by a common bearing and attitude [*Einstellung*] toward philosophical problems, who take and bear separate responsibility for everything they claim to have discovered within this attitude, including any theory of the nature of this "attitude."[20]

This circle of researchers (the "Göttingen circle") began with a loose association of responses to the work of Edmund Husserl, often deemed the Father of Phenomenology. However, Scheler is right when he characterizes phenomenology as philosophers joined by a *common insight* rather than by a predefined method. Although Husserl used the language of method, Scheler points out that method ("the consciousness of the unity of the investigatory procedure") arises as a secondary consideration in the development of knowledge: indeed, he argues that there is not an accepted definition of many long-standing subjects of study, such as mathematics or physics.[21] Outside of Husserl, there is not inordinate focus on method among phenomenologists.

Instead, most phenomenologists hold to *the phenomenological attitude* as the root of right philosophy. Scheler defines the phenomenological attitude as "an attitude of spiritual seeing in which one can see [*erschauen*] or experience [*erleben*] something which otherwise remains hidden." He continues that method generally thinks about facts, but phenomenology deals with new facts themselves, "a procedure of *seeing*" before getting "fixed by logic."[22] Phenomenology is rooted in the act of perception, and the phenomenological attitude embraces that encounter between subject and other that occurs prior to language.

The focus on experience, and a way of seeing, is necessarily joined with a "spiritual posture" or disposition [*Geisteshaltung*] of openness to what the person sees. The posture is necessary preparation for philosophical inquiry, which Scheler roots in the act of loving, an open encounter: "*a love-determined movement of the inmost personal self of a finite being toward participation in the essential reality of all possibles.*"[23] Love, Scheler argues, is the act that reveals, more than reason could, the essential value of the other. To see another in love is to see much more than to see another through analysis or objectification. Most important, John Paul will add, it is to see as Christ sees.[24]

Another influence on John Paul II, Gabriel Marcel[25], addressed this phenomenological attitude: the focus on experience and seeing, spiritual posture, and the primacy of love from similar yet different perspectives. Marcel was a Catholic, a largely freelance philosopher, a respected playwright, and a trained concert pianist. His life was shaped, he says, by his mother's death when he was a child, and the experience of working for the Red Cross in World War I. His job was to work with French families who were searching for missing loved ones in the war. The other influence on his work was his slow journey to accepting the Catholic faith, after a childhood marked by little religion of any sort. These influences yielded base questions for his philosophy, marked by being with others: Why do the people we love die? What does it mean to be faithful in relationship? And how do I live?[26]

Like Scheler, Marcel approaches reality through the phenomenological attitude. Although he doesn't use the word "attitude," he offers substantially similar language with his distinction between primary reflection (scientific reflection on problems to be solved) and secondary reflection (the state of wonder before mystery). Although both forms of reflection have their place, Marcel was afraid that secondary reflection—that is, the phenomenological attitude—was lost in an age where scientific method was seen to be the answer to all encounters. Indeed, "the answer to all encounters" doesn't even make sense as a sentence: we answer questions, and we respond to encounters. Further, Marcel worried, appeals to mystery were seen, increasingly, as an escape from rigorous thinking. Marcel lamented this reality, arguing that life is to be explored rather than solved, and our relationships to God and each other are defined as mysteriously rich rather than as a burdensome problem. To Marcel, mystery is not the unknowable, but the place where subject and object distinctions begin to lose their hard edges: "A mystery is something in which I am myself involved, and it can only be thought of in a sphere where the distinction between what is in me and what is before me loses its meaning and its initial validity."[27]

Marcel mirrors Scheler when he speaks of the human position taken to the world as mystery: instead of the "spiritual posture" or disposition [*geisteshaltung*] of Scheler, we have the complementary term "*disponibilité*," inadequately rendered in English as "availability." *Disponibilité*, notes an interpreter, "seems to demand to be understood as an attitude…. The notion clearly has a bodily signification, referring to a direction we take, a way we face, or even more graphically, to a way in which our face is turned."[28] However, there is more to this positioning than direction:

> …the attitude of availability is dispositionally opposed to an attitude which seeks "to dispose of" persons and things…. "To dispose of" is to exercise a power over having. We can dispose of only what we have power over, of whatever we have at our disposal: methods, instruments, information, categories….We can never dispose of *presence*; if we treat persons as things over which we have powers of disposal, they will invariably withhold their presence from us…. Availability is an opening upon the presence of another, not a way of access to certain goods he possesses.[29]

Disponibilité is both a decision for dispositional openness to another, as well as a way of association that enables and facilitates this non-objectifying relationship.[30] If we were to move back to Scheler again, that way of association is the "love-determined movement," upon seeing another, that opens one to the value of the other.[31]

Finally, Marcel rightly is heralded for his distinction between being and having as opposing ways of defining the human person,[32] which influenced the Second Vatican Council as well as the anthropology of Karol Wojtyla (especially in *Love and Responsibility*)[33] and John Paul II (harkened in many encyclicals, especially *Evangelium Vitae, Laborem Exercens*, and *Centesimus Annus*).[34]

John Paul II is seen echoing many of the themes struck by Scheler and Marcel: his personalist focus on "*the fundamental dimension of man's existence, which is always a co-existence,*"[35] his definition of humanity created to the image of God as a capacity for relationship to God, and his emphasis on approaching the human other through the eyes of love and value, not use. His use of phenomenological attitude seems evident in how he handles the "first sight" of Eve by the man Adam: it is, because it was filled with the light of God, a look of wonder, a look where one says to the other, "This is one I can love."[36]

But John Paul II, though a friend to the phenomenological attitude, is still speaking as a theologian and pastor of the Church. The phenomenological attitude is brought in to enrich, through attention to experience, the revelation and doctrine of the Church. I would hold that the phenomenological attitude does more than "shade in the picture," because there are elements of the Theology of the Body that are arguably new teaching.[37] But the phenomenological attitude is less a dialogue partner and more a tool to understand the reality in which we participate. John Paul clarifies his use of phenomenology in the Theology of the Body literature as a means of understanding human experience: "Yet,... our human experience is in some way a legitimate means for theological interpretation..."[38] But as he notes in an earlier text, written before his pontificate, "...[I]n all of this, the phenomenological method plays only a secondary assisting role.... At the same time, these investigations convince us that the Christian thinker, especially the theologian, who makes use of phenomenological experience in his work, cannot be a Phenomenologist."[39] In the end, the theologian, *qua* theologian, is not a phenomenologist, but can and should work out of the phenomenological attitude.

The Move To The Contemplative Attitude

The phenomenological attitude, however, is not the only attitude employed. Contemporary spiritual direction literature places at the center of spiritual direction a disposition and practice called "the contemplative attitude." While this is not identical to the phenomenological attitude, there are some striking similarities. The contemplative attitude also bridges in interesting ways the gap John Paul notes above between phenomenology and theology.

The contemplative attitude is the proximate goal of the practice of spiritual direction: the director should live out of a contemplative attitude, and foster the directee's ability to be present in a contemplative attitude, because this is where a person can perceive God. Contemplation is a putting aside of self-interest and distractions, and turning attention to God, Who is present in the moment. It assumes at its core that Christ is present where two or three gather, and that the Holy Spirit is present as the true director of human souls. The spiritual director serves God as one who is used by the Holy Spirit to nudge someone's attention to depth and mystery, to ask the person how they perceive God's work in his/her life. The director is fundamentally one who sees and listens in the light of God for another's spiritual awareness and growth. In fact, it is not just seeing and hearing, but watching and listening, which are quite different.

The contemplative attitude takes as its cue attention, which leads to absorption. We learn to place ourselves in a posture (*disponibilité*) that opens us to God. We watch for God, we learn to sense His presence. And, having sought, we "see" God, and prayer is effortless. We stay there, like Mary of Bethany,[40] and we watch, we listen. We become absorbed in the reality of God.

"Seeing," in the contemplative attitude, is sometimes referred to as "gazing," a word John Paul uses frequently within the Theology of the Body audiences.[41] Gazing refers to a focused attention held in wonder and has many references in Scripture.[42] It opens attention to beyond what is seen, but focuses upon the visible with intensity. Patricia Byrne, SSC, expands: "To gaze, therefore, has a passive as well as an active dimension. When one gazes, one has the sense of being drawn in, and in this way being held by someone or something.... Gazing is an activity that takes time; it cannot be rushed. It needs space, and there must be some element of distance if one is to gaze, to contemplate. Perhaps there is a paradox here, of being absorbed in and, at the same time apart from...."[43] Byrne continues that gazing is central to the contemplative attitude in spiritual direction, the "look which 'sees' the hidden mystery in the encounter, while...being alert to the real person of the directee."[44]

The other aspect of the contemplative attitude is the insistent focus on the fullness of reality through the notion of presence to another. So many people have defined the contemplative attitude as a "long, loving, look at the real" that no one is sure where the definition began. However, Marcel regarded the act of beholding the presence of another to be so critical that he called it "that exchange which is the mark of all spiritual life."[45] Ralph Harper adds "all presence has authority, a force and radiance, unreserved yet unpredictable. One whose presence makes others come alive is one who is alive and real. Real life has its marks: immediacy, fullness, and something like the annulment of time."[46] It may be noted that this sounds much like the absorption that comes with "the gaze."

Like the phenomenologists, those who practice the contemplative attitude in spiritual direction in many ways go back to the call of first sight at creation, Marcel's cry that deep reflection begins with wonder, the "spiritual seeing" with which one can see the value that at first blush is hidden. The reason spiritual directors serve to point toward these realities? *Spiritual sight, once found, yields a clarity of desires that compels a response to God.* Seeing the fullness of reality enables the directee to see his life as a calling from God, and enables him or her to respond. At the most fundamental level, spiritual directors "[help] directees pay attention to our self-revealing God; second, [they help] directees recognize their reactions and decide on their responses to this God."[47]

The Role Of Carmelite Spirituality

The contemplative attitude leads neatly into John Paul's other distinctive source material for his Theology of the Body: the influence of St. John of the Cross and Carmelite spirituality in general. John Paul II was, unknown to many, a Carmelite tertiary, currently known as a third order Carmelite.[48] He was introduced to the spiritual theology of St. John of the Cross by a layperson, Jan Tyranowski, before entering an underground seminary as a young man in Soviet-controlled Poland. Years later, his dissertation in theology was titled "The Question of Faith According to St. John of the Cross."[49] In many ways, his theology never strayed from the formative influence of the insights of Carmelite spirituality: "Wojtyla read in phenomenology a Carmelite sensitivity to the lived experience of personal subjectivity....Buttiglione makes a similar point when he says that Wojtyla 'read in St. John of the Cross a kind of phenomenology of mystical experience.'"[50] John Paul II's Theology of the Body is his effort to live out the calling of the third order Carmelite and make present the riches of Carmelite mysticism for all people, especially laypeople. He sees it as a way to "pray always" in one of the most tangible, physical realities of our lives: as ensouled bodies living out the vocations of marriage or celibacy.

Prayer As Initiated By The Holy Spirit

Carmelite spirituality focuses on the encounter with God through prayer, and interpreting the received experience of prayer, to live out the greatest commandment: you shall love the Lord your God with all your heart, soul, and mind.

Prayer—as understood by the doctors of prayer John of the Cross and Teresa of Ávila—is a universal call, always a gift of the Holy Spirit, and always initiated by the Holy Spirit. That prayer is initiated by the Holy Spirit is not only a Carmelite anchor, it is a root teaching of Christianity.[51] John and Teresa make that teaching explicit in their expressive writings and poetry on infused prayer, that is, prayer given by God.

The challenge for many seeking to grow in their prayer relationship to God is how to practice receptivity—to not control the relationship to God. As we learn to pray, as children or adults, we feel very much in control. I'm going to recite an Our Father now, or a rosary, or sing this song. I'm going to go to Church now, to a prayer group, or take a nature hike. Although John and Teresa never doubt the reality of free will—and freedom is essential to an authentic relationship with God—they will say that decisions to pray, and how to pray, are responses to an initial prod from the Holy Spirit, and a person's prayer response begins with simple attention. Prayer, best understood, is complete openness before God, allowing God to do great things through you. Moving from discursive prayer (praying with words) to infused prayer (receiving and attending to God's presence) is hard to describe and hard to teach. But it is essential to growth in holiness, because it is God's will for every single human being.[52]

Detachment From All Created Things

The other element of their teaching on prayer, besides being a personal call to respond to God's grace, is a forceful description of the reality of desire for God in competition with all other desires, good or evil. Unfortunately, it is easy to read into Sts. Teresa and John a kind of superhero mentality toward the spiritual life: if you do this, then this, then this, you'll cross the finish line and be in union with God. This unsubstantiated misreading only proves how desirous we are of being in control. A love relationship with God is not a checklist, and union with the Beloved is no calculus derivation. What John and Teresa speak of is that the closer we draw to God, the more we desire nothing but God. *Vice versa*, the more we shed unnecessary attachments in desire for God, the more we are open to God's love. We simply need to put aside the desires that take our eyes off of God—which although simple, is not necessarily easy.

What makes the talk of attachments and detachments difficult for many contemporary readers, and necessary to understanding the Theology of the Body, is a singular challenge: perceiving how pleasure is a good in itself. God created the world as good, and yet, ultimately, we must be willing to detach from it. Once we are wholly committed to God above all things, we can recognize that the world was given to us as gift, to attract us to God. It should be cherished as God's work, beautiful in itself and for itself. All the created universe is presented for our enjoyment— as long as we are ordered to God, and as long as our relationship to the universe is ultimately ordered to God. This insight is put humbly and less esoterically in Paul's language within the second letter to the Corinthians: "Whether you eat or drink ... do it all for the glory of God."[53]

Ignatius of Loyola, a rough contemporary of Teresa,[54] presented the same insight succinctly in his "First Foundation," with which he begins *The Spiritual Exercises*. A modern reading of the opening is presented here:

> The goal of our life is to live with God forever.
> God, who loves us, gave us life.
> Our own response of love allows God's life to flow into

us without limit.

All the things in this world are gifts of God,
presented to us so that we can know God more easily
and make a return of love more readily.

As a result, we appreciate and use all of these gifts of
God insofar as they help us develop as loving persons.
But if any of these gifts become the center of our lives,
they displace God and so hinder our growth toward
our goal.
In everyday life, then, we must hold ourselves in
balance
before all of these created gifts insofar as we have a
choice
and are not bound by some obligation.
We should not fix our desires on health or sickness,
wealth or poverty, success or failure,
a long life or short one.
For everything has the potential of calling forth in us
a deeper response to our life in God.

Our only desire and our one choice should be this:
I want and I choose what better
leads to the deepening of God's life in me.[55]

There is a very positive sagacity in this: *everything* is given as a means to know God. Everything is gift, everything is ordered to God, our Creator and Redeemer: but only in as much as we see God as the center. And the temptation to displace God, for most people who have not advanced far through the darker periods of prayer, is constant.

The created world is a two-edged sword: it reflects God's light, and is created to lead us to God. But as fallen human beings, we make elements of the reflected light gods in themselves. Creation can draw us to or lead us from God, but ultimately, it depends on our posture before God. John of the Cross or Ignatius's insights about the goodness of the created order boils down rather simply: put God first.

The focus on receptivity found in Carmelite spiritual theology—through prayer, through attention, through clearing out the clouds of sin, through reordering attachments that are good but not God—is an absolute assumption within all of John Paul II's thought, including the Theology of the Body literature. You freely offer yourself to God through offering yourself to the one whom you were called by God to marry, to be united in one flesh—or through offering yourself directly to God for the kingdom of heaven. This detachment for another makes room for you to receive the First before all created things: the "irradiation" of the Holy Spirit.

> The reality of the gift and of the act of giving, which is sketched in the first chapters of Genesis as the constitutive content of the mystery of creation, confirms that the irradiation of Love is an integral part of the same mystery.... Only Love creates the good, and in the end it alone can be perceived in all its dimensions and its contours in created things and, above all, in man. Its presence is the final result...of the hermeneutics of the gift....

> This consistent giving ... *bears witness to rootedness in Love.* The first verses of the Bible speak of it so much that they remove all doubt. They speak not only about the creation of the world and about man in the world, but also about grace, that is, the self-communication of holiness, about the irradiation of the Holy Spirit, which produces a special state of "spiritualization" in that first man.[56]

When he and other interpreters use the language of "the law of the gift," "the law of *ekstasis*," "or the hermeneutic of the gift"[57]—three phrases pointing to the same donative movement of union with God—this is clearly a Carmelite influence he is presenting to a largely secular audience.

An Engaged, Transforming God

This spiritual theology (Carmelite theology and John Paul's theology) also presumes the intimate engagement, power, and involvement of God in our world and in the details of our very lives. There is nothing in this theology that is in the least bit Deist. Our God is a giver of good gifts, and His will for us is that we may receive the most complete and astounding of all gifts, to share in His likeness through a union of love.[58] This very nature of self-giving is seen in the Trinitarian nature of the Godhead. As the One who knows all things knows, we are each and every one wounded and sinful persons, and each person is enticed to the full love and healing of God in a way unique to that person. To that end, God has a specific will for each one of us, a will that brings healing to our specific illnesses, physical and spiritual, and our greatest hope is fulfilled when we cooperate with that will—a will that is never against our best desires, because it leads us to our God of Love.[59]

This is a theology that respects the human being's free will: indeed, much of John of the Cross's work deals with that very freedom and how we choose to use it. But it also assumes Thomas Aquinas's well-known statement that the only truly God-absent free choice we make is to say no to God. God is there, enticing, luring, loving, teaching, befriending, correcting. Omnipresence as a doctrine does not necessitate personal relationship. The Carmelites go well beyond simple omnipresence to assuming that the God of the covenant is always a God in relationship to us, and that His love impels us and makes us strong.[60] Every prayer, every action for God, is a response to His first love for us. Even receiving God's love requires the help of God, in the preparation and in the moment. God both prompts and facilitates our life-response to divine love. We choose to cooperate with God's help, but we do nothing in this great and growing exchange of love entirely on our own, except abandon it.

The God Of Relationship

The twin themes of receptivity and the omnipotent goodness of God lead, not surprisingly, to the language of spiritual betrothal and marriage in both John of the Cross and Teresa of Ávila. Although the spousal imagery of a wedding between God and humanity is rife throughout Scripture (e.g., Hosea, Song of Songs, Isaiah, Ezekiel, Revelation), the Carmelite doctors of prayer do put their particular stamp on the analogy. Human beings, individually, are called to a complete and total cleaving to God. This is no less than the first commandment: you must love the Lord, your God, with all your heart, soul, and mind. This does not mean simply acknowledging God's existence or doing good in the name of God. It means putting God before all things, in every movement of your life. In a relationship of prayer that is attended and nurtured, the normal development is toward a sense of betrothal:[61] God asks for permanent and complete devotion (and in turn offers that attention to you in a felt sense). This leads, in people who do not run the other way, to a "spiritual marriage."

Other mystics have used different language to describe the same spiritual movement: the anonymous author of *The Cloud of Unknowing* speaks of the soul being "oned" with God, for example. Ignatius's union is filled with military metaphor of absolute service to the King. But there are clear advantages to the analogy of marriage. One only has to think of the traditional wedding vows—I promise to be true to you, in good times and in bad, for better and for worse, in sickness and in health, all the days of my life—to sense the enormity of the gift given, and the gift one is impelled to give to God.

It is not surprising, then, that John Paul II embraces this insight into relationship with God through the language of the body as created for relationship, the "sign" of marriage. Although John Paul is not conflating the two senses of marriage,[62] the thematic similarities are striking.

Spiritual Betrothal and Marriage	Earthly Marriage
Life is promised and lived as gift to another.	Life is promised and lived as gift to another.
Self-centered desires are purified over time to live out a full-hearted response to love.	Self-centered desires are purified over time to live out a full-hearted response to love.
The way of God's will for that person is fulfilled.	The way of God's will for that person is fulfilled.
There is an overflowing into new spiritual life.	There is an overflowing into new life, physical and/or spiritual.

The Carmelite influence may be boiled down to this: the interior life of the human being is as real as any other seen and felt reality. The human being, not as body and soul but as body/soul, is called to "spiritual marriage" with God in specific and discernible ways. This internal *sight calls to response*. And a fully open response leads to God's first desire and our best desire: union with God.

***

From John Paul II's background in phenomenology and Carmelite spirituality, we see a constellation of lights at play: the influence of the phenomenological attitude ("an attitude of spiritual seeing in which one can see or experience something that otherwise remains hidden"), the importance of *disponibilité* as a posture of openness to God, the personalist insight on the fundamental dimension of human coexistence, human value discovered and discerned in the light of God through love, the providence and initiative of a personal God who wills good for us, the constant and fruitful activity of the Holy Spirit (especially given way in the prayer lives of believers), the essential spiritual move of detachment from created things in order to receive them as gifts ordered to God, and the language of covenant, chosenness, betrothal, and spiritual marriage. These lights join, connect, and frame the papal audiences John Paul called "a Theology of the Body."

What Is Theology Of The Body?

This book assumes little knowledge on the part of the reader of John Paul's Theology of the Body literature: however, the more you have read it, hopefully the more you will appreciate the nuances in what follows. There are many secondary sources on the audiences, some popular, some more academic.[63] However, I am trying to present this material in such a way that readers new to the subject may have the grounding to appreciate the constructive extension that follows. To that end, I offer a very brief synopsis of John Paul's purpose, structure, and animating insights in the audiences, and encourage readers to read the texts themselves as well as some of the secondary literature, should you desire a deeper understanding.

Michael Waldstein identifies the overarching purpose of the Theology of the Body correctly, I believe, when he says that "...the purpose is to show the divine plan for human spousal love, to show the goodness and beauty of the whole sexual sphere against its cheapening in the 'objective, scientific' way of looking at nature. God's plan and its renewal by Christ, the redeemer, is imprinted deeply within the bodily nature of the person as a pre-given language of self-giving and fruitfulness."[64] There are multiple, complementary purposes in this thick text—for example, to better illustrate the sign of the created human body, to lead people in the secular world to see God imprinted within lived experience, to better flesh out the call to celibacy as a call to unite oneself to God and his kingdom, to further root the teachings presented in *Humanae Vitae* in a personalist framework—but the text's prime purpose is exploring what John Paul II calls the "*spousal meaning of the body*," the observation and teaching that the human being is called to commit himself or herself fully in covenantal relationship, whether that is embodied in sacramental marriage or a celibate life ordered to union with God.

The animating insight within this text is how the spousal meaning of the body reveals the reciprocal dynamic of *gift*: as ensouled bodies, we are created to receive God in word, sacrament, and prayer. And like Christ, we are called to give ourselves fully and completely to God the Father. This is every human being's personal act of faith, hope, and love, and it is expressed through the acts of our very bodies. Because John Paul wants to say that we speak a "language of the body," even a "gospel of the body" that reflects God's Trinitarian communion and love prior to the written revelation, he reflects upon the creation of man and woman through the "*hermeneutics of the gift*."[65] We understand the creation of the human being as ensouled body through its interpretation as a specific gift of God, with its own beauty, wisdom, and call. The call to love as God loves involves a yielding and openness that is rooted in the relationship of the Father and Son in unity with the Holy Spirit. We are called to communion through the dynamic of the gift.

John Paul II introduces our creation and call to communion through the prelapsarian triad of original solitude, original nakedness, and original unity: a structure that recognizes these particular moments of human existence as holding the value and meaning of the human being.[66] All three, as moments offered in the Adam and Eve narrative, lead to a first *communio personarum*,[67] or *communion of persons*: the solitude is offered at self-knowledge, a consciousness of distinction from the rest of creation in the light of God; the nakedness is offered as a recognition of similarity and difference, capacity and desire to live with and for another, to freely give yourself as gift; and the unity is the desire realized in self-giving love and fruitfulness. Who we were created to be is essential in understanding how lived experience changed with the Fall, what redemption does and does not promise, and how we are called to live now. We were created for communion with each other and with God, we fail in communion with each other and with God, and we are called to live in a redeemed order of communion with each other and with God.

The original nakedness of humanity, argues John Paul—the lived world of the prelapsarian human being—"signifies the original good of the divine vision."[68] There is an openness and vulnerability without fear, and recognition of common humanity (Gn 2:23: "Here at last is flesh of my flesh and bone of my bone"). There is no distinction in the text between the bodiliness and spirit of each person: not that body and spirit are identical, but they so intertwined that they are not seen as separate. Each person's value is seen by the other in the light of God's mystery:

> Seeing each other reciprocally, *through the very mystery of creation, as it were,* the man and the woman *see each other still more fully and clearly* than through the sense of sight itself, that is, through the eyes of the body. They see and know each other, in fact, with all the peace of the interior gaze, which creates precisely the fullness of the intimacy of persons.... At the same time, they "communicate" based on the communion of persons in which they become a mutual gift for each other, through femininity and masculinity. In reciprocity, they reach in this way a particular understanding of the meaning of their own bodies. The original meaning of nakedness corresponds to the simplicity and fullness of vision in which their understanding of the meaning of the body is born from the very heart, as it were, of their community-communion. We shall call this meaning "spousal."[69]

For men and women who are called to marriage, that gift is reflected in a real way in the gift that a man and woman give to each other in their committed life together, expressed most fully in the bodily commitment of sexual intercourse. They open themselves to each other in an exclusive way, and open themselves to the possibility of new life from concrete acts of love. Sexuality, as created by God and often experienced by people who live in healthy marriages, is a truly beautiful gift of God that reflects how God calls us to commitment and yields fruitfulness. I will also argue that it is a source of healing, as all vocations truly lived are. But the key is gift: we understand our lives as gift, our vocation to marriage as gift, our mutual offering of self as gift, our children—should there be any—as gift. Recall Ignatius's first foundation: "All things in this world are gifts of God presented to us that we may know God more easily, and make a return of love more readily." Recall John of the Cross, on how one must detach oneself from mutable goods to fully embrace immutable good to receive again all mutable good. Or St. Thérèse de Lisieux, another Carmelite with a simpler way of speaking but not living, exclaiming "everything is grace."[70] John Paul's Theology of the Body is a concrete way of understanding that all was initially given as gift, that the original creation of man and woman was the realization of holiness, i.e., being "set apart" for each other, and through that, for God. The spousal meaning of the body is a language that captures that possibility and reality: we are created to live exclusively and fully for another.[71]

John Paul summarizes what he calls an "adequate anthropology"[72] at the end of the first chapter, which focuses on Genesis and the creation of Adam and Eve:

> Man appears in the visible world as the highest expression of the divine gift, because he bears within him the inner dimension of the gift. And with it he carries into the world his particular likeness to God, with which he transcends and also rules his "visibility" in the world, his bodiliness, his masculinity or femininity, his nakedness. A reflection of this likeness is also the primordial awareness of the spousal meaning of the body, pervaded by the mystery of original innocence.

> Thus, in this dimension, a primordial *sacrament* is constituted, understood as a *sign that* efficaciously *transmits in the visible world the invisible mystery hidden in God from eternity.* This is the mystery of Truth and Love, the mystery of divine life, in which man

> really participates. In the history of man, it is original innocence that begins this participation and is also the source of original happiness. The sacrament, as a visible sign, is constituted with man, inasmuch as he is a "body," through his "visible" masculinity and femininity. The body, in fact, and only the body, is capable of making visible what is invisible: the spiritual and the divine. It was created to transfer into the visible reality of the world the mystery hidden from eternity in God, and thus be a sign of it.
>
> …Original innocence, connected with the experience of the spousal meaning of the body, is holiness itself, which permits man to express himself deeply with his own body, precisely through the "sincere gift" of self (*Gaudium et Spes*, 24:3). Consciousness of the gift conditions in this case "the sacrament of the body": in his body as man or woman, man senses himself as a subject of holiness.[73]

The challenge, argues John Paul, is that we live in a fallen state, marked by the "hardness of our hearts": we do not see the other in the light of the mystery of creation, but through the much more limited and warping eyes of concupiscence.[74] We often experience our sexuality as a conflict, a landscape of traps marked by the boundary of shame, and are tempted to selfishness rather than self-gift. Sexual intercourse, in particular, can become an occasion to focus on what one can get—or disastrously worse, take—rather than what one can give to the vowed other.

But our present reality, although fallen, is not hopeless. The language of the body, imprinted at creation, remains. When we live according to the law of the gift, according to the revealed goodness of the call to marriage or to celibacy, we find "the gospel of the body." We find the gospel of the body because we find ourselves, as we were created in truth, to be a visible proclamation of our loving God. And the ensouled body is ultimately redeemed: the doctrine of the transformed (or resurrection) body firmly rejects the concept that the body is a structure of convenience to be shed in the fullness of union with God. We can live in the light and hope of that redemption, and should see and act through that lens. John Paul elaborates:

> Christ's words, which flow from the divine depth of

the mystery of redemption, allow us to discover and strengthen the bond that exists between the dignity of the human being (of the man or the woman) and the spousal meaning of his[/her] body. On the basis of this meaning, they allow us to understand and bring about the mature freedom of the gift, which expresses itself in one way in indissoluble marriage and in another by abstaining from marriage for the kingdom of God. On these different ways, Christ "fully reveals man to man himself and makes his supreme calling clear" (*Gaudium et Spes*, 22:1). This vocation is inscribed in man according to his whole psycho-physical composition precisely through the mystery of the redemption of the body.

Everything we have tried to do in the course of our meditations in order to understand the words of Christ has its definitive foundation in the mystery of the redemption of the body.[75]

The Theology of the Body audiences divide into two major sections: the first part, which establishes this "adequate anthropology," is a decidedly sacramental exploration of the human being, a theological anthropology. The second part, which focuses on marriage, is decidedly moral theology. This book, without ignoring the second part, will focus on extending the first. As Waldstein notes, John Paul does not present Jesus as a moralist, but as first and foremost the Redeemer.[76] To that end, we are going to focus on the ensouled body as a created, fallen, and redeemed sign of the radical, healing love of God, seen and experienced through the bodily experiences of childbirth, impairment, and death. The person's own body, and seeing the body of another, is a gift—and as such, an encounter. *Sight calls to response.*

The insights borne in this unusual set of texts are many. However, the interpretive key is this: the human body is best approached as a gift. We are created to receive that gift but also impelled to offer that gift to God, to "make a return of the good God has done for me." As John Paul II often cites from *Gaudium et Spes* 24, "[Man]...cannot fully find himself except through a sincere gift of himself." When this occurs, we see anew (or as John Paul often says, "re-read") the "pre-given language of self-giving and fruitfulness" that points to the nature of God.[77]

The "Language Of The Body" And Signs

The *thesis* of John Paul II's audiences is that the human body is a sign: "The body, in fact, and only the body, is capable of making visible what is invisible: the spiritual and the divine. It has been created to transfer into the visible reality of the world the mystery hidden from eternity in God, and thus to be a sign of it."[78] However, it is not the body as matter alone, but the human person as body and soul, a unified being without separation. When John Paul II uses the term body, he usually uses the term as a way of observing the experience of being bodily, and what that incarnate reality points us toward. As he says elsewhere: "The visibility of the Invisible belongs thus to the order of signs, and the 'sign' merely indicates the reality of the mystery, but does not 'unveil' it."[79]

Christopher Cullen helpfully proposes that Augustine's teaching on signs (offered as a means of interpreting Scripture as a God-given sign) can be used to understand better John Paul II's employment of the word "sign": not because John Paul uses Augustine's structure of sign, but because Augustine's clarity of teaching on this topic can be a lens to discern how John Paul is utilizing the term. A sign, according to Augustine, is "a thing, which besides the impression it conveys to the senses, also has the effect of making something else come to mind" and is a form of communication that requires the capacity for rational thought.[80] Particularly, Augustine makes a distinction between natural and intentional signs: natural signs "make something else known without the intention or desire of signifying," while intentional signs "are signs that the living give to communicate information of various sorts."[81] Then, within intentional signs Augustine makes a distinction between proper (literal) or transferred (metaphorical) signs. The ensouled human body, in John Paul, seems to function as both natural and intentional sign: it is the primordial language for communicating the call to union with God. Cullen extends this: "the sign is the human body; the signifier, God; the recipient, the human being. John Paul seems to speak of the signified in a two-fold way: as 'the nuptial meaning' of the body and as 'the communion of persons.'"[82] As primordial sign, its existence bears within it, through its creation, the intrinsic meaning of pointing to God.[83] Of course, usually this is called the creation to the image of God.[84]

That said, John Paul II does not make explicit use of Augustine in this work and does not define the term "sign" explicitly, either. In the second half of the audiences, his preferred term is the "language of the body," which can speak to the potential for a particular behavior or refer to the behavior itself.[85] And in *Evangelium Vitae* (written over a decade after these audiences were delivered), John Paul refers to human sexuality as "the sign, place, and language of love," [86] by which Daniel Jamros, S.J. suggests (with some seeming exasperation) that the Pope had not yet landed on a single term that "captures the essence of the body."[87]

However, I would call attention to Jamros' telling use of the word "captures." A sign that captures God is not a functional sign at all. The referent always overwhelms the sign, whether that sign is God-made or human-made. John Paul clarifies:

> We only wish to observe that man, in his present state of existence in the body, experiences many limits, sufferings, passions, weaknesses, and finally death itself, which relates his existence at the same time to another or different state or dimension....[88]

A sign, or language, at its root relates what is seen or heard to what is greater than itself—like a parable or a poem does. With the fundamental touchstone of the Theology of the Body literature being mystery, the last thing John Paul II wants to do is concretize that, and by that move, lose it. John Paul manages, like his beloved St. John of the Cross, to find God in all things, but he recognizes that to see that beauty rightly means to see with the help and light of God's revelation, which overcomes all fallen ways of sight.

When we talk about the sign of the ensouled body, I would encourage us to hold the phrasing lightly: indeed, as John Paul seems to do. His use of multiple terms (sign, language, place) underlines the fact that the term points to the referent, and the terms are insufficient in themselves. His use of language and sign is not foreign to the world of logic, but it does not primarily inhabit it. There is an analogical imagination being employed here, a contemplative attitude that strives to place phenomenological "seeing" at the service of revelation and human experience. This, I would hold as a Catholic theologian, is "living in reality." In the next three chapters, the book will explore what it means to be "living in reality" through the experiences of giving birth, living with impairment, and dying.

If this is indeed catechesis,[89] it is a catechesis that has more in common with the parable than with the question and answer format catechisms. The General Directory for Catechesis presents the idea that catechesis must be in concert with divine pedagogy—God's teaching work. The parables of Jesus, the poetry of inspired Scripture, the writing of spiritual doctors such as Teresa of Ávila and John of the Cross (who also expressed his deepest insights through poetry): these are all forms of catechesis. The catechesis is the offering of traditional doctrine; the theology is the seeking of understanding, pushing closer to that horizon which is God.

I also posit an unusual but possible understanding of catechesis as the teaching work of another pastoral venue. *Perhaps the Theology of the Body is presented as a catechetical spur to spiritual direction.* The Theology of the Body is certainly, as I have argued, informed by some of the greatest spiritual directors of the ages (John of the Cross and Teresa of Ávila), and in harmony with others (Ignatius of Loyola, and as we will see in a later section, Francis de Sales and Jean-Pierre de Caussade). And the effort to teach people to see, to re-read the language of the body in relationship to others, and to open themselves to a deeper communion with God is profoundly within that field of ministry. Teaching is not the primary purpose of spiritual direction, and in fact can twist spiritual direction awry if the meeting is conducted as a tutoring session. But helping another to recognize God's action in one's life is certainly a kind of teaching. It is the sort of teaching a field guide does on a hike, without a detailed map but following a star (the Christ). Even the formal *Catechism of the Catholic Church* devotes one of its four major sections to the lived doctrine of prayer. Given the deeply emotional reader reactions to the audiences, the almost *lectio divina* style of scriptural reading, and the repetitive meditative quality of some of the texts, I would say that we can consider the Theology of the Body audiences to be John Paul's gift of spiritual direction to the secular world. Encounter at your own risk.

Extending The Theology Of The Body: Giving Birth, Living Impaired, And Dying

John Paul's insights into the hermeneutic of the gift offer a way to re-read the language of the body, in the light of original blessing and redemption, that leads us to Christ. God's plan and its renewal by Christ are imprinted deeply within the bodily nature of the person as a pre-given language of self-giving and fruitfulness, as Waldstein neatly summarized. The everlasting mystery we are called to enter expresses itself in the visible order and, therefore, is first communicated in the sphere of the sign. Our challenge is to read those signs, given to us, to understand our calling in the midst of a fallen world. It is a challenge of confusion and blurred sight, rather than rational debate.

The challenge of the Theology of the Body for theologians is that to speak of the re-reading of the body is not to work in the realm of metaphor. Metaphor has an honored place in religious language, but to speak of the ensouled body as a pre-given language is more primal than metaphor: the creation of the human being, by a God who graciously communicates in every means possible His desire for union with humanity, is its own sign that points to God, a pre-verbal language that is seen most clearly through the lens of Christian revelation. As "first language," the sphere of the sign must be taken seriously as essential to understanding God's plan for the universe. John Paul reflects on this reality to evocative effect in the second half of the audiences: what it means to be man, woman, called to marriage, or not called to marriage. But as spiritual sign, there are other primal human experiences that benefit from the insights of the Theology of the Body: the act of giving birth, the reality of being limited (or impaired), and the process of physically dying. Indeed, if the ensouled body *is* natural and intentional sign, then these realities not only could have meaning, they *do* communicate meaning. The question is not "are they meaningful?", but *"what do they mean?"*

The text continues as a constructive project: what would it mean to interpret childbirth, impairment, and dying as primordial spiritual signs? How could the background and insights of the Theology of the Body literature help us to perceive the spiritual reality of these three experiences? My presumption is that these realities are not on the same level as John Paul's reflection on the sign (and sacrament) of marriage. But they are vocational realities, like marriage. They are calls to God. And I will argue that they were designed or shaped by God to draw us to God-self, through entering the depths of the law of the *ekstasis*. They express the reality of our call to receive and to give. As such, they are spiritual signs to ourselves and the world of God's continuous, enticing love.

These chapters are structured in a way similar but not slavish to John Paul II's manner of presentation: each chapter begins with an analysis of how the reality is culturally presented, then offers the rooting Scriptures (and attending doctrines) that help inform a Christian view of the experience, and finally attempts to "re-read" the experience as intended by God, with the help of phenomenological attitude and contemplative Carmelite insights. Each chapter answers the question: how is this event of the ensouled body created as a sign that points to God and draws one to union with God?

I begin with the most natural extension of the audiences' reflection on marriage: perceiving the spiritual sign of childbirth.

ENDNOTES

1. John Paul II, Homily of April 8, 1994, #6. http://www.vatican.va/holy_father/john_paul_ii/homilies/1994/documents/hf_jp-ii_hom_19940408_restauri-sistina_en.html.
2. See Susan Windley-Daoust, *The Redeemed Image of God: Embodied Relations to the Unknown Divine* (Lanham, MD: University Press of America, 2002), 88-90, and Maurice Merleau-Ponty, *Phenomenology of Perception*, trans. Colin Smith (London: Routledge, 1962), 374.
3. Theodore Prescott, "Edward Knippers: A Profile," *Image* 3 (1993), accessed October 9, 2012, http://imagejournal.org/page/journal/articles/issue-3/prescott-profile.
4. Ibid. The best-known exception is his painting "The Prize," which depicts Herodias's daughter presenting Herod with the severed head of John the Baptist. Herodias and Herod, arguably drunk and high, are clothed. Salome is naked, but her positioning manages to combine sexual availability and repulsiveness. John's sightless eyes are before her, closed.
5. Knippers, Edward, "Artist Statement by Edward Knippers," *Theology Forum*, blog, November 3, 2008, http://theologyforum.wordpress.com/2008/11/03/art-incarnation-%C2%BB-artist-statement-by-edward-knippers/.
6. Ibid. Emphasis added.
7. For example, smoke as reaching to God, see Ps 141:2: "Let my prayer be counted as incense before you." For smoke as presence: the smoke enveloping Mount

Sinai signaling the presence of God in Ex 19:18.

8. A more philosophical take on this phenomenon—art that bends toward Cubism, an attempt to catch reality the moment it is seen, fractured and without form—see Maurice Merleau-Ponty's seminal essay "Cezanne's Doubt" in *Sense and Non-Sense*, trans. Hubert L. Dreyfus and Patricia Allen Dreyfus (Evanston, IL: Northwestern University Press, 1964).

9. Edward Knippers, "On Art and Incarnation (5): On art and 'not playing in the shallows,'" *Theology Forum* (blog), Kent Eilers, November 7, 2008, http://theology-forum.wordpress.com/2008/11/07/edward-knippers-%C2%BB-art-incarnation-5-on-art-and-not-playing-in-the-shallows/.

10. John Paul II, *Letter to Artists*, 1999, #13, http://www.vatican.va/holy_father/john_paul_ii/letters/documents/hf_jp-ii_let_23041999_artists_en.html.

11. Timothy Gallagher, OMV, *Meditation and Contemplation* (New York: Crossroad, 2008), 17. Gallagher offers here a "standard" version of these instructions, which are repeated with slight variations throughout the exercises.

12. There is a reason that the Spiritual Exercises are meant to be done with a spiritual director or a person of Christian wisdom. If there is any question that the imaginative prayer is not the work of God, then someone immersed in the Christian tradition can advise on this. Obviously imaginative flights that take one to sinful realities or understandings of God that do not mesh with Christian revelation would not be considered helpful prayer, and the director can help you understand what happened there. But in my limited experience, and that of others, a misguided imaginative prayer really doesn't happen as often as you may guess within the framework of the *Spiritual Exercises.*

13. Another excellent example of Ignatius's visuality and highly honed appreciation for expression through the senses may be found in his love of the prayer called the *Anima Christi:* "Soul of Christ, sanctify me. Body of Christ, save me. Blood of Christ, inebriate me. Water from the side of Christ, wash me. Passion of Christ, strengthen me. O good Jesus, hear me. Within thy wounds hide me. Permit me not to be separated from thee. From the wicked foe defend me. At the hour of my death call me. And bid me come to thee. That with thy saints I may praise thee. For ever and ever." Ignatius did not write the prayer, but used it repeatedly as part of the Exercises.

14. Karol Wojtyla,[Evaluation of the Possibility of Constructing a Christian Ethics on the Assumptions of Max Scheler's System of Philosophy] *Über die Möglichkeit eine christliche Ethik in Anlehnung an Max Scheler zu schaffen*, ed. Juliusz Stroynowski, *Primat des Geistes: Philosophische Schriften* (Stuttgart-Degerloch: Seewald, 1980), 184, cited within *Man and Woman*, Introduction, 75.

15. Benedict XVI, *Jesus of Nazareth* (New York: Doubleday, 2007), 92. Pope Benedict continues in this passage on Mt 5:8, "Blessed are the pure in heart, for they shall see God." "Man's fundamental affective disposition actually depends on just this unity of body and soul, and on man's acceptance of being both body and spirit. This means he places the body under the discipline of the spirit, yet does not isolate intellect or will. Rather, he accepts himself as coming from God, and thereby also acknowledges and lives out the bodiliness of his existence as an enrichment for the spirit. The heart—the wholeness of man—must be pure, interiorly open and free, in order for man to be able to see God." Many thanks to Fr. Andrew Beerman for pointing me to this passage.

16. For a fuller treatment of this theme, see the recent dissertation of Thomas Petri,

O.P., "Locating a Spousal Meaning of the Body in the Summa Theologiae," dissertation (Washington, DC: Catholic University of America, 2010). The relationship between Thomism and John Paul II's personalism is increasingly being paid real attention. Janet Smith presented a paper at the USCCB's conference, "Intellectual Tasks of the New Evangelization" (September 15-17, 2011), detailing some of the differences and similarities between the philosophical branches. Both she and Petri argue that there is a complementarity in the philosophies, although different foci and obviously different language. Petri goes so far to say that the Theology of the Body material corrects through attention and embellishment certain weaknesses in Thomism. While I am happy to allow them there is a complementarity, I will be focusing on advancing the too-unrecognized phenomenological and personalist influences. Catholics tend to see Thomism everywhere; we don't see as often the influence of contemporary philosophies. John Paul II also complicates the matter a bit by using phenomenological insights, but not citing them to a particular philosopher. That is, he *does* phenomenological work within a theological context, rather than study it within the Theology of the Body literature.

17. For more, see the Rev. Dr. Thomas McGovern, "The Christian Anthropology of John Paul II: An Overview," *Josephinum Journal of Theology* 8(1): 132-147 (Winter-Spring 2001), 134.

18. In general, I would argue that the personalist movement grew out of the phenomenological impulse; they are sibling philosophical movements and share some similarities in theme and content. Both were reactions to the increasingly mechanistic view of the world offered by the Industrial Revolution, as well as philosophical pragmatism.

19. "An Evaluation of the Possibility of Constructing a Christian Ethics on the Basis of the System of Max Scheler" translation of Karol Wojtyła, *Ocena możliwości zbudowania etyki chrześcijańskiej przy założeniach systemu Maksa Schelera.* (Lublin: Tow. Naukowe Katolickiego Uniw. Lubelskiego, 1959).

20. Max Scheler, "Phenomenology and the Theory of Cognition," trans. David Lachterman, *Selected Philosophical Essays* (Evanston: Northwestern University Press, 1973), 137.

21. Ibid., 136-7.

22. Ibid., 137.

23. Max Scheler, "The Essence of Philosophy and the Moral Preconditions of Philosophical Knowledge" trans. Bernard Noble *On the Eternal in Man* (New York: Harper & Brothers, 1960), 74.

24. If philosophy is a quest for essences, Scheler's contribution is that seeing in love reveals more than reason or logic, and only when reason and logic are driven by love is philosophical knowledge of essences gained. Scheler's insights seem to offer phenomenological reflection as an art more than a science.

25. For a brief overview (in Spanish), see Juan Luis Lorda, *Antropología Del Concilio Vaticano Segundo a Juan Pablo II* (Madrid: Palabra, 1996), 43-5.

26. Windley-Daoust, *The Redeemed Image of God*, 74.

27. Gabriel Marcel, *Being and Having: An Existentialist Diary*, trans. James Collins (New York: Harper and Row, 1965), 117.

28. McCown, Joseph, *Availability: Gabriel Marcel and the Phenomenology of Human Openness* (Missoula, MT: Scholars Press, 1978), 7.

29. Ibid., 10-11.

30. I cover *disponibilité* in greater detail in *The Redeemed Image of God*, 102-7, and

McCown's *Availability* is an excellent resource on Marcel's use of the term.

31. Both Scheler and Marcel expand on this insight, Scheler through defining hatred as a closing of the person to the value-givenness of the other (see his *Formalism in Ethics and Non-Formal Ethics of Values*, trans. Manfred Frings and Roger Funk [Evanston: Northwestern University Press, 1973], 261ff), and Marcel through *via negativa* metaphors that help define this particular posture of availability: encumbrance and crispation (see Windley-Daoust, 104).

32. Marcel, *Being and Having*.

33. Pope John Paul II, *Love and Responsibility*, trans. H.T. Willetts, revised ed. (New York: Farrar, Strauss and Giroux, 1981).

34. Although Marcel is not mentioned explicitly, the theme is certainly present. See *Evangelium Vitae* #22-23, *Laborem Exercens* #12-13, *Centesimus Annus* #36.

35. John Paul II, *Crossing the Threshold of Hope* (London: J. Cape, 1994), 35-6.

36. *Man and Woman*, 14.4.

37. Arguably, the most distinctive teaching is John Paul's proposal that the human being becomes an image of God "not so much in the moment of solitude as in the moment of communion" (*Man and Woman* 9.3).

38. *Man and Woman*, 3.4.

39. *Man and Woman*, 75, translating and quoting John Paul II, *Primat des Geistes: philosophische Schriften*, Juliusz Stroynowski, ed. (Stuttgart-Degerloch: Seewald, 1980), 196.

40. Luke 10:39.

41. Philosophically, Emmanuel Levinas is the one who introduces the power of the gaze of the Other. His intersubjectivity argues that gaze of the Other is, in fact, a call. His philosophy of "the Face" owes much to his Jewish roots, and John Paul II cites him as an important source of his theology. See *Crossing the Threshold of Hope*, 35-6.

42. Not all these references to the gaze are positive, but they all refer to a concentrated manner of seeing the depth of the other: 2 Kgs 8:11, Ps 11:4, Ps 27:4, Ps 39:13, Prv 4:25, Song 1:6, Is 47:13, Mi 4:11, 2 Cor 3:7, Rv 11:9.

43. Patricia Bryne, SSC, "The Gift of Presence: The Elusive Core of the Spiritual Direction Relationship," *East Asian Pastoral Review* 38, no. 1 (2001): 5-56.

44. Ibid.

45. Gabriel Marcel, *Homo Viator* (New York: Harper and Row, 1962), 50.

46. Ralph Harper, *On Presence* (London: SCM Press, 1991), 4.

47. William Barry, S.J. and William Connolly, S.J. *The Practice of Spiritual Direction* (New York: HarperOne, 2009), 48.

48. John Paul II mentioned this affiliation in a letter to Cardinal Ballestrero, OCD, dated September 14, 1981, and was known to wear the mark of the Carmelite order, a brown scapular, his entire life. Secular Carmelites take vows, as their (often cloistered) nuns, brothers, and priests do. It is a vocation dedicated to a life of holiness within the family of the Carmelites but bearing an active apostolate to the secular world.

49. The dissertation was published in English under the title *Faith According to Saint John of the Cross* (San Francisco: Ignatius Press, 1981).

50. *Man and Woman*, Waldstein introduction, 81.

51. From the *Catechism of the Catholic Church* #2567: "God calls man first. Man may forget his Creator or hide far from his face; he may run after idols or accuse the deity of having abandoned him; yet the living and true God tirelessly calls each

person to that mysterious encounter known as prayer. In prayer, the faithful God's initiative of love always comes first; our own first step is always a response. As God gradually reveals himself and reveals man to himself, prayer appears as a reciprocal call, a covenant drama. Through words and actions, this drama engages the heart. It unfolds throughout the whole history of salvation."

52. There is some debate as to whether John of the Cross and Teresa of Ávila held that the life of prayer and holiness they describe is universal—that is, meant for everyone. One of John Paul's professors, Reginald Garrigou-LaGrange, O.P., held that the Carmelite doctors did mean to express a universal call to holiness regardless of state of life, and John Paul himself upholds the clear teaching of the Second Vatican Council that there is indeed a universal call to holiness (see Lumen Gentium, Ch. 5).

53. 1 Cor 10:31.

54. There is some mystery as to whether Ignatius's writings directly influenced Teresa's: she does not quote them, but she does not quote many writings at all beyond Scripture. Ignatius died approximately 30 years before Teresa, and there was no personal contact. We do know that the Jesuit St. Francis Borgia encouraged Teresa in her contemplative prayer in 1555. Whether he directed her through any elements of the *Spiritual Exercises* (composed 1522-24) is not known.

55. This rendition comes from David Fleming's modern reading of *The Spiritual Exercises, Draw Me Into Your Friendship: A Literal Translation and Modern Reading of The Spiritual Exercises* (St. Louis, MO: Institute of Jesuit Sources, 1996), 27.

56. *Man and Woman* 16:1.

57. The "law of the gift" is George Weigel's phrase from *Witness to Hope* (New York: HarperCollins, 1999), 136; the "law of ekstasis" is Wojtyla's term in *Love and Responsibility*, 126, and the "hermeneutic of the gift" is from the audiences themselves, *Man and Woman*, 13:2, 16:1.

58. Jas 1:17 "Every generous act of giving, with every perfect gift, is from above, coming down from the Father of lights, with whom there is no variation or shadow due to change." James's letter is also telling in the verse that precedes this one, on temptation coming from our own desires.

59. This is also, clearly, not process theology, which affirms the absolute love of God but not the omnipotence. Process theology tends to speak of divine purpose rather than will. See John Cobb and David Griffin, *Process Theology: An Introductory Exposition* (Philadelphia: Westminster Press, 1976).

60. 2 Cor 5:14.

61. In Teresa of Ávila's *Interior Castle*, this would occur in the sixth mansion.

62. Teresa of Ávila, in defining spiritual marriage, speaks of it being distinctively different from earthly marriage: "...corporeal union is quite another thing and the spiritual joys and consolations given by the Lord are a thousand leagues removed from those experienced in marriage." *Interior Castle* 5.4.

63. The most popular presentation of the audiences in English has been Christopher West's *Theology of the Body for Beginners*, revised edition (West Chester, PA: Ascension Press, 2009). Some of the more meaty popular sources include: West's *Theology of the Body Explained: A Commentary on John Paul II's "Gospel of the Body"* (Boston: Pauline Books and Media, 2003); Carl Anderson's *Called to Love: Approaching John Paul II's Theology of the Body* (New York: Doubleday, 2009); J. Brian Bransfield's *The Human Person According to John Paul II* (Boston: Pauline Books and Media, 2010); and as helpful preparatory work to under-

standing the audiences, Edward P. Sri's *Men, Women, and the Mystery of Love: Practical Insights from John Paul II's Love and Responsibility* (Cincinnati: St. Anthony Messenger Press, 2007). Select academic sources include: Mary Shivanandan, *Crossing the Threshold of Love: A New Vision of Marriage* (Washington, DC: Catholic University of America Press, 1999), and Michael Waldstein's monograph-length introduction of the most recent English translation of the audiences, *Man and Woman He Created Them: A Theology of the Body*. There are many more very helpful academic treatments of John Paul II's anthropology in general, which include his Theology of the Body: Rocco Buttiglione's *Karol Wojtyla, The Thought of the Man Who Became Pope John Paul II*, trans. Paolo Guietti and Francesca Murphy (Grand Rapids, MI: Wm. B. Eerdmans Publishing Co., 1997), and Juan Luis Lorda, *Antropología del Concilio Vaticano Segundo a Juan Pablo II* (Madríd: Palabra, 1996). The best short treatment of John Paul II's anthropology, including the Theology of the Body, that I have encountered is the Rev. Dr. Thomas McGovern's "The Christian Anthropology of John Paul II: An Overview," *Josephinum Journal of Theology* 8, no. 1 (Winter-Spring 2001): 132-147.

64. *Man and Woman*, Introduction, 105.
65. *Man and Woman*, 13.2.
66. "While Genesis expresses this value in a purely theological (and indirectly metaphysical) form, Genesis 2, by contrast, *reveals, so to speak, the first circle of experience lived by man as a value.*" *Man and Woman*, 9.1.
67. This phrase comes from Vatican II's *Gaudium et Spes* 12: "But God did not create man as a solitary, for from the beginning "Man and Woman he created them" (Gen. 1:27). Their companionship produces the primary form of interpersonal communion [*communio personarum*]."
68. *Man and Woman*, 13.1.
69. Ibid. Other English translations, and subsequent interpreters, substitute the word "nuptial" for "spousal." While nuptial certainly has a greater poetic sensibility, the word in Italian is *sponsale*, and spousal is indeed the more accurate translation.
70. Thérèse de Lisieux, *St. Thérèse of Lisieux, Her Last Conversations*, trans. John Clarke (Washington: Institute of Carmelite Studies, 1977), 57.
71. There has been some debate in recent years on how the Theology of the Body should be presented. Some, such as Bishop Jean Laffitte, have argued that the catechesis must be presented within the full mystery of God's love for humanity, from creation to the Eschaton, in order to avoid an undue focus on the sexuality. He also argues, rightly, that John Paul II is not talking about some mystic sexuality (that all sexual contact brings us to God) but that "sexuality has a mystical perspective and dimension." The gift of sexuality is part of the gift of the sacrament of marriage, and there is a dimension of the mystery of God within it. See "Interview With Bishop Jean Laffitte On Theology of Human Love," *Catholic News Agency,* accessed October 11, 2012, http://www.catholicnewsagency.com/document.php?n=1057.
72. An "adequate anthropology"—not his most helpful terminology—is defined as "an understanding and interpretation of man in what is essentially human." It relies on "essentially 'human' experience." Because of this, it is neither defined by supernatural revelation per se, nor seen in a purely biological fashion. In short, his adequate anthropology is an anthropology informed by a phenomenology. See n. 23 in *Man and Woman*, 13:2.
73. *Man and Woman*, 19:3-5.

74. John Paul understands concupiscence as a corrupt desire that objectifies and uses the other for selfish ends. In particular, sexual concupiscence consists in the detachment of desire from the spousal meaning of the body. See audiences 39-41.

75. *Man and Woman*, 86.8.

76. *Man and Woman*, Waldstein introduction, 127.

77. Ibid.

78. *Man and Woman*, 19.4

79. *Man and Woman*, 97.5.

80. Augustine, *De Doctrina Christiana*, 2,1.1. He continues on natural signs in 2, 1.2: "Now some signs are natural, others conventional. Natural signs are those which, apart from any intention or desire of using them as signs, do yet lead to the knowledge of something else, as, for example, smoke when it indicates fire. For it is not from any intention of making it a sign that it is so, but through attention to experience we come to know that fire is beneath, even when nothing but smoke can be seen. And the footprint of an animal passing by belongs to this class of signs. And the countenance of an angry or sorrowful man indicates the feeling in his mind, independently of his will: and in the same way every other emotion of the mind is betrayed by the tell-tale countenance, even though we do nothing with the intention of making it known." Conventional, or intentional, signs are addressed in the rest of book 2: "Conventional signs, on the other hand, are those which living beings mutually exchange for the purpose of showing, as well as they can, the feelings of their minds, or their perceptions, or their thoughts. Nor is there any reason for giving a sign except the desire of drawing forth and conveying into another's mind what the giver of the sign has in his own mind." (2,2.1) Most of the book is dedicated to understanding the role of sign in Scripture. Source: James Shaw, trans. First series, vol. 2., *Nicene and Post-Nicene Fathers*, ed. Philip Schaff (Buffalo, NY: Christian Literature Publishing Co., 1887). Revised and edited for New Advent by Kevin Knight. http://www.newadvent.org/fathers/1202.htm.

81. Christopher Cullen, S.J., "Between God and Nothingness: Matter in John Paul II's Theology of the Body," in *Pope John Paul II on the Body: Human, Eucharistic, Ecclesial: Festschrift Avery Cardinal Dulles, S.J.* John M. McDermott, S.J. and John Gavin, S.J., eds. (Philadelphia: Saint Joseph's University Press, 2007), 71.

82. Ibid., 72.

83. Cullen argues that John Paul II's "body language" functions as intentional sign. Daniel Jamros, S.J., also argues for natural sign in "Sign, Subject, and Style: A Response to Fr. Cullen" in *Pope John Paul II on the Body*, 82. There is an argument for both, but I would agree that the point of the Theology of the Body is that God created the human being, intentionally, as sign.

84. Although, just to make it challenging, John Paul does refer to the body as the sign of the image of God. Sign and image are not identical terms. Jamros, 84.

85. Jamros, 83.

86. *Evangelium Vitae*, #23.

87. Jamros, 83.

88. *Man and Woman*, 3.4, n.8

89. John Grabowski, in the foreword to the original compilation of the audiences, cautions the reader that encyclicals are higher forms of catechesis than audiences. I would agree, while noting that John Paul II's encyclicals, including his multiple Catholic social teaching encyclicals, are in harmony with the theology of the au-

diences. The ambiguity of the level of authority of the audiences gives us (and John Paul II, I suspect) some room to explore with interpretation within Christian anthropology and doctrine. See John Paul II, *The Theology of the Body: Human Love in the Divine Plan* (Boston, MA: Pauline Books & Media, 1997), 20.

CHAPTER 2
The Gift of the Birthing Body

The Vocation To Motherhood

 KEY CONCEPTS

> **This chapter** on childbirth begins with a cultural critique of the current medical practices in giving birth, which many say are unnecessarily medicalized and divorced from any positive (never mind spiritual) associations. A phenomenology of natural childbirth (a birth with few medical interventions) yields a more powerful experience of a Theology of the Body "language of self-giving and fruitfulness." The chapter faces the experience of pain, and how it is interpreted (both in the Christian tradition and in human experience), but it also faces the experiences of being overcome, yielding, availability to God, self-abjection, hospitality, and tenderness. This chapter looks at those experiences with a contemplative attitude and insights from the Theology of the Body: all the experiences, in different ways, signal the human being's call to give oneself in love. In an important way, we are called to some form of spiritual motherhood or fatherhood, and this bodily experience gives witness to that.

We know that the whole creation has been groaning in labor pains until now; and not only the creation, but we ourselves, who have the first fruits of the Spirit, groan inwardly while we wait for adoption, the redemption of our bodies. [...]

Likewise the Spirit helps us in our weakness; for we do not know how to pray as we ought, but that very Spirit intercedes with sighs too deep for words. And God, who searches the heart, knows what is the mind of the Spirit, because the Spirit intercedes for the saints according to the will of God. —Romans 8:22-23, 26-27

> *...[H]e said to me, "My grace is sufficient for you, for power is made perfect in weakness." So, I will boast all the more gladly of my weaknesses, so that the power of Christ may dwell in me.* —2 Corinthians 12:9

> *There is no fear in love, but perfect love casts out fear; for fear has to do with punishment, and whoever fears has not reached perfection in love.* —1 John 4:18

All of the Theology of the Body literature explores the creation of the human body as a sign that points to union with God. We are encouraged to live in *disponibilité*, to interpret what we see through the hermeneutic of the gift. The natural extension of the communion of persons, presented by John Paul II as part of the creation to the *imago Dei*, is the fruitfulness of the marital union, which is shown in a very concrete way through the conception and birth of a child.

In this chapter, we are exploring childbirth as a gift of God that points to God. As John Paul encouraged, in his use of phenomenology, we are making use of human experience[1] to shed light on a scriptural reading and the teaching of the Church: that we are called for union, and that love is fruitful. Of course, the child is a gift of God to the parents and the world. But we will focus on the remarkable *act* of giving birth. Birth, I will argue, was given to us as a way to see how all souls, pregnant with the Holy Spirit, are transformed by cooperating with the Spirit, letting God "make all things new." Some experience and see this act directly, and others indirectly, but it is a gifted call to all. All calls demand response, and giving birth is both a call from and a response to the Holy Spirit.

One aspect of this reflection is that there is a spiritual reality at work in birth. This should be obvious, given we are speaking of the God-given work of an ensouled body. But, too often, this spiritual reality is not obvious or even acknowledged. The other aspect of this reflection is that the process of giving birth—that is, a birth that is typical and unhindered by impairment or illness—parallels the process of spiritual yielding and cooperation with God. It is an ideal ground for learning receptivity and activity. I would go so far to say that the process is given to women by God as a way for both women and men to be able to recognize how to respond to the Holy Spirit.

A large part of the gift of birth is how it helps us define motherhood as a call. God does not call all mothers through birth—adopting is no less a call to motherhood—but birth is a concrete example of how God works through ensouled bodies to give sign to what it means to be a mother, and for attending fathers, important formation on what it means to be a father as well. These are both particular vocations, and rooted in the universal vocation to holiness. It is the flowering of the first *communio personarum* John Paul addresses in his reflection on the creation of Adam and Eve. To reflect upon the sign of birth, and the call to motherhood and fatherhood, helps us understand what it means to be "the Family of God," as African Catholics are striving to name the Church.[2] The Theology of the Body—when extended—ultimately reflects on what it means to be placed into core community, in immediate and Church families.

> A father to the fatherless, a defender of widows,
> is God in his holy dwelling.
> God sets the lonely in families,
> he leads out the prisoners with singing....[3]

Living In Reality? Childbirth Seen As Disease

Before "re-reading" the natural sign of birth, we need a reading of the signs of the times: how childbirth is presented through predominant medical practices of the West. What is clear is that we have become more likely to name childbirth as disease—as Marcel would say, a problem to be fixed—rather than part of the normal, but very real, mystery of life.

To discuss childbirth is to discuss a lived reality where angels indeed may fear to tread. On the one hand, from time immemorial, women have regaled women on the details of giving birth, sharing everything from well-polished war stories to halting, hesitating stories of wonder and beauty. On the other hand, since the advent of moving the act of giving birth into the supposedly more sure hands of doctors and hospitals, women have had less to share: birth was taken out of their hands, a medical event managed by the advent of pain relievers and other gadgets. Most conversations around a pregnant woman's impending birth revolve around choosing drug options and whether she will choose an elective Cesarean section, and many memories involve just how bad the pain was before consenting to an epidural. In the meantime, hospitalized childbirth does not seem to improve infant or maternal mortality rates in itself. And the United States, according to a 2010 report, had a Cesarean section rate of 32 percent[4]—a 53 percent rise from 1996 to 2007, and as many acknowledge, may be far greater than any discernable high risk would necessitate.

Although medical intervention can indeed be a lifesaver, and pain relief in itself (natural or medical) can be a concrete help, there are real losses involved with the evaporation of shared natural birth stories. My point in this section is to explain briefly how childbirth in America got to this place, and "read" what these likely well-intentioned medical practices spiritually communicate to mothers and fathers.[5]

A Short History Of Childbirth In America

Prior to childbirth becoming a medical event, women were usually attended by lay midwives, that is, women who were experienced in helping other women give birth. They had no medical degrees, simply experience and willingness to help, and people asked for their help based on word-of-mouth recommendations. Sometimes other family members were involved in helping a woman give birth, especially if a midwife was not available. With the advent of public sanatoriums in the 19th century, the increasing faith in the abilities of medical professionals and the superiority of modern medicine, and the promise of pain relief, women began to give birth in hospitals.

The initial outcome of this move to hospitalized childbirth was not good. Increasing numbers of women and children died of "childbed fever," or puerperal sepsis. The reasons for childbed fever were not well understood in the second half of the 1800s or even the early 1900s. Although doctors were aware that housing numerous sick people with contagious diseases in the same institution was a recipe for disaster, sanitation methods were slow to be seen as a preventive cure to hospital-borne diseases. Childbed fever was a bacterial infection that was spread through one doctor doing cervical checks for many women, to see if a woman was fully dilated and ready to push. Doctors, moving from a sick patient to a patient giving birth, did not realize that going from woman to woman to "just check" without washing hands thoroughly could cause her death. Even 60 years after discovering that cleaned hands, or newly created rubber gloves, would diminish the spread of bacteria, many doctors resisted the clean-hands drill, and childbed fever still accounted for 40 percent of maternal deaths in many American and European hospitals.[6] Treatment (and a lot of treatment for childbirth in this era is more than a bit chilling) involved giving the woman a vaginal wash of weak carbolic acid, which likely just pushed the infection into the uterus and hastened her death.[7] Rather than give society pause—hospitals were supposed to make childbirth safer, and the opposite seemed to be happening[8]—the number of maternal deaths in hospitals only seemed to underline the reason women went to hospitals: childbirth is indeed dangerous.

Many of the first women to go through hospital births were young late-1800s immigrants, separated from most family and social structures, poor, and willing to accept the way it was done in their new country. In rural areas and on the frontier, midwives were slower to yield ground. But being lay midwives, they did not have access to the era's siren call for all people in pain—chloroform. Also women on the frontier were less likely to have the support of mothers and sisters to help them through this event. Doctors, despite the costs, became more and more the desired go-to person for a woman in labor.[9]

However, most doctors failed to use the hard-won knowledge particular to midwives—that is, what normal birth looks like. This gap in knowledge led many doctors to their *de facto* mode of operation: pain indicates something is wrong. Something wrong is disease, not health. And you attack a disease. In the worst hospitals, every birth began to look like, and be treated as, a medical emergency rather than a natural act of life. In addition, hospitals became aware that sanitary conditions in a hospital are essential to good health. While this realization made "childbed fever" less common and decreased the maternal death rate dramatically, the way sanitation was applied also led to a variety of innovations and interventions that made giving birth considerably more difficult for women. First, husbands and supporting family were denied entry: they were introducing too many germs. Birthing women were positioned in "easy access" to the baby for the hands-dripping-wet-but-newly-cleaned doctor—lying flat on their back, feet in stirrups. Never mind that this position, other than putting a woman upside down on her head, is the worst possible position for birth, as well as the most painful position for labor—the woman doesn't have the advantages of gravity or movement on her side. The position also slows down labor precipitously. But the flat on back position allowed other possibilities—quick drug administration (depending on the era, a medical cocktail called "twilight sleep," ether, or an epidural), a quick hook up to an IV for fluids or Pitocin[10], convenient fetal monitoring. When the pushing stage occurred, the doctor could easily do an episiotomy[11] to hasten birth (and sometimes did without consent). Indeed, if a woman needed an emergency C-section, she is set up and ready to roll (literally—on the bed, down the hall to the ER). All these innovations are potential advantages if the birth is a medical emergency, but highly problematic if it is not.

It would not be fair to lay all criticisms at the doctors' feet, however. More than anything, birth stories of the first half of the 20th century indicate obstetricians used their best judgment as people trained to treat disease suddenly finding themselves in a delivery room. Protocol typically used in surgery was used in childbirth, with mixed results. And most importantly, women *flocked* to the hospitals for the pain relief. Women were not only asking for doctors, they were lining up and even going into debt to afford the pain relief promised in hospital births.

Regardless, a number of people in the 1950s and '60s began to question some of the childbirth procedures that were becoming standard practice. When stories of women in "twilight sleep" emerged (such as needing to be strapped in a bed wearing a football helmet to prevent self-injury while giving birth, the unnerving post-op reality of not being able to remember anything about the birth, the increasing rate of children born with depressed nervous system reactions[12]) people began to suggest that perhaps natural childbirth was a reality whose time had come—or, really, whose time had returned.

A number of unmedicated childbirth responses arose at the same time: the Lamaze method of childbirth, which historically has focused on breathing and visualization techniques to distract oneself from pain, and The Bradley Method® of husband-coached childbirth, which focuses on understanding the process and working with your muscles through relaxation. Obstetrician Grantly Dick-Read's *Childbirth Without Fear*[13] was published, which argued neurologically that women who went into the birth process unafraid had considerably less pain. The Leboyer method of welcoming a newborn—which corrected common medical practices after birth that cause the newborn pain and separation from the mother—gained in popularity.[14] And Michel Odent, a surgeon in France, pioneered the practice of water birth in the Western world, where the mother takes advantage of the weight-distributing properties of water immersion to labor with less pain.[15] Additionally, a new medical profession, the certified nurse-midwife, increased in presence and popularity, as well as the re-creation of "doulas"—women trained to help a woman labor, who work outside of the hospital establishment but alongside the laboring mother. Some hospitals began to establish stand-alone birth centers—less technology, more home-style comforts, with the option of being moved to the hospital if there are complications.

Many things changed, but not all for the better: despite the growing awareness that medical interventions sometimes created more problems than they solved, doctors were reluctant *not* to use every tool in the medical bag, if for no other reason than the advent of the litigious society and the harsh (and real) possibility of being sued for millions of dollars.[16] And of course, they *want* to address concrete, unquestioned problems. The difficulty is discerning between what is indeed a medical problem, and what falls within the boundaries of typical. The baby's heartbeat dipped during a contraction, but then rose to normal again. Typical or not? The mother's labor is progressing fairly steadily, but much more slowly than the average of one centimeter per hour. Typical or not?

A Typical Pregnancy/Childbirth Experience Today[17]

A typical gestation and childbirth in the United States looks like this: when you are pregnant, you see the doctor or midwife at eight weeks. You will be interviewed about your family genetic history and your situation in life, along with questions like: "Is this a wanted pregnancy?" You will likely be asked this apart from your husband, who, you never know, may be abusing you, and the nurse wants an honest answer. You may be offered a CVS (chorionic villus sampling) test, if you have a family history of a genetic disease, or perhaps an amniocentesis to screen for birth defects. Medical staff may push the amnio option hard if you are over age 35, because the possibility of child defects increases with maternal age. You meet with your providers monthly, then every other week, and they check your glucose level and the baby's heartbeat. There may be an ultrasound to see how the baby is developing and to determine when the baby is due.

Before the due date arrives, you will have made a decision, based on a variety of factors, as to whether to get a C-section or whether you will attempt a vaginal birth. You will likely have created a birth plan—procedures and methods you want to do in the hospital, who will be present, etc. You will have decided whether you will have labor induced or not.

After laboring at home for hours (unless you are induced), you will go to the hospital when the contractions are four minutes or less apart, each lasting one minute, for at least one hour's duration (hence, the prenatal mantra "4-1-1"). Once at the hospital, things can go in many different directions, but the following scenario for a normal hospitalized birth is typical: you will be checked for progress, and if you are far enough along, you will be offered an epidural. If you accept that, you will be laboring in bed, with a fetal monitor strapped to you, and your baby's heartbeat seen on a screen nearby. You'll be relatively sensation-free from the lower back down, passing time with your husband. You may get an IV drip of Pitocin to "move labor along." When you get to the pushing stage, you will be urged to push in tandem with your contractions, which can be tricky. (The epidural may be turned off at this point to help you feel the urge to push). Possibly there will be an episiotomy if the pushing stage seems long or there is fetal monitor feedback that the baby could be in distress. Finally, you give birth! You are relieved and excited. You will be allowed to hold the baby for a while, unless the baby is in medical trouble. The cord will be cut (maybe by your husband), and you will deliver the placenta. The baby will be washed and swaddled, perhaps receive a vitamin K shot, and you will get to hold him, perhaps nurse him, as you are stitched up.

For many women, this scenario is unbelievable bliss. A (likely) healthy baby, in a reasonable amount of time, *and* a relatively pain-free delivery? Compare this to the delirious young woman who died of childbed fever in the typical warehouse hospital of the 1880s—clearly many things have improved. And women in the United States have voted with their feet on this: most women request medical help, especially the epidural, to give birth. The C-section rate in the United States has risen steadily for years, and there are doctors who seriously suggest that *all* births should be C-sections.[18] Labor and delivery wards are remarkably quiet places these days, people note: most women are plugged in, hooked up, and chatting comfortably throughout delivery.

The controversy around the appropriate practice of childbirth can be ferocious, and my intention is not to wade into those agitated waters, or question people's choices, especially those made under duress. Clearly there are circumstances where the interventions are needed to assure a safe and healthy childbirth, although it also seems clear the interventions are not needed nearly as often as they are performed.[19] But there are a number of challenges inherent in the medical *status quo* regarding childbirth. First, clearly childbirth has been treated as a problem: both the pain of it, and the unknown quality of it. Atul Gawande, an associate professor at Harvard Medical School, addresses the broad scope of challenges with some clarity when he says that labor and delivery wards in hospitals have succumbed to the industrial revolution of childbirth: full of functions, machines, probable outcomes, statistical analysis, and reliability procedures. What is lost, he notes with a bit of sadness but no real indignation, is the long tradition of helping others give birth as a craft, a gift nurtured and offered from generation to generation.[20] What bothers many is the reality that with the "industry" of birth, the dignity of the mother, child, and process can easily be misplaced. The spiritual sign is ignored. Everyone wants a healthy child and mother—but the tragedy of trying to secure these goods through some of the current practices is that we become blind to perceiving childbirth as a foundational vocational experience where the ensouled body, when properly "seen," leads us to union with God.

A Phenomenology Of Natural Childbirth

John Paul II used phenomenological insights to sketch an anthropology that illumines the spousal meaning of the body: a communion of persons that points and leads to union with God. The body and its activities reveal the soul. When the ensouled body acts in harmony with God's will, the body and its activities reflect the God in whose image he or she is made. If childbirth is given to us as a spiritual sign, an extension of that spousal meaning, then a phenomenological analysis particular to giving birth should bear its own fruit. To begin with this exploration, I want to focus on the method of natural childbirth called "The Bradley Method®," called such after obstetrician Robert Bradley. Convinced that women can and should give birth with a minimal amount of medical intervention and pain, he devised a method of giving birth that relies on knowledge of how the body works, learning to work effectively with your muscles, relying on the paradoxical strength of relaxation, and recognizing external and internal signs that make clear where a woman is in the labor process. In short, he presents the female body as a remarkably created miracle, designed to give birth with work, receptivity, encouragement, and knowledge. I ask your indulgence as I go into the process in some detail, because some physical particulars will be important to the "spiritual seeing" discussed later and are typically unknown unless you have been present at a natural childbirth. If there is anything to the hypothesis that John Paul's Theology of the Body serves to catch the people of our age through parabolic language, we need the familiarity with the material of childbirth for this extension of the parable.

Physical And Emotional Signs Of Giving Birth

First Stage Of Labor

A medical observation of a typical Bradley birth looks like this: when the first stage of labor—the gradual opening of the woman's cervix to approximately 10 centimeters in diameter—begins, the uterus contracts (or flexes) like the very large muscle that it is. The uterus draws the cervix in, gradually stretching the cervical opening like a turtleneck sweater over the baby's head (assuming this a typical presentation, not breech). The uterine muscle contracts and retracts, a bit more with each flex, until the cervix is completely dilated. The contractions last about 30 seconds to one minute or a bit more, and then (almost always) the laboring woman gets a two to five minute rest before the next contraction.

Physically, a contraction is observed as a rising and receding wave of sensation,[21] a kind of "hardening" of the muscle from the outside, which starts off slowly and rises to a peak, and then recedes. The contractions are mild at the beginning of the first stage. At the end of the first stage, the contractions get increasingly intense, and many women say there is pain involved in the contracting.

The Bradley Method® teaches those attending a childbirth to be aware of emotional stages as well. The emotional marker for the first part of the first stage is usually happiness and excitement: the woman is glad that "today's the day" and usually able to do whatever else she was doing for a while. The latter part of the first stage is marked by the woman getting somewhat introspective, drawing into herself and getting more serious about working with the contractions. The length of this stage varies widely, making a reading of the signs particularly important.

Transition

The most difficult part of a normal childbirth is the movement from first to second stage, called transition. The cervix is usually at eight centimeters or more, and the contractions may feel (or more rarely, truly be) on top of each other with no "break" in between contractions. The woman's uterus also may be trying to push the baby out, so there are competing muscle movements: contracting and retracting to open the cervix, and pushing from the "top" of the uterus down.

Physically, this will likely be felt in a way most women call painful, often (although not always) incredibly painful. It is always felt as very intense, because the uterine muscle is working at maximum capacity, putting in an extra dose of drive before reaching the finish line of full dilation. The cushion of water between baby and cervix often breaks at this point, if it has not already. This both creates an increase in direct pressure of the baby's head on the cervix—the cushion of water, distributing the pressure, is gone—and is usually felt as a big jump in intensity and, often, pain. Sometimes, although not always, there are signs of neurological reaction to sudden pain—trembling, hot and cold flashes, nausea and vomiting. Regardless, nearly all birthing women are glad it is a very short stage, lasting from 10 to 30 minutes.

The emotional signpost for transition from first stage to second stage is self-doubt. Sometimes the mother will say "I'm not able to do this." Or perhaps a doula is telling her that she's doing great, and she may vigorously shake her head no. She could come across as disoriented and frightened if she is taken aback by the intensity or pain.

The Second Stage Of Labor

The second stage begins once transition is over, and the cervix is fully open: the pushing stage. Usually there is a quiet space before the pushing contractions start. The uterine muscle is working in a different way now, like a piston to push the baby out, and the woman feels an urge to cooperate with that pushing sensation. Once again, there are big flexing movements that are felt externally as the midsection of the body tightening, while the baby travels down the birth canal—moving forward with a contraction, and slipping slightly back as the mother rests. The woman feels a very tight, numbing sensation when the baby's head crowns, and with a few more controlled pushes, the baby is out, to the enormous felt relief of the mother. The umbilical cord is cut and clamped after it stops pulsing oxygenated blood to the newborn. If placed tummy down on the mother's body, the baby will eventually, of his own accord, try to inch up to the mother's breast to nurse.

Emotionally, the signposts of the second stage mirror the first stage, but in quicker succession because the second stage itself can be anywhere from three hours to mere minutes long. When the pushing begins, the mother is excited and happy—baby is coming soon, and that transition is over! Midway through, she becomes serious with the hard work involved. At the very end, there could be self-doubt, especially with the unfamiliar sensation of nerves being compressed while the baby's head is crowning around the mother's perineum. The pressure serves as a natural anesthetic, but it is a strange, intense, and unfamiliar sensation. Finally, with the delivery of the baby, and holding the baby afterward, there is typically incredible relief—as if you didn't fully know how hard your body was working, the pressure building, until the work was instantly done—and joy that seems to go well beyond the endorphin rush that is part of childbirth.

The Third Stage Of Labor

The third stage of birth, which occurs as the mother is holding the baby, or the newborn is attended by others, is the delivery of the placenta, which is another very short pushing stage, seemingly effortless compared to what the woman has just lived through.

First Observations On Physical And Emotional Signs

These external observations, and the ability to recognize patterns, bring to mind a curious reality: the human being is the only mammal who does not give birth alone.[22] Most mammals retreat to a quiet, dark place and appear to not want or need contact. Birth is also an easier endeavor for all other mammals, because of the way the newborn descends in a mammal with a cervix tilted for a creature that moves on four limbs. In the human being, the baby descends the birth canal like a key in a lock: there is an optimal position for the baby (head down, anterior presentation), and the baby actually twists down the birth canal, and is delivered "face down." Women can and do give birth with less optimal positioning (breech births, and posterior presentations), but it does create challenges, and, sometimes, serious medical complications. Regardless of presentation, from time immemorial, women have given birth with the help of others. The woman may be doing the hard work that only she can do, but the others enter into a process that involves physical, emotional, and spiritual help. The Bradley Method® encourages the interrelational process of giving birth, and sets up that significant other who helps "read the signs" to be the woman's husband. More on that later in the chapter.

I offer this as a description as to what natural childbirth looks like: signs received and engaged. Most people cannot see past the pain, and others will not see past the medical data. One vision yields to fear, the other vision yields to a reductionist view of what is happening.

But there is also a "spiritual seeing" of childbirth by laboring mothers:

> I felt as though my husband and I were with God at the dawn of creation. Nothing in my 9 years in religious life, which I continue to value highly, brought me as close to a sense of God creating and loving his creation ("And God saw that it was good") as that morning when the air was as pure as the day after a storm and God's power and love flooded the room. It remains, along with the delivery of my second child, the most deeply spiritual experience of my life. –Kathy Pesta

> I always viewed myself as weak when it came to pain, but through each childbirth God showed me how strong I can be when I unite myself to Him. –Sandy Smith

> …[F]or the most recent birth I was fortunate to have had Sr. Maureen at my side; she is an RN and Hospital Massage therapist for laboring women. My favorite quote from her was, "they (RN's and Dr.'s) still think birth is a medical event!?" –Amy[23]

> I was pregnant at the age of 16 and sent away to live in a Home for Unwed Mothers in Chicago run by the Salvation Army. When I went into labor in the middle of the night, I walked to the hospital, which was in the same building as the sleeping quarters. I was alone and terrified. We were not allowed any pain medications. When I lied down [sic] on the hospital bed, I started praying Hail Marys and I didn't stop until hours later when I gave birth to a little baby girl. I recall being surprised that there was so little physical pain during

this process. To this day, I rely on Hail Marys to get me through difficult times…. [Then describes a typical but somewhat painful hospital birth of her son, years later, with her husband present.] Interesting, Susan, that I've never looked at these two births next to one another. Surprising that I had almost no pain whatsoever in the first case when I was essentially alone with the Virgin Mary, and normal birthing pains when my husband accompanied me during the birth of my son.[24]

While pain brings discomfort and fear, I think my greater fear was always missing the opportunity to feel this amazing rite of passage. To be fully immersed in the moment that my children entered the world. To understand what it is that women all over the world and through the ages have experienced. To think of it as something to "get through" instead of something in which to deeply plunge scared me. Natural birth required the greatest of me – trust, surrender, and awareness in full.[25]

Given the well-documented and zestfully described experiences of pain, it bears examination that there are many women who describe a natural childbirth as one of the spiritual high points of their lives: not just the incredible gift of the new son or daughter, but *the gift of the physical experience of giving birth*. There is a "spiritual seeing," as Scheler would have put it, or a "secondary reflection" (Marcel) on the experience of childbirth that is rooted in wonder and mystery. To see the beauty of the process of childbirth, to see birth as a sign, requires the openness that is *disponibilité*. But that openness is challenged by the specter of extreme pain as the inevitable experience and problem of childbirth. Since we are examining how "God's plan and its renewal by Christ, the redeemer, is imprinted deeply within the bodily nature of the person as a pre-given language of self-giving and fruitfulness"[26]—how the ensouled body is a sign pointing to God—we need to take seriously that this experience was given to women as an opportunity to spiritually grow, to come closer to seeing God's face. But to examine that seemingly audacious concept seriously, we need to look squarely at the experience of, and at some theological explanations for, pain in the context of giving birth.

Pain In Childbirth: A Defining Reality, Or Not?

The Neurology Of Pain In Childbirth

The point of exploring a theology of childbirth is not to address pain *per se*. Pain that is the result of illness or medical impairment is firmly a theodicy issue: why does a good and all-powerful God allow suffering? This is a real issue, and we will address it later, in the chapters on impairment and dying. The more immediate issue here is: how we can address the *wonder* of childbirth, when most in the Westernized modern world define childbirth via the lens of pain?

Grantly Dick-Read, a British obstetrician, published a groundbreaking text in 1942, *Childbirth Without Fear: The Principles and Practice of Natural Childbirth*.[27] Dick-Read, who has enjoyed more appreciation by the medical field since his death in 1959 than he did beforehand, argues clearly that women who are in pain during childbirth should have access to medical interventions and anesthetics: in this age, he says, there is no excuse for women to give birth in excruciating pain. But he argues just as strongly that most women could give birth with work and effort, but not excruciating pain, if they were able to approach childbirth without fear. The experience of pain in a normal, uncomplicated birth is a result of what he calls the Fear-Tension-Pain syndrome.

The Fear-Tension-Pain syndrome is based in neurological science. Pain is a real experience, but it also has a subjective component and is notoriously difficult to measure: anyone who has been in a hospital recently is familiar with the periodic query by a nurse to "put a number" on his or her pain, as part of the medical team's effort to offer pain management. Part of the pain equation is neurological. Briefly put, Dick-Read argued that most women in the modern Western world are taught to be afraid of the pain of childbirth. When one encounters the new, intense, and unusual muscle movements called contractions, if one is prepped for fear, the body's reaction is to physically brace itself. By tensing the body's muscles, the body does the opposite of what it is supposed to do—open up. Muscles working in two different directions produce a pain reaction. Once that pain is experienced, it can become a vicious cycle of increasing fear, bracing tension, and resultant pain. In addition, the muscular tension created by the fear affects the circulation of the blood within the uterine muscle, which hinders the effectiveness of labor.[28]

This insight is what Robert Bradley used to create a method of laboring safely and without pain: fear dissipates with the practice of physical relaxation (which I will argue later is a physical manifestation of *disponibilité*). Bradley Method® parents take 12-week courses on practicing relaxation techniques—recognizing and releasing tension in any muscle of your body. One book's popular presentation of the method states "*Relax as if your life depended on it!*"[29] While I think that phrasing could draw one to fear rather quickly, the point is made: not being afraid of labor and being able to release tension is utterly essential to a pain-reduced natural childbirth. And the relaxation requires a deeper exercise than just responding to a nurse's suggestion to "just relax." It is a difficult, new, radical situation in which to be relaxed. Beyond the relaxation exercises, the "coach" (the woman's husband) and/or a doula is mandated to guard the woman's peace—keep it quiet and pleasant in the laboring room, help her recognize the physical signs of tension and release them, give back rubs to alleviate the distraction of back pain. Bradley recommends laboring at home, since most women are more relaxed there. Music and a cheerful attitude can help, as well as lots of encouragement.

The question people always raise is how, exactly, can you know that the pain is part of the Fear-Tension-Pain syndrome, or a result of something truly amiss? This is a difficult question, whether a woman is attempting an unmedicated childbirth or not. As this is not a textbook for birth attendants, I will respond simply: if a woman has the "full box of natural tools" for tension management and she is in excruciating pain, something may well be abnormally wrong. Trained attendants will be able to recognize the difference between normal pain and abnormal pain. There are indeed observable signs that indicate the woman should seek medical intervention immediately (bleeding during labor, for example, or pain that does not stop at the end of a contraction). Other times, pain may be an indication of complications in the baby's position, and various decisions will have to be made regarding natural or medical interventions. But Dick-Read and Bradley both argue: for uncomplicated childbirths, that is, the majority of childbirths, women do not have to labor in unending pain. In serious and strenuous effort, yes. And most women find transition difficult and painful at points. But by and large, childbirth does not have to be endless pain in the way we have been taught to assume that it always is.

The Theology Of Pain In Childbirth

Theologically, the treatment of childbirth has been a very mixed story. Throughout Scripture, children consistently are said to be a blessing from God.[30] Childbirth may (or may not) be another story. Theology has had its own challenges as to whether pain should be named a defining reality in childbirth after the Fall.

Scriptural Sources On Pain In Childbirth

There is no prelapsarian childbirth recorded in Genesis. But it gets infamous mention early on, after Adam and Eve eat of the fruit of the tree of knowledge of good and evil, against God's express direction:

> To the woman he said, "I will greatly increase your
> pangs in childbearing;
> in pain you shall bring forth children,
> yet your desire shall be for your husband,
> and he shall rule over you."
> And to the man he said,
> "Because you have listened to the voice of your wife,
> and have eaten of the tree about which I commanded
> you, 'You shall not eat of it,'
> cursed is the ground because of you;
> in toil you shall eat of it all the days of your life;
> thorns and thistles it shall bring forth for you;
> and you shall eat the plants of the field.
> By the sweat of your face you shall eat bread until you
> return to the ground,
> for out of it you were taken;
> you are dust, and to dust you shall return" (Gn 3:16-19)

There are three quick interpretations gained from a very casual reading of the passage: 1) God makes childbirth painful, 2) Eve and all women get cursed by God as a punishment for sin, and 3) Adam seems to get the lighter punishment. Indeed, there are Christian women who have taken this assigned punishment so seriously that they have refused any pain management during birth, saying it negates God's intended punishment for fallen humanity.[31]

A close reading of the passage, even translated, resolves one problem with the casual reading above: Adam and Eve are *not* cursed by God. The serpent is cursed. The ground that Adam tills is cursed. Adam and Eve are not cursed. The consequences of their actions come from their breaking of the express command of God as recorded in Genesis 2:16-17:

> "And the Lord God commanded the man, 'You may freely eat of every tree of the garden; but of the tree of the knowledge of good and evil you shall not eat, for in the day that you eat of it you shall die.'"

It does not say "when you eat of it, I will kill you" or even "I will make you mortal." Eating from the fruit of that tree is an act that leads to death. The issue is less the disobedience (although that occurs), but the root of the disobedience: The human beings wanted to change their role in the relationship with God. Adam and Eve wanted to be like God, not in a way of imitation of holiness, but in a grasp of taking what is not theirs to have, superior knowledge befitting the Divine; they turned away from trusting their Source and elevated their lesser desires. In wanting to be like God, they made themselves "gods." In their state of original innocence, grasping to be God, ironically, made them less like God. The destruction of right relationship with the God of all life results in a withering, an (eventual) physical death.[32]

The "sentences" of God upon humanity have more to do with the consequential breaking of many primal relationships than imposed punishments: the woman, Eve, will now bear children in toil and (perhaps?) pain. Her urge (and what that refers to is much debated) will nonetheless be for her husband, despite the trial of birth. Her primal relationships to husband and child are struck to the core. Adam's transgression yields a broken relationship to the entire earth, tilling and harvesting in toil and sweat. Even the snake loses its honor as most cunning and is reduced to enmity with humanity. Relationships remain, but are left in shreds.

Another problem with a casual reading of the passage is the assumption that God makes childbirth painful (as a consequence or punishment for sin). This problem is resolved with an examination of the original Hebrew. The Hebrew word that is translated "pain" is *issabon*. However, childbearing is not the only spot where that term, and the related term *eseb*, is found:

To Eve:

> To the woman he said, "I will greatly increase your pangs (*issabon*) in childbearing; in pain (*be'eseb*) you shall bring forth children..." (Gn 3:16).

To Adam:

> ...[C]ursed is the ground because of you; in toil (*issabon*) you shall eat of it all the days of your life... (Gn 3:17b).

Both Adam and Eve receive pronouncements that part of the result of sin is in this Hebrew root, *eseb* (*issabon* comes from the root *eseb*). *Eseb* is a word commonly used in the Hebrew Scriptures—but every other time but one, it is typically translated toil.[34] While toil certainly refers to exertion and hard work—and pain and exhaustion can be a part of that, as well as frustration and sorrow—the first meaning of *eseb* is *not* pain; it is work. In the Septuagint, the word is translated into the Greek *lupe*, which does not refer to physical pain; instead, it refers to emotional challenge.[35] *Lupe* is also used (and mistranslated) in the New Testament in John 16:21-22:

> When a woman is in labor, she has pain (*lupe*), because her hour has come. But when her child is born, she no longer remembers the anguish (*thlipsis*) because of the joy of having brought a human being into the world. So you have pain (*lupe*) now; but I will see you again, and your hearts will rejoice, and no one will take your joy from you.

Thlipsis is a word that means applying pressure, compressing (which is a remarkably accurate descriptor for labor contractions). Once again, pain *could* be a consequence of pressure. But it is not the root meaning of the word.[36]

The translations of *eseb* and *lupe* to the single English word "pain" indicate a certain "reading into" the passages borne on preconceptions that childbirth must be painful. Even the King James Version gets the translations more correct than most modern translations, by using the words "sorrow" or "anguish" rather than "pain."

What does this mean? The results of making one's lesser desires a god—and fracturing the fullness of relationship to the true God—involve a consequential cracking of primal relationships: mother to child, spouse to spouse, humanity to the rest of creation. The effort to live out the truth of those relationships—tilling and harvesting, unity in "original nakedness," and giving birth[37]—will be marked by toil, rather than a workful ease. While the consequences of the original sin are absolutely tragic, they are not *defined* by pain. The sensed dissociation, i.e., the rupture of felt relationship between one's own body and soul and one's relationship to God and others, is the consequence of original sin that *opens the door* to the possibility of pain. Something stands between the original sin and pain. John Paul's Theology of the Body helps point to what that "something" is: fear.

Fear, Sin, And Childbirth

So far, we have a reading of Scripture that seems to indicate that pain in childbirth is possible, but not certain, and that painful childbirth is not a "curse from God." We also have Scripture that describes the first words of the fallen Adam as "I heard You, but I was afraid..." (paraphrase of Gn 3:10). Of all the consequences of that first sinful act—the broken relationships to God and humanity, as well as all the consequences listed as part of Catholic doctrine[38]—the primal experiential consequence seems to be not pain, but *fear*.

For such a common experience, fear (as a sense of peril or uneasiness) has a shocking lack of direct theological reflection.[39] People comment that the most common phrase found in the Bible is "be not afraid," usually uttered by God or an angel after a manifestation of the Divine or the spiritual world. That implies, of course, that people were often afraid in these situations. Rudolf Otto, in *The Idea of the Holy*, locates fear as a descriptor of a numinous experience, but focuses on what some call a "holy fear," or awe. While holy fear and fear of peril do have some common felt experiences, they are not identical. Given that the fear of Adam (and Eve) led them not to honor God but to hide, we will focus on the experience of fear as felt peril.[40]

John Paul II approaches fear as an experience indirectly in the Theology of the Body audiences, through shame. He spends a great portion of the audiences discussing shame as a "boundary experience" that marks the change in landscape from original nakedness to original sin, that shame flowered as a reality with the original sin.[41] The experience of shame is essentially relational and reveals the fallen human condition: our sense of alienation from our true selves, from other persons, and from God. Shame indicates a sensed rupture between the spiritual and bodily human being: the harmony that once existed between body and spirit is gone.

> "I was afraid, because I am naked".... These words reveal a certain constitutive fracture in the human person's interior, *a break-up, as it were, of man's original spiritual and somatic unity*. He realizes for the first time his body has ceased drawing on the power of the spirit, which raised him to the level of the image of God. Its shame bears within itself the signs of a certain humiliation mediated by the body.[42]

> ...[Shame] contains such cognitive sharpness that it creates a fundamental disquiet....In this sense, the original shame of the body ("I am naked") is already fear ("I was afraid") and pre-announces the unrest of the conscience....[43]

But shame as experience can be "swallowed up" in covenantal love, when one lives according to the sign of the body in truth, as a call to self-gift, receiving, and union.[44]

John Paul II argues that the experience of shame precedes fear, a "loss of certainty that the body of the person is a 'sign', an image of God in the visible world."[45] Regardless of which came first, there is certainly much common language between the lived worlds of fear and shame. The following elements of shame come from sociologist Helen Merrell Lynd's classic *On Shame and the Search for Identity*:[46]

Elements of Shame (Lynd's language)	Elements of Fear (my language)
exposure	dangerous vulnerability
incongruity	lack of meaning that fosters a sense of peril
threat to trust	threat to safety
involvement of the whole self	involvement of the whole self
difficulty to communicate shame	difficulty to communicate anything beyond fright

Whether the experience of shame causes fear, or fear is manifest through shame, clearly fear is a prime experiential consequence of original sin, and this primal fear has something to do with the felt dissociation within each person as soul and body. British theologian H.A. Williams, in the context of exploring modern resistance to the doctrine of the resurrection of the body, sets out the central problem with clarity:

> What then is the experience which has led us to regard the resurrection of the flesh as "grossly materialistic" in a pejorative sense, i.e. as totally undesirable?

> ….It is the experience of fear. Primarily it is fear full stop. But free-floating fear must find an object and the object is found in what is closest at hand—in myself as flesh and blood, in myself as body. The body, after all, is vulnerable. At any moment, it may be injured or destroyed. And what will physical passions do if given half a chance? Because we are afraid of our own bodies we have constructed a theory which dissociates the body from the essential man…*Fear is the experience at the source of all dualistic theories about man. The theories reinforce the fear and the reinforced fear in its turn seems to confirm the theories. Hence the staying power of the dualistic theory of man.*[47] [Italics added.]

Moving back to fear in childbirth: the *shape* of fear is usually defined by its object. A fear of intimacy is demonstrated by a backing away from deep relationships. A fear of failure is seen as a withdrawal from trying to achieve something difficult. And a fear of God's call is seen in shrinking away from the call, redefining the call's terms, or attempting to "get ahead of God" and take control. It may mean change on your part, less being "in charge." This fear of the unknown terms of God's call is usually manifest as *resistance*. And if entering into giving birth is an experience of God's call, the fear of the *terms* of the call often results in women resisting, which increases pain.

The pronouncement in Genesis on "intensifying toil in childbearing, in toil shall you bring forth children" is rooted not only in the Fall's dissociation of the laboring woman and the rest of creation, but also in the inheritance of fear as a border experience that marks our fallen reality. Some pain is a likely reality in childbirth, not a direct curse. God does not wish upon us what is evil, but pain often is rooted in fear, and fear exists as a consequence of our original and actual sin.

The issue here is not to make Christian women feel guilty about giving birth and experiencing pain—outraged, confused, and sputtering "But I *do* have faith!" After all, there is pain that occurs when something medically goes wrong that would occur absolutely regardless of a woman's faith life, and it is the sign that medical intervention may be needed. But there is pain that occurs through physically resisting the fear of the unknown terms of the call to giving birth. ("How can I possibly do this? This could be painful; this could be harder than I can manage.") Experiencing that fear, and responding by bracing oneself for pain, is not sinful. But there is an opportunity here: childbirth calls women to open themselves more greatly to trust in the power of the Holy Spirit as the Lord and Giver of life, to embrace the reality that their bodies are created to do this very thing, giving birth to a child, with God's help. We need to cede absolute control of a process that is often beyond a person's mental control, and recognize that we cooperate with God's work here. If we don't have the faith this seems to call for, we can recall that Christ mentions that the disciples themselves didn't yet have faith the size of a mustard seed. But I would hold that most women are not challenged to see that God is actively calling you to motherhood *through the process* of giving birth. True, as soon as a child is conceived, a woman becomes a mother, whether that child lives or dies before birth. But there is something about the yielding to and cooperating with an ultimate Power much greater than your own that is the road of every call. Laboring women are called by God to this moment, and assisted by God no matter what the circumstances of the birthing.

This requires a "spiritual life is in the details" approach that is the way of the Carmelites, a willingness and risk to see the God of all creation to be the God of this particular act of procreation. What would it look like to see Jesus Christ actively in authority over a woman's fertility and childbirth? Although it is amazing what science can report to us, there is much about birth we do not know. How do we honor that mystery? Catholic theology arguably does a fine job in honoring the value of the child, and the vocation of motherhood in general, but how do we honor the mystery of giving birth itself? *We can honor the mystery by seeing gestation and birth as part of God's plan for the human being's renewal in Christ, an expression of the "pre-given language of self-giving and fruitfulness." We need to take seriously that this experience was given to women as an opportunity to spiritually grow, to move closer to seeing God's face, and as a semi-public sign for all to see how we are called to cooperate with God.*[48] When we see God's work in the created manner of giving birth, we can see that all souls, pregnant with the Holy Spirit, are transformed by cooperating with the Spirit, letting God make all things new. Childbirth is not intended as something to soldier through, or a tragic circumstance of getting to the baby. Childbirth is designed to be an occasion of healing renewal, of participation with God's plan for love and life, and a gift—a fiery gift—in learning to trust in God's providence.

A Theology Of Childbirth: Living In (Spiritual) Reality

It is striking to me that there is so very little written on a theology of birth: in academic, devotional, or *any* kind of literature.[49] There does seem to be a strong "tap into your body's strength" ethos among many doulas and midwives, but that is not quite a spirituality. If the underlying message given by current medical practices is "you can't do this without medical help—we are the source of your security and peace" and the midwives' reaction is "you are strong and you can do this by yourself—trust your body," an extension of the Theology of the Body reacts to both, saying "God is the ultimate source of your strength, security and peace, seen through the sign of giving birth with the help of God and others." Giving birth is a bodily sign of fruitfulness and union with the Holy Spirit, and a privileged ground for giving and receiving grace. We will be looking specifically at how natural childbirth is given as a means of cooperating with God. Certainly women *can and do* cooperate with God in a medically managed childbirth, and, sometimes, using medical interventions in giving birth is wise and even life-saving. But the clarity of the spiritual sign typically is best seen in natural childbirth, and that will be my focus: the call to attending the present moment, practicing *disponibilité* through yielding, embracing weakness, engendering hospitality, and expressing tenderness.

The Present Moment

The spiritual lens of natural childbirth is found in the principle of beholding. To behold is to see, but specifically to call attention to the remarkable. As Christians, we need to allow ourselves to behold the act of giving birth as cooperation with God's desire, which is a hard, life-transforming work. When we behold, we see that giving birth requires attention and openness, a deliberate move to allow the event to unfold: changing you, changing your body, and cooperating with the life-giving and life-altering process. *Giving birth compels your attention to behold the Holy Spirit in the present moment.*

Jean-Pierre de Caussade, an 18th century Jesuit priest, gave a series of talks at a French convent, which subsequently were written by the nuns and published posthumously as *The Sacrament of the Present Moment*.[50] His argument is that the path to holiness is easy to understand and not an achievement of spiritual techniques or intellectual knowledge: instead, according to our state in life, we are to find the will of God in the present moment. Stephen Rossetti picks up on this insight when he holds that we can only find God in the present, not in the past, nor the future.[51] He notes (as a psychologist) that most people spend their mental time in the past or future—any place but the present. Both will argue that God has a particular will for each person in this moment: and more than at any other moment in your life, this process of labor is where God calls the pregnant woman to step into motherhood. And there is no other rule than to accept the present moment as a place where God wants you.[52]

For example: one of the great mysteries of birth is that doctors are not certain what exact confluence of scientific realities causes a woman to go into labor. One can ascertain when a baby is full term and try to read certain physical signs, but that's about it: there is no clear marker that indicates when a mother will give birth until labor begins. The timing of birth is mysterious. Now, certainly it is convenient for mothers to schedule an induction of the birth. (You can arrange your work schedule, arrange childcare, etc.) Occasionally it is medically advisable.[53] But if it is not...what does that say about allowing the birth to happen in God's own time? What happens when you take that control?

So much of whether childbirth is an event to survive or an experience that brings you closer to God through your vocation to motherhood involves *our response to fear*. Fear of danger is a legitimate reaction, and it can be protective in a helpful way. Fear of pain is understandable, because it hurts. But pain does not necessarily mean something is wrong with the birth: it could mean that something is wrong in the *way* the mother is giving birth (through physical position, or her psychological approach to it). The key to embracing the present moment is to not be afraid of the normal processes of childbirth.

The opposite of fear is not so much courage, but *trust*: trust that God is present and will give you what you need in the moment. De Caussade illustrates this trust—this ceding of control to fully cooperate with God's will—in evocative language:

> In this state of joyful self-surrender the only rule is the present moment. In this our soul is as light as a feather, liquid as water, simple as a child, as easily moved as a ball in following these nudges of grace. Such souls have no more consistence and rigidity than molten metal...so these souls are pliant and easily shaped to any form that

God chooses to give them.[54]

These images are, interestingly, some of the same images used in The Bradley Method® for relaxing the muscles and allowing the uterus to contract and do its work, unimpeded: imagine yourself as liquid, imagine riding a wave, receive the birth of your child and allow it to happen. In addition, there is at least one other person there helping you focus on accepting and relaxing through the contractions: your husband (or birth coach). His (or her) role in this present moment is to attend to your process of opening up: caressing a brow to release tension, checking the laboring mother for relaxed positioning, maybe physically supporting the woman during contractions if she is laboring standing up, and lots of encouragement.

To be fully present at the time of giving birth is to move into mystery. And that does take courage. But more, it takes trust: trust in someone outside of oneself. And since our primal relationships—body and soul, mother and child, human to creation—have suffered a felt dissociation as a consequence of original sin, trust requires a radical move to embracing God's will. Fear is a potent distraction from the call to trust.

As I said in the first chapter, receptivity in prayer is hard to explain and hard to teach. But giving birth in this manner "teaches" receptivity to the work of God beautifully. It is a gift, fiery indeed, but a gift nonetheless: it calls our attention to God. Childbirth as a bodily sign presents the "law of the gift" in an exquisitely designed manner.

Disponibilité

As John Paul has said, "the fundamental dimension of man's existence is a co-existence,"[55] and the woman carrying a child in her womb could not be a more radical representation of that insight. The fact of co-existence compels a response in the mother: a choice between openness to the other or closure. *Disponibilité*, or an attitude of "availability," models this well.

In an effort to define *disponibilité* through its opposite, Gabriel Marcel suggests antonyms such as encumbrance and crispation. Encumbrance is a physical word: when one is encumbered by material concerns, emotions, whatever—one is unable to participate in the sacrament of the present moment. Crispation is an even stranger word, which refers to a hardening and shrinking within:

> To describe a shriveling and contraction, which are consequent upon a withdrawal into the self. The guiding image of the process of crispation is that of the crustacean animal who secretes around himself a shell which hardens with time, locking the world out as it locks itself in....[56]

This is a wonderfully sensate way to speak of the "hardening of heart" referred to in Scripture. But even more concretely, it is a word that describes the fear reaction that results in resisting the opening of the cervix: a bracing or counter-hardening of the uterine muscle that results in real pain.

The present moment, when giving birth, calls for a disposition of openness of the womb. The challenge is manifest in the form of physical resistance. Most resistance, I would hold, is a resistance to the possibility of pain, manifest as fear. But if we are encumbered by the fear of pain, and shrivel within and "harden our shell" to avoid it, the physical resistance can move to becoming a spiritual reality in the ensouled body. The phenomenon of resistance is well known within spiritual direction literature and refers to the directee's unconscious maneuvering to avoid seeing God's action in his/her life—even when the directee holds that he/she *wants* to see God's action in his/her life.[57] In childbirth, the resistance has a much more physical tenor. Ignatius places resistance squarely in the arena of spiritual warfare: the enemy "uses discouragement and deception... dissatisfaction... [and] doubts and anxieties" to detract us from our attempts to "pursue the lead of God in our life."[58] Resistance in all forms draws us away from the sacrament of the present moment; indeed, according to Ignatius, that is exactly the point. The Evil One does not want us to be fully present to the work of the Holy Spirit.

Disponibilité is a disposition and attitude that prepares one to behold the work of God in the present moment of giving birth. Relaxation is simply a physical tool to keep the worst of pain at bay and allow you to respond to God's call to give birth. It is the moment after the call where the prophet responds, "Here I am, Lord." *Disponibilité* is a concrete disposition for the hard work of love, which, when perfect, casts out all fear. But the "how" of *disponibilité* is far from obvious. To that end, I offer a more familiar idea: the practice of yielding.

To yield is a rich verb, especially in this context. Yield, after all, can mean to bear or produce. We speak of a field that yields a crop. Yielding, as a word, implies fruitfulness.

But yielding is an art, especially in this framework. Many spiritual theologies speak of the goal of surrender to God (although the 12 steps associated with Alcoholics Anonymous don't use the actual word "surrender," many advocates for AA do). Although surrender can be a word that holds great meaning—the total gift of oneself to another—I am going to suggest that a better word, which one gets to practice many times in giving birth, is "yielding."

Many women I know are challenged by the word "surrender," and not without reason. Many women spend a lifetime building up a notion of self-worth in a society that seems determined to diminish the value of women. (You're not smart enough, or truly an individual, or you have no identity beyond your sexual nature.) Even those women who have a healthy self-image, who recognize that their value is multifaceted and comes from God—to "surrender" the details of that identity, even to God, requires a radical act of trust. We see how corrupt the other options are, and if we cannot trust God with our basic identities, we're working without a net. Surrender, as a spiritual move, assumes that a person's primary sin is pride. Although women can be prideful, it is not typically their primary sin.[59] Many female theologians have argued, rightly, that a woman's typical sin is more likely to be self-diminishment. The confusion for many women is discerning from whom we receive our true identity. All these reasons make surrender a powerful, but potentially burdened, word.

Surrender is also a loaded term when a woman is giving birth. For a spiritually strong woman who is surrounded by like-minded people in a safe place for giving birth, surrender to God is a potent and welcome act. That is a situation where the best meaning of the word is clear. But using the word surrender in any other circumstance invites unhelpful connotations. For example, the act of giving birth could cause a woman who has been sexually abused to have flashbacks to the abuse, of being forced to submit to someone against her will. Or if a woman is surrounded by medical personnel callous or unsympathetic to the kind of birth she is trying to have, and treating the birthing mother like a medical object, the idea of surrender may have very uncomfortable undertones.

The art of yielding describes more explicitly than the hammer strike of surrender how to practice the attitude of *disponibilité* in giving birth. Yield refers to right of way. It is not to give up, *but it is to give place to another: to yield a right of way, to yield one's concerns for another's*. To yield is to bend, move, stretch for another. It requires flexibility, not dissipation.

Emilie Griffin's modern classic on prayer, *Clinging*, has a chapter devoted to the experience of yielding. As she pithily says, "Hard to think about, easier to do."[60] Yielding is, first and fundamentally, a response. If childbirth is a call, it is seeing God's work, sensing the call placed upon you, and responding by making way. Yielding is *disponibilité* in action: openness to God, responding to God. And a laboring mother is called to yield to God's work, opening and pushing along, with every single contraction: short rest, sense the contraction beginning, and yield again. One doula calculated that in the average labor, there are 314 contractions.[61]

Yielding, in childbirth, means to stay with the present moment. God is there, and you are needed there, not someplace else. It means not resisting, but gracefully (and it will take grace) allowing the process to happen and cooperating with it as well as possible. Some moments will be cherished. Some will be difficult. In a normal childbirth, all these moments are where God expects you to be. You have been inserted in the mystery of creation as an active agent. There is a purpose to all of it.

Yielding, in birth, does not mean waiting around in endless pain for it to end. It means participating in the physical yielding of your cervix to make a path for someone else. It means taking the occasional cues of discomfort (or, yes, pain) as a sign to move to alleviate that pain, to create a "corrected" path. For example, when a laboring woman shifts her hips standing up while having a contraction, that is yielding. When a husband applies back pressure to allow the laboring mother to maintain a challenging labor position that is optimal for the baby's descent, that is yielding. To move to medical interventions when a woman consents that is in her child's best interest, although perhaps not her personal preference, that too is yielding. Yielding is giving place, not giving up.

The natural sign demonstrated here is a call to yield to the work of God in one's life. It is less about our initiative and more about how we "make way" for God's word first, and respond to it. Yielding requires attentiveness to the call, allowing it, cooperating with it. To yield is to be in responsive relationship with God, making room for His will for your life. Yielding helps you to behold God's work rather than your own.

Self-Abjection

If yielding is best understood as physically and spiritually "giving place," self-abjection may be best understood as "giving in" (although not giving up). "Abject" is a hard word to embrace, but there are few words that better describe the utter poverty experienced during a labor's transition than abject. Remember, this is the point in the labor that is marked by self-doubt, increased intensity, and possible pain and disorientation. The uterine muscle is completing the opening of the cervix in a burst of energy, often while beginning the pushing contractions simultaneously. A muscle being pulled two ways is, at minimum, an intense sensation.

Self-abjection is the experience of yielding in the extremes. St. Francis de Sales speaks to the need to love our weakness in order to magnify the glory of Christ. Our weakness reminds us that we rely on God, which when acknowledged, allows a privileged space for God to break in.

One of the physical techniques to promote relaxation—an openness to birth and an openness to God—is to encourage "sounding" the most intense contractions. Ideal "sounding" is basically a low groaning. Screeching and shallow breathing indicates you have fallen into the fear-tension-pain cycle and sets you to spiral within it. A coach will suggest to lower the pitch of your voice and try to do relaxed, deep breathing, not for propriety's sake, but to facilitate the opening of the cervix, diminish some of the pain, and counter the undeniable challenge to fear. Groaning, rather than screaming, inexplicably seems to help women cooperate with birth. But there is no question: groaning is a physical sign of self-abjection.

St. Paul knew something of that abjectness himself—"whenever I am weak, then I am strong" (2 Cor 12:10)—and expressed it using the language of groaning in birth in writing to the Romans:

> We know that the whole creation has been groaning in labor pains until now; and not only the creation, but we ourselves, who have the first fruits of the Spirit, groan inwardly while we wait for adoption, the redemption of our bodies. For in hope we were saved. Now hope that is seen is not hope. For who hopes for what is seen? But if we hope for what we do not see, we wait for it with patience.
>
> Likewise the Spirit helps us in our weakness; for we do not know how to pray as we ought, but that very Spirit intercedes with sighs too deep for words (Rom 8:22-26).

Remarkable: when we are weak, the Spirit helps us; we do not know how, but the Holy Spirit groans to God through us. Paul is using his culturally entrenched experience of being around women giving birth (men may not have commonly been present, but all births were home births, and certainly groans carry through walls) to express how the early Christians were waiting in hope for the fullness of redemption, as the Holy Spirit serves as our Advocate.[62] But if childbirth is recognized as a call to which we respond, the point where we do not know how to pray (or *respond*) to God as we ought, the Spirit groans through us. Coaches and attendants are usually on high alert during transition, holding the laboring mother's hand, mopping a brow. At this point, when we cede our illusion of control and consent to our weakness by allowing others to help, we are at our most human. We yield, and open ourselves to God's help as we give everything we have to participate in the mystery of new life, in living out our calling to motherhood.

We have not been wrested of control. One could try to be "in control" in the same way that one can stand in front of a tidal wave: go right ahead, but it isn't a healthy move. Yet it is the person's choice. It is better to not be afraid and try to relax, to let it happen, groan (it is surprisingly hard work to go with the churning, thunderous flow), for a short while.

Hospitality

Many people are familiar with the story of Servant of God Dorothy Day (1897-1980), co-founder of the Catholic Worker, a radical movement dedicated to serving the needs of the homeless and vulnerable through depending on God's providence. As a young adult, Dorothy—a strong-willed young woman in love and living with a man named Forster Batterham, writing for socialist and communist papers in New York City, and joining marches for women's suffrage and worker's rights—found herself pregnant. In fact, she was pregnant for the second time; she had an abortion of an earlier pregnancy by another man. This pregnancy, wholly unexpected since she had thought she was barren after the earlier abortion, she was determined to bear, despite Forster's objections and her own precarious financial situation. While pregnant, she decided that the baby must be baptized in a faith she wished she could fully embrace herself. She was attracted to Catholicism, sitting in the backs of churches full of people she was trying to stand in solidarity with, the working immigrant poor of New York City—but she hesitated to become Catholic, in significant part because it would mean the end of her relationship with Forster. When recounting this story, Jim Forest, a friend of Dorothy Day as well as her biographer, said "And this birth, the birth of Tamar Teresa, was a turning point, the beginning of her ministry of hospitality. It all began with the hospitality of the womb."[63]

The striking beauty of this insight—that the radical hospitality of the Catholic Worker began with the hospitality of the womb—is also a sad comment on modern realities. More than any time in history, we can deny children the hospitality of the womb. Much of the first trimester, in many clinics, is spent determining whether to extend the hospitality of the womb or not to any given child. At this writing, a new noninvasive prenatal test for Down syndrome has been developed, which detects

Down syndrome with accuracy at nine weeks gestation, and is planned to be available at relatively low costs in 2012.[64] While some will take the test, receive a "positive" for Down syndrome, and use the remaining months to prepare for a child with special needs, it is likely that most will choose to abort the child.[65] It is a new and fearsome control, and one that denies not only the dignity of the child, but also the spiritually formative powers of maternal hospitality: the crucible of otherness.

The "crucible of otherness" is the other side of John Paul II's vision that "the fundamental dimension of man's existence is a co-existence." And it is an ancient insight, going back to the early church desert fathers and mothers:

> The desert tradition teaches us that we are to submit ourselves to the crucible of otherness. Encountering others only for their usefulness to us or for their similarity to us does not require us to change. Encountering the other as wholly other creates the "heat" that softens the heart. When we encounter the other more as they are, and less as we would have them, we become open to dis-illusionment—the process of detachment of our projected desires from the other and our sense of entitlement that the other fulfill them. Transformation requires that we give others 'authority' over our spiritual formation and access to our hearts.[66]

The desert fathers and mothers of the early church have a fierce reputation for asceticism and solitude, earned by following a call to detach themselves from familial relationships, move to the desert, and devote themselves to a life of prayer. But the ironic piece of this: precisely after they set themselves apart, they were sought as guides, interrupted for "a word," and constantly expected to extend hospitality to the stranger... which they did. This accommodation of the other as wholly other forms us in ways we cannot control nor fully expect.

The hospitality of the womb leads us to the crucible of otherness in different ways. This "crucible of otherness" is found in three ways in childbirth: the otherness of the process of giving birth, the otherness of the child, and the Otherness of the Holy Spirit.

The Otherness Of The Birth Process

The otherness of giving birth, encountering the experience on its own ground, is important. When facing something so huge, so life-altering, and wrapped in fear—of course we want to control it. If not avoid it, at least shape it. So much of birth is planning (if only subconsciously) the perfect experience, trying to achieve the painless birth with aromatherapy and soothing music at the end. A reasonable effort to avoid pain is good for both the mother and the baby, but forcing the birth process to be something in your imagination could be rejecting a real gift. Giving birth is nothing like what you can imagine. Even as your body was created to do this, it is stretching, opening, working, and pushing in intense and unprecedented ways. It is a new experience of who you can be, and who you are.

The Otherness Of The Child

The otherness of the child is also part of the formative crucible of otherness. You don't know to whom you will be called to give birth. Even if you know some things—gender, maybe even a genetic abnormality—you do not know the character of your child. All you know is that he or she *is*, and you are his or her mother.

In 2010, a woman in Florida gave birth to a daughter with Down syndrome. The DS diagnosis was unexpected. Due to a beautifully written and photographed blog post on the birth, expressing the shock, fear, despair, and powerful love she felt in the hours after birth, her experience became known worldwide:

> [....] Two hours went by, and I was off the wall in pain, begging for an epidural. But the anesthesiologists were busy. I looked around the room and tried to take it in . . . the candles, the music, the lavender oil I'd brought that wafted through the air. I remember telling myself, "You are about to meet your new daughter." Then I heard the sounds of the song we'd chosen to play as I delivered our baby, "When You Love Someone" by Bryan Adams. And I began to cry.
>
> My husband, my friends, my dad, the nurses, all of them smiling, cameras flashing. I pushed, and pushed, and

pushed, then finally watched as the tiniest little body came out of me, arms flailing, lungs wailing. . . and then, they handed her to me. And I knew.

I knew the moment I saw Nella that she had Down syndrome and that nobody else had realized it yet. I held her and cried. I panned the room to meet the eyes of anyone who would tell me she didn't have it. And all I can remember of those moments is her face. I will never forget my daughter in my arms, opening her eyes over and over as she locked eyes with mine and stared, boring a hole into my soul.

Love me. Love me, she seemed to be telling me. I'm not what you expected but, please, love me.

That was the most defining moment of my life. [....][67]

Later, she was interviewed on the experience by many major news outlets. When asked if she would have preferred knowing ahead of time that Nella had Down syndrome, to prepare herself and perhaps avoid the hard hours of grief after Nella's birth, she said no. What was healing, what made it possible, was that I was able to love her.[68] The crucible of otherness can be intense. But it also can be healing.

The Otherness Of The Holy Spirit

The Holy Spirit, we recite every Sunday, is the Lord, the Giver of Life: and as such, is the raw power within childbirth. When we cooperate with the power of God, amazing things—like new life—can happen. The Holy Spirit gives us the power to get through what seems impossible, but it means putting aside your desires, yielding absolute control, and deep trust. When the desert fathers say "transformation requires that we give others 'authority' over our spiritual formation and access to our hearts," it means that we assent to the Holy Spirit as the Lord, the Giver of Life, in that particular present moment. We allow the Spirit to know our heart, and work through and with our laboring selves, at that space and time.

I want to be careful *not* to propose that childbirth is an inherently mystical experience, and by that, I mean that the laboring mother may not have a felt experience of the immediate presence of God. I do think that is possible, and people sometimes speak of it. God will grant the mystical wherever God wills. But the larger point is not about the felt experience of the Holy Spirit, but the reality of the Holy Spirit as the power of God that brings forth new life. Personally, I think we can sense the work of the Holy Spirit in childbirth better *after* the birth process: in like manner as the centurion at the Crucifixion recognized Jesus as the Christ, we may say "truly, this event was the work of the Holy Spirit!"

As Ignatius says in the First Foundation, we are not called to "fix our desires on health or sickness, wealth or poverty, success or failure, a long life or short one. For everything has the potential of calling forth in us a deeper response to our life in God" (see Ch. 1, pg 20). There is a danger in hoping that childbirth will be the painless spiritual ground for giving and receiving grace: we all know childbirth can be, for medical, emotional, and spiritual reasons, tragic and incredibly difficult. Women and children do die. However, childbirth can be, and I would say is created to be, a privileged sign of giving and receiving grace. And if it expresses its fallen nature through pain, illness, complications, even death: God is there, in that moment. It is charged with the Holy Spirit.

Some Catholic women, to join their suffering with the suffering of Christ, do often approach childbirth as a time to "offer it up," and contemporary literary writer Matthew Lickona describes his wife's decision to approach birth this way very well:

> My wife has delivered all four of our children without medication. She does this for a number of reasons, not least of which is her belief in St. Paul's claim "in my flesh I complete what is lacking in Christ's afflictions for the sake of his body, that is, the Church" (Colossians 1:24). She offers her pain of the labor to God for the health of her baby and her mother's return to the Catholic Church. The catch is that, when things get really bad— when the low growl she makes when bearing down on a contraction gives way to a wavering cry, endlessly rising in pitch and volume—she cannot pray. She cannot think....My wife, my pillar of strength and stability, is lost in a miasma of pain.[69]

This willingness to embrace this cross indeed fits Ignatius's "a deeper response to our life in God." I would simply encourage this move to embrace pain not to be the first move. Childbirth, unless something is going wrong, is not unending pain (although the example above described an abnormally fast labor, a 90-minute start-to-finish birth, which is inevitably very hard). But if pain is unavoidable, then offering the pain to God is a beautiful move. It is pain on behalf of the other, willingly undergone. It is, for a time, to lay down one's life for a friend: your son or daughter. *That* is the hospitality of the womb.

Love And Tenderness

The last element that deserves theological reflection is the reality of tenderness. The moment when the baby emerges is such a felt change—after stretching, stretching, more stretching, and suddenly, the intensity vanishes as quickly as a candle is blown out. The pain you perhaps didn't recognize as pain evaporates in an instant. In most circumstances there is a flurry of activity, checking baby, perhaps suctioning amniotic fluid out of baby's nose and mouth, quickly checking the mother, and then placing the baby on the mother's body with a warmed, clean towel over both. Then, there is usually "the look."

In a typical unmedicated childbirth, a healthy newborn will move from some distress at the birth (think of all that is new—breathing, cold, unmuffled noise, and unfiltered light) to—when held, especially by the mother—a state of quiet alertness.[70] The newborn's eyes slowly wander, and find the eyes of the one holding her. A newborn child cannot see well—but can see perfectly objects that are about 10-12 inches away, the exact distance of the mother's eyes to a cradled newborn in arms.[71] The state of quiet alertness, a state of open receptivity and focus, occurs off and on throughout the first few weeks of life. But it is typical for it to happen within a half-hour of birth. After a period of approximately 40 minutes of held quiet alertness, and perhaps an attempt to nurse (where the gaze into eyes continues), the baby usually falls into a deep sleep.[72]

It is difficult to put to words the tenderness of this moment. Scripture may hint at it: "...when her child is born, she no longer remembers the anguish because of the joy..." (Jn 16:21).[73] The phenomenon is well-known, and many current hospital delivery practices try to honor that first hour as a privileged time for bonding, to express tenderness. Interestingly, John Paul II had a great deal to say on the particular phenomenon of tenderness.

Tenderness, according to John Paul II, is nothing like "sickly sentimentality."[74] Rather, tenderness is something we feel for another when we become conscious of the ties that unite us.[75] In particular, tenderness springs between people who are close to each other, the tendency "to make one's own the feelings and mental states of another."[76] It seeks to be expressed. When John Paul reflects on tenderness, he speaks of the phenomenon within the experience of romantic love: tenderness between two people attracted to each other is a natural good that deserves proper expression when within a proper relationship, and should never be used as a license for objectification. There is, says John Paul, a "right" to tenderness within a married relationship. But there is no reason these basic insights into the phenomenology of tenderness should not be expanded to the "ties that bind" relationship within the human family.

The moment of this receptive gaze, and similar moments afterward, are a gift. They are not automatic or even necessary to familial bonding. But the state of quiet alertness does seem to be built into the natural childbirth process. And the look expresses the spiritual ties that bind the mother and the child, including the father, who sometimes is embracing both. The spiritual nature of tenderness is elaborated by John Paul II:

> It is especially in relationships between two human beings that one of them is able to, and feels the need to, enter into the feelings, the inner state, the whole spiritual life of the other—and is able and needs to make the other aware of this.[77]

And later in the same text,

> Tenderness is the ability to feel with and for the whole person, to feel even most deeply hidden spiritual tremors, and always to have in mind the true good of that person.[78]

I think of the typical broken conversation that occurs immediately after birth: "Hello, little baby. Oh, you are beautiful. I'm your mama. Sh, sh, it's okay. It's okay." All these broken statements hold everything you want your newborn to know. You are cherished, you are my child, and despite everything feeling new to you, it's going to be OK. I don't know if the child needs to hear the words, and obviously newborns cannot understand language (although I would say they can understand tenderness). But the mother, out of tenderness, needs to say it; and communicates these basic ideas through warmth, touch, comfort, and attention. She wants to enter into the child's inner state and comfort it. And this is God's healing at work—not just for the child, but also for the mother herself.

The beauty of John Paul's description of tenderness is that it is not simply emotion. It is rooted in vocation and relationship. It is expressed through bodily gestures—the embrace, the gentle touch, the gaze—because this spiritual sign expresses the renewal of the person in the Holy Spirit through the acceptance of vocation: I am your mother (or father), and you are my child. But the vocation is a gift given only through and within the Fatherhood of God. One of the most unexpected and poignant references to the presence of God at birth occurs in Psalm 22, the prayer Jesus uttered in shorthand ("My God, my God, why have you abandoned me?") from the cross:

> On you I was cast from my birth,
> and since my mother bore me
> you have been my God.
> Do not be far from me,
> for trouble is near
> and there is no one to help. (Ps 22:10-12)

If it is reasonable to assume that Jesus of Nazareth, as an observant Jewish man who prayed the psalms every day of his life, was praying this particular prayer at his death, it not only says that God is the power that presides over giving birth ("drew me forth from my mother's womb"), but that we are in some way "thrust upon God" after the moment of birth: not just Jesus, but all of us. After birth we find our place and security in the world through the loving attention of the mother and father, who accept their vocation through the bonding expressions of tenderness. Mothers and fathers are not God; they accept their vocations from God. But we are the ones who are created to express God's love and blessing upon these vulnerable children. We are the ones who communicate: "You have value and worth. You are desired by God and by us. You are loved."

This section, I expect, is difficult to read for adopted children, for children born in medical emergencies or tragic circumstances, and for women who simply didn't have this kind of moment after birth for any given reason. I want to be clear the purpose in describing this is that it is a typical experience of unmedicated birthing mothers and children, and may be designed so as a spiritual sign. It is not absolutely necessary. Newborns, whatever the circumstances of their birth, deserve and usually get the comfort they need in American hospital settings. Children deserve to be cherished, and although you (as infant) may never know the experiences of that first hour, you likely were cherished. But: I would also hold that if you were not physically cherished by a mother, or as a mother you could not physically cherish a child, the Holy Spirit rejoiced at your first infant breath and was present to you (or your child) in a way we cannot fully know or describe. God can overcome all less-than-perfect, even desperately tragic, circumstances of birth. And as we have seen in the psalm above, there is a greater familial relationship pointed to here, God as first receiving parent: "Upon you, O God, was I thrust from the womb…since my mother bore me you are my God." There are multiple paths of healing, and this section and chapter are meant to pay attention to just this one.

Tenderness is a close cousin of compassion: that is, to suffer with. The Hebrew word for womb, or uterus, *rekhem*, comes from the same root as the Hebrew word for compassion: *rakhamim*. We know that Scripture speaks of God having *rahum*, womb-like love, translated as mercy and compassion.[79] God has offered us the hospitality of the divine womb, so to speak, with every act of love. Likewise we are called to the womb-like love of compassion: the call to stay in the present moment, to open and yield to God's initiative, to cooperate in His divine work, to put Love first, and to cherish the vulnerable is a call that is stamped as a spiritual sign onto our bodies as women.

What Theology Of The Body, Extended, Says About Spiritual Motherhood (And Fatherhood)

The hermeneutic of the gift holds that every life is given the greatest of all gifts: a call to follow God. If the body is stamped at creation with a pre-given language of self-giving and fruitfulness, the response to the call is to offer one's life in gratitude to its Source, our loving God.

The body giving birth gives a woman essential practice in yielding to grace, and the gift of the power of God. But even more so, it acts as a sign of the spiritual life: how all souls, pregnant with the Holy Spirit, are transformed by cooperating with the Spirit, letting God make all things new. That requires putting aside fear, putting on trust, accepting grace and other helps. That requires allowing God to lead, work within you, and transform you. Scripture cites the analogy of birth frequently, and whether *pain* is correctly translated or not, the *process* of birth is one cited as one we all must embrace:

> When a woman is in labor, she has pain, because her hour has come. But when her child is born, she no longer remembers the anguish because of the joy of having brought a human being into the world. So you have pain now; but I will see you again, and your hearts will rejoice, and no one will take your joy from you (Jn 16:21-22).

According to John, *we are all in labor.* We are all at the point of salvation history where God is pushing through us to the second coming. This requires attention, acceptance, cooperation with God's will, and allowing "birth" to happen. Perhaps the gift of the natural birth process is that it helps us to experience, see and express God's work in us, as God's people and as an individual child of God.

Although there is no example of a birth before the Fall, it is reasonable to expect that given the original call to be fruitful and multiply, birth as a sign points to the embodied soul's cooperation with the work of the Holy Spirit, embedded in the realm of pre-historical experience. Our fallen experience of birth is indeed fallen, and we see "through a glass darkly" as the King James Version so regally states it. But like all encounters with the Holy Spirit, birth can give us a taste of what that original life in the Spirit would have been like: and more important, what our journey into holiness involves and bears in the realm of redemption. The sign of birth is a sign of the Spirit-led dynamism of reciprocal giving. As such, it is an ideal place to recognize that the law of the gift is in many ways the law of the call, the theology of vocation.

Mary As Spiritual Mother

When I say that there is no prelapsarian experience of birth, some Catholics may immediately point out: what about Mary, the mother of God? Was she not born without original sin? Would she not have experienced birth in a prelapsarian manner?

The answer is yes and no. We have no clue from Scripture, which simply reports she gave birth to her firstborn son. The *Protoevangelium of James*, an apocryphal piece that describes the birth of Jesus in some detail, was not accepted into public revelation for a reason: it's not reliable. Mary, as a member of the human race, suffered the realities of aging, pain, and injury.[80] This seems, at least, to open the door to the possibility that she could have had a typically painful delivery of Jesus. But others conjecture that since the consequence of original sin for women seems to say that pain will be intensified, and Mary was not subject to original sin, then the consequence of pain must have been absent from the birth. Indeed, what the birth could have looked like is shrouded in additional mystery by the perpetual virginity of Mary, a "real and perpetual virginity even in the act of giving birth" to Jesus Christ.[81] For many, this argument revolves around how to speak of Mary's purity and humanity in a fallen world.[82]

In the end, we cannot know what the birth of Christ looked like, but we do know *how Mary received* the conception and birth of the Son of God: and this gives us all the insight we have about her as a person, and her call to motherhood. That is, she did not give in to fear, and lived out her vocation in utter fearlessness. At the annunciation, being approached by an angel and the Holy Spirit, she asks a simple clarifying question (How can this be...?) and then responds "I am the handmaid of the Lord, let it be done to me according to your word." No flash, no drama, only humble assent. In an age of historical-cultural criticism, we know that the stakes were high for her personally, in her culture: she was betrothed to Joseph but not living with him, and this seemingly illicit pregnancy could result in being stoned to death. Additionally, if it is true that she was dedicated as a child to the Temple as a virgin (as some legends offer), this pregnancy would look to the world like another grievously broken vow. It's hard to see how anyone in such circumstances would have received this "good news" well.

But the encounter with the Holy Spirit may have assured her and strengthened her to travel 50 miles to tell the other person mentioned in the annunciation, a cousin with another miraculous pregnancy, Elizabeth. And her words are not "I'm afraid," "I'm so worried," or even "I'm confused" but:

> ...My soul magnifies the Lord,
> and my spirit rejoices in God my Savior,
> for he has looked with favor on the lowliness of his
> servant.
> Surely, from now on all generations will call me blessed;
> for the Mighty One has done great things for me,
> and holy is his name. (Lk 1:46-49)

That is, her response to Elizabeth's awe-filled "you had faith" was to redirect Elizabeth's awe to God: "Look! Look at the goodness of God! Look at what God has done! In me, in Israel, in all the small ones of this world!"

Mary's acceptance of the pregnancy, the child, and her vocation to motherhood is rooted in a fearlessness that comes from a harmony of body and spirit, and total trust in God. If she was indeed without fear— that psychological consequence of dissociation—then *perhaps* she saw the birth of her son (whatever that would look like) as work, as effort, as cooperation with the Holy Spirit, but not pain. That is, *perhaps* she did not anticipate or experience pain because she did not give in to fear, from her acceptance of the annunciation onward. Perfect love cast out all fear.

For Mary, accepting motherhood meant to focus her energy and attention—in her case quite literally and directly—on God, fearlessly and without reserve. This was her untarnished experience of motherhood. So what does this say about the rest of her vocation, as spiritual mother to all humanity? What does it mean for her to be *the* spiritual mother?

One of the most famous icons of Madonna and child is the Virgin of Tenderness, the patron of Russia. The icon, initially written[83] in 12th century Constantinople, features Mary cradling the baby Jesus near her face as he clings to her. Jesus gazes lovingly at her eyes while Mary, gesturing to the infant Son of God, gazes serenely at you, the viewer of the icon. Spiritually, this icon communicates beautifully one of the central tenets of Mariology: everything in Mary's life was dedicated to leading others to the Son of God. And that she was given to us, pure gift, as a

spiritual mother. A witness, yes, a sister, yes, a model for Christian discipleship, yes: but the primary relationship between Mary and the people of God is one of motherhood. Indeed, in this picture, she is holding him up for us to see. But what a phenomenology of birth shows us is striking: *the state of quiet alertness so common to the first hour of birth is the state with which she beholds us.* She looks at us with the mother's gaze: Mother of God and spiritual mother of you as well.

Recently, there has been considerable discussion in certain religious circles about spiritual motherhood, that some women are called to spiritual motherhood (via the consecrated life of virginity) while others are called to physical motherhood (giving birth to children). I am ambivalent about making a strict division between the two. Just as we are all called to union with God, all women are called to *some* aspect of spiritual motherhood. This is not a competition between better calls. All calls are to union with God. God graciously chooses the way that best heals *you*, the path that is perfect for each of us as individuals and for the life of the world. Arguably, you can say that the consecrated life is a more *direct* path; giving your life to God through forsaking the life of building a family, embracing a life free of primary familial relationships, is a witness for the life to come when human beings will "neither marry nor be given in marriage" (Mk 12:25). There is a freedom for love of God and neighbor through accepting a commitment to a celibate life. Catholic teaching (as well as the Bible, for all the beauty it holds about children and family) holds that the consecrated life is a more spiritually direct route to union with God.[84] We can say, then, that women who have dedicated themselves to the consecrated life are embracing a spiritual motherhood, modeling the fullness of the spiritual motherhood of Mary, both her total yes to God and the promise that God brings spiritual fruitfulness out of union. Women who are mothers of children can embrace a spiritual motherhood through the avenue of physical motherhood: as ensouled bodies, giving birth and mothering children is indeed a spiritual (as well as physical) act. The difference is not that one group is asked to give their lives to God, and not the other. We are all called to the law of the gift. But married men and women are called to give their lives to God through giving themselves to the other—and then giving their lives to the children to whom they become parents—and we can see it is not a direct giving to God. It can be utterly *complete*, but it is not *direct*. It is, however, a very full and rich journey. It is fruitful in a beautiful way that builds God's family on earth and sanctifies the people of God.

When women give birth, we are cooperating with a vocational call: the call to motherhood. It is not the only way to motherhood; adoptive parents are no less parents than birth parents and move through their own "labor" to foster healthy attachment.[85] They are no less called by God. In fact, they are called by God to "care for the orphan," as scriptural a call as one could hope to find. As for mothers who are birth mothers, but have given the child up for adoption, they too are living a call. They are bearing new life, and putting that child in a loving, secure home puts the needs of the child first in a radical and perhaps very painful way. They are putting the needs of the child first *and* answering a family's fervent prayers. It is a sacrificial love of the first order and should be honored as such.

The birth is not the only or essential moment of motherhood, but it is stamped on the female body as a very important way to know who God is. Fruitfulness is a natural consequence of a life of union. It may be hindered by illness or impairment, but that does not deny that fruitfulness is a natural consequence of union.

Through a theological reflection on the phenomenon of natural childbirth, we can see that spiritual motherhood is a call to which we respond by trust in God, fearlessness, cooperation with the Holy Spirit, and fruitfulness. The response yields room for the Holy Spirit to act in us and in the world. It transforms through seeing the value of human beings in cherishing love.

Spiritual Fatherhood

The claim that birth is a sign does mean that the sign bears meaning for men as well as women. What does the sign of birth have to say to men, and the call to spiritual fatherhood? Can a woman's experience of birth have anything to say to a man?

The official name of the movement often called "The Bradley Method®" is the "American Academy of Husband-Coached Childbirth." Robert Bradley—reportedly a devout Catholic[86]—argued against medical convention that husbands should be present with their wives throughout labor, and with the birth of their children.

Bradley's theory crystallized when one of the women, moments after delivering—as her husband paced in the waiting room—grabbed the doctor to thank him with kisses and hugs.

"Oh, thank you, thank you for showing me how!" she said.

"It hit me like a sledgehammer," Bradley later wrote. "What on earth was this lovely woman kissing me for? Why was I the object of gratitude as a labor coach while her young lover sat uselessly in the waiting room, fearful and anxious [...] deprived by isolation from the most meaningful emotional experience of their lives together? The more I thought about it, the more ridiculous it seemed."

This recommendation not only bucked medical practices, but also challenged a long-standing practice in many cultures that childbirth was women's work, and properly attended by women. Much of the modern history of obstetrics could be read as a battle of the sexes: women were midwives (theoretically men could and can be midwives, but this rarely happened). Only men were ob-gyn doctors for many years, and it is safe to say there was a fair amount of sexism in the treatment of the midwives.[88] Midwives, shunned, sometimes returned the favor by giving little weight to the doctors' recommendations and going their own way. One could argue that the gender tensions go back to Exodus 1, where the Egyptian midwives Shiprah and Puah creatively buck the Pharaoh's command to infanticide and allow the newborn sons of the Hebrew slave women to live.

In the midst of this, Bradley cut through multiple cultural expectations and raised what seemed to be a crazy concern to almost everyone: why isn't the father present, and helping, at the birth of his child? There may be occasional legitimate reasons why this is impossible, but a father present at the birth of his child does seem ideal, and natural. Bradley, in fact, has the father of the child much more than present: he is "coaching" the laboring mother. Coaching may not be the best word, but it is intended to communicate a kind of observational involvement. During the first and second stage of labor, he is watching his wife very intently, having conversation when she desires it, encouraging, praising, providing back rubs, even literally supporting his wife's weight when she has a contraction standing up. And yes, before the joke is made, he is possibly the recipient of many brutal squeezes of the hands.

Catholic theology has a long tradition of the father as the provider and protector of the family, and there is an element of this in his role within attending childbirth as well: the husband is encouraged to protect his wife's space and wishes, and to provide help as is possible. But what most Bradley Method® fathers seem to walk away with is the same lesson learned by their laboring partners: the challenge of practicing receptivity. While the laboring woman practices receptivity to birth by accepting it and cooperating with it, the attending husband is there to see to her needs, their child's needs, and not his own. What is challenging for many attending husbands is to see their wives in such a difficult process, and not be able to make that "go away." There is receptivity to God's plan unfolding here in the process of labor, and the husband is not able to "fix" it, control it, or do anything but honor it. His role is to support his wife for better or worse, and usually a birthing event is felt as a combination of the two. A husband's physical support as his wife gives birth seems a vital element of the marriage covenant ("will you accept children lovingly from God…?") that shouldn't be quickly ceded to even the most caring medical professionals. The husband/father has a role in the family that does not disappear when the going gets tough.

There is a transcendental beauty held in this moment, when a couple works together to give birth to this child, desired by God, into the world. Every family is the holy family in such a moment, bound by joy. God is present at every childbirth. But when a husband attends his wife's birth of their child, they naturally invite God into the vocation to holiness that began with the vows of their marriage. Living out the vocation honestly creates a space to see God's work.[89]

I hesitate to read too much into what a birth father's presence and participation at his wife's labor and the birth of his child has to say about spiritual fatherhood, mostly because I expect that people more familiar with living out the fullness of the role of spiritual fatherhood (that is, priests) would make more salient connections. But I see possibilities. The spiritual process of birth highlights that we must pay attention to the unfolding event, that part of spiritual fatherhood is listening and beholding the work of God in the other. Part of spiritual fatherhood is naming the signs of progress in the other. Part of spiritual fatherhood is standing ground, not running away when the other is in "transition." Part of spiritual fatherhood is heralding the impending birth. And the joy of spiritual fatherhood is in welcoming the spiritual birth of another, indeed, a spiritual birth that you may see more clearly than the other does. So much of fatherhood is about observation in love, a facilitation of the life of the other that puts your life aside. There is great gift, but also great sacrifice, and the role of the father accompanying the mother at the birth of his child can crystalize that reality.

In Scripture, it is clear that childbirth was experienced as a part of life. Husbands attending a woman's birth may not have been typical due to Jewish law, but after all, we are talking about a culture of people who lived in close quarters and didn't have hospitals. People, women and men, *knew* childbirth. Families would have handed down knowledge on how to give birth well. By contrast, today, many mothers hand down to daughters the experience of "I was unconscious and met you a few hours later," and fathers, "I was worried and bought cigars." When other cultures have taught what it means to be a mother or father, there is an "on the ground" reality that was known. Can we speak of what it means to be a spiritual mother or father without any experiential knowledge of this God-given reality? I don't mean to say that everyone needs to experience childbirth, but that we live in a culture that diminishes, mocks, and sanitizes an experience that is central to many people's understanding of the vocation of parenthood. To put it bluntly, can we even read the Bible correctly and translate toil when it is toil and pain when it is pain? Childbirth, as a semi-public sign in receiving God's grace, is important: designed by God for our good, but tarnished by sin, and almost completely smothered by cultural mores and expectations. When we are able to perceive the spiritual sign, and welcome it, we live in a healing moment, where the unitive relationship between God and humanity is embraced.

Our Own Vocation To God's Family

The three applications of the Theology of the Body made in this book—giving birth, living impaired, and dying—are joined by more than a connection to the hermeneutic of the gift. I argue that they all, seen rightly, illumine a call embedded in our ensouled bodies and animated by the Holy Spirit to God's family. This is no saccharine sentiment: the Theology of the Body is in many ways a theology of vocation. Edith Stein, also known as St. Teresa Benedicta of the Cross, wrote in her *Essays on Woman* that every human being has a threefold vocation: a universal vocation as a beloved child of God; a gendered vocation as a son or daughter of God; and an individual vocation, which begins with a call to a state of life and moves from there, i.e., marriage, or consecrated life, or diaconate/priesthood, then perhaps to mother or father, activist, teacher, or other possibilities.[90] We are all born to God's family and called to be family to each other.

The ancient call to be brothers and sisters to each other sounds like a wooden bell in a culture where families are, by definition, broken. Many have written of the challenge of accepting the Fatherhood of God, in the experience of children with an abusive father or the motherhood of Mary, given all the mixed messages we receive about the value of motherhood. Part of the prophetism of the body, as John Paul sometimes called it,[91] is the message of the spiritual value of fatherhood and motherhood. How beautifully we have, body and soul, been created for this gift. How we are called to participate in the mystery of creation, the intensity of labor, the joy of new life. When we participate with our vocational call, the path is not made perfectly straight, but there is nothing ultimately to fear.

One embodiment of the Church that explicitly names the call to be God's family is the Church in Africa. John Paul II's Post-Synodal Apostolic Exhortation *Ecclesia in Africa* notes the work of the African bishops over four weeks in 1989, and underlines with enthusiasm the synod's call to image the Church as God's family: a way of understanding Church and relationships that is culturally derived, but also scriptural and universal. The Church as God's family could be profoundly compatible with the purpose behind the images of Church asserted by the Second Vatican Council's Dogmatic Constitution on the Church, *Lumen Gentium*: "By her relationship with Christ, the Church is a kind of sacrament or sign of intimate union with God, and of the unity of all mankind."[92]

Not only did the Synod speak of inculturation, but it also made use of it, taking the *Church as God's Family* as its guiding idea for the evangelization of Africa. The Synod Fathers acknowledged it as an expression of the Church's nature, particularly appropriate for Africa, for this image emphasizes care for others, solidarity, warmth in human relationships, acceptance, dialogue and trust. The new evangelization will thus aim at *building up the Church as Family*, avoiding all ethnocentrism and excessive particularism, trying instead to encourage reconciliation and true communion…. "It is earnestly to be hoped that theologians in Africa will work out the theology of the Church as Family with all the riches contained in this concept, showing its complementarity with other images of the Church."[93]

We are called to be family, to answer calls to spiritual motherhood, spiritual fatherhood, at different times within our life journey. If the anthropology within the Theology of the Body were extended to name the body as a pre-given sign of self-giving and fruitfulness, we can see how childbirth points to all human beings' renewal in the Holy Spirit, a sign that points to the path of holiness through a fearless openness to God, yielding space to the Holy Spirit, and being hospitality. This cooperation with the Holy Spirit leads to transformation, healing, and fruitfulness. It is often crowned in tenderness and joy. No, not every birth looks like this. Probably most don't in their entirety. But there is much reason to believe childbirth was meant to look like this, and even in its fallen reality, reflects the call to transformation and fruitfulness in the Holy Spirit.

If John Paul II's Theology of the Body speaks to the universal vocation to union to God through the sign of marriage, the call to be spouse, this extension points to the gendered vocation to life and fruitfulness through physical and spiritual motherhood and fatherhood.[94] It is both a natural extension of the meaning of the first sign as well as a commonly experienced consequence and gift.

In the next two chapters, the extension of the key themes of the hermeneutic of the gift in the Theology of the Body continues to expand the notion of vocation to God's family through theological reflection upon spiritual brotherhood and sisterhood in the phenomenon of impairment, when the body is prevented from living in ways we expect, and spiritual elderhood, theological reflection upon the phenomenon of dying, particularly, watching a loved one die.

ENDNOTES

1. As John Paul II says: "We only wish to observe that man, in his present state of existence in the body, experiences many limits, sufferings, passions, weaknesses, and finally death itself, which relates his existence at the same time to another or different state or dimension...." *Man and Woman*, 3.4, n.8.
2. See John Paul II, *Ecclesia in Africa* #63.
3. Pss 68:5-6, NIV translation.
4. F. Menacker and B.E. Hamilton, "Recent trends in cesarean delivery in the United States" *NCHS Data Brief*, No. 35. Hyattsville, MD: National Center for Health Statistics, (March 2010).
5. Many books, mostly by fairly outraged women, have been written on the state of medical childbirth in the United States (and much of the Western world). Four representative examples: Jennifer Block, *Pushed: The Painful Truth about Childbirth and Modern Maternity Care* (De Capo Press, 2007); Marsden Wagner, *Born in the USA: How a Broken Maternity System Must Be Fixed to put Women and Children First* (Berkeley and Los Angeles, CA: University of California Press, 2008); Tina Cassidy, *Birth: The Surprising History of How We Are Born* (New York: Grove/ Atlantic Monthly Press, 2006); and Naomi Wolf, *Misconceptions: Truth, Lies, and the Unexpected on the Journey to Motherhood* (New York: Anchor Books, 2001). There is also a popular and provocative documentary created on the subject, *The Business of Being Born*, DVD, directed by Abby Epstein. (Los Angeles: New Line, 2008). It is a complicated story, fed by sociology, the scientific revolution, religious attitudes, psychology, feminism, and flat out sexism. My narrative simply will address how birth got moved into hospitals in the United States, and, for better or worse, what a typical experience of a hospital birth is today.
6. Cassidy, 57-63. Louis Pasteur's theory of living microbes and Joseph Lister's principles of antisepsis emerged in the 1860s, but the hand washing was slow to take hold as a practice, and the statistic above is compiled from the 1920s.
7. Cassidy, 56.
8. The New York Academy of Medicine released a study in 1933, *Maternal Mortality in New York City*, which cited that poor hospital care led to the majority of mother and infant deaths. Soon after, a White House report found that despite the rapid and dramatic increase in hospital births over home births, mother/infant mortality was not declining overall (Cassidy, 61). Although modern midwives have been embraced by modern medicine in some regions of the Western world, they still have an uphill battle in terms of reputation. See this December 2011 posting comparing same-week news stories of a midwife hailed as a heroine of public health in Indonesia, compared to a lay midwife saving a woman and infant's lives in an emergency birth in California, and then getting arrested for practicing medicine without a license: Stacia Guzzo, "The Paradoxical Perception of Midwifery in American Culture," *Feminism and Religion*, blog, December 13, 2011, http://feminismandreligion.com/2011/12/13/1722/.
9. Cassidy, 36-49. The relationship in the early 1900s between lay midwives and the medical establishment was appalling, to put it mildly. Although it is clear that lay

midwives varied in their abilities (as did obstetricians), most historians now see that they did not deserve to be criminalized as a group by states that saw doctors as the new wave of public well-being and the authorized protectors of public health. As many saw it, doctors were reputedly better educated and trained, sworn to the Hippocratic oath, and could administer new drugs that made childbirth less painful. To dispute that began to be seen as a criminal act, akin to child abuse.

10. Pitocin is a synthetic hormone used to induce or speed up labor, created to mimic the natural hormone oxytocin. It is the most commonly used medical intervention in hospital childbirths to help induce or speed up labor, especially if the mother is in bed (which slows labor) and has an epidural (which compensates for the increased pain due to the quicker and stronger contractions).

11. An episiotomy is a surgical incision made in the perineum—the tissue between the vaginal opening and the anus—during childbirth.

12. Cassidy, 90-4.

13. Grantly Dick-Read, M.D., *Childbirth Without Fear: The Principles and Practice of Natural Childbirth.* Second revised edition. (New York: Harper and Row, 1959). The text was initially published in Britain as *Revelation of Childbirth,* (London: William Heinemann, 1944).

14. Frederick Leboyer, *Birth Without Violence,* 1st American ed. (New York: Knopf, 1975).

15. Michel Odent, "Birth Under Water," *The Lancet* 322, Nos. 8365-6 (December 31, 1983):1476-7, ISSN 0140-6736, 10.1016/S0140-6736(83)90816-4, http://www.sciencedirect.com/science/article/pii/S0140673683908164.

16. One of the reasons stated baldly for the dramatic increase in the Cesarean rate is due to providers' fears of malpractice claims and lawsuits. See Theresa Morris, *Cut It Out: The C-Section Epidemic in America* (New York: New York University Press, 2013), chap. 1.

17. This brief account of the gestation and birth process is simply to give those who have not given birth or been near a person doing so what exactly the medical process is like for many women. What is written here is a combination of many sources, including my own experience and the experience of women I know. If you prefer a medical resource for what this experience may look like, I suggest the text written by a medical doctor and registered nurse team: William Sears, M.D., and Martha Sears, R.N., *The Birth Book: Everything You Need To Know To Have A Safe And Satisfying Birth* (Boston: Little, Brown and Company, 1994.)

18. Atul Gawande does not go quite that far, but discusses the issue with sympathy in his fascinating book *Better: A Surgeon's Notes on Performance* (New York: Picador Press, 2008), 192ff.

19. This is my opinion, based on research. A summary of the argument may be found in Marjorie Tew, "Do Obstetric Intranatal Interventions Make Birth Safer?" in *BJOG: An International Journal of Obstetrics & Gynaecology* 93, no. 7 (July 1986): 659–74.

20. Gawande, 192.

21. Interestingly, "birth" also has an etymological root in the word *wave: bara,* the root, is Old Norse for wave, billow, or bore. Vangie Bergum, "Birthing Pain," *Phenomenology Online,* http://www.phenomenologyonline.com/sources/textorium/bergum-vangie-birthing-pain/, (accessed October 12, 2012).

22. This was mentioned as the single element that clearly distinguishes the birth of a human being from the birth of other mammals, including chimpanzees. Joseph

Milton, "Chimps Give Birth Like Humans," *Nature: International Weekly Journal of Science*, April 19, 2011, doi:10.1038/news.2011.247. Although there are a few records of preference for solitary childbirth in a few cultures, these observations are debated (for example, first births may be typically accompanied, and there is some question as to whether laboring women are truly alone or not allowing the men access). Evolutionary science points out that the way human women give birth appears to naturally necessitate help in a way our closest relatives on the evolutionary chain (chimpanzees and other primates) do not. Wenda Trevathan, "Need For Assistance With Childbirth," (*CARTA: Center for Academic Research and Training in Anthropogeny*), http://carta.anthropogeny.org/moca/topics/need-assistance-with-childbirth (accessed September 19, 2013).

23. These first three descriptions were online comments on my article "A Fiery Gift: a meditation on birth and the spiritual life," *America Magazine*, October 5, 2009, http://www.americamagazine.org/content/article.cfm?article_id=11891.
24. Anonymous, personal interview, November 28, 2011. Name withheld on request.
25. Untitled blog post, *Baby McL*, January 4, 2009, http://babymcl.blogspot.com/2010/01/joseph-winslette-mclaughlin-born-dec-21.html
26. *Man and Woman*, Introduction, 105.
27. Grantly Dick-Read, *Childbirth Without Fear: The Principles and Practice of Natural Childbirth*, 2nd rev. ed. (New York: Harper and Row), 1959.
28. Dick-Read, 39-48. This is also part of the reason water labors—that is, laboring in a large pool of water—are statistically shown to be more comfortable for the laboring mother, and pain is reported with much less frequency. Water is inherently relaxing and produces a more relaxed state in the mother. See Michel Odent, "Birth Under Water."
29. Susan McCutcheon. *Natural Childbirth the Bradley Way*. Rev. ed. (New York: Plume, 1996), 77.
30. Most memorably in Ps 127.
31. Colleen Carpenter Cullinan, "In Pain and Sorrow: Childbirth, Incarnation, and the Suffering of Women," *Cross Currents*, 58 (Spring 2008):1, 99. I will discuss this article in more depth at the beginning of chapter 3, since its analysis has as much to do with impairment as childbirth.
32. For every reader who has said this passage seems unfair to humanity because the serpent tricked Eve: note Gn 3:2-3, where Eve very correctly and precisely renders the command of God to the serpent. She knew what God said, and knew who God was and is, and still preferred a creature's rebuttal. There is no trickery here (although the serpent is cunning in its language). St. Paul also famously argues that death is a consequence, a "fruit," of that sinful act in Rom 6:23: "For the wages of sin is death, but the gift of God is eternal life in Christ Jesus our Lord." Other scriptural references to death as a consequence of sin: Jas 1:15, and Gal 6:7-9.
33. As Phyllis Trible notes, *issebonek* refers to pain or toil in general. Carol Meyers' *Discovering Eve* exegetes the passage word by word, emphasizing what a grammatically and linguistically challenging passage it is, but saying more strongly than Trible that the Hebrew is rightly translated "toil." Helen Wessel notes explicitly that the words used for the woman's and man's sentences are the same root, and most naturally translated toil. Wessel argues that the use of the word *pain* has no cause other than a reading of our own cultural understandings onto the Hebrew text. Phyllis Trible, *God and the Rhetoric of Sexuality*, (Philadelphia:

Fortress, 1978), 127; Carol Meyers, *Discovering Eve: Ancient Israelite Women in Context* (New York: Oxford, 1988), chap. 5, and Helen Wessel, "Biblical and Talmudic Images of Childbirth," *Encyclopedia of Childbearing: Critical Perspectives*, ed. Barbara Katz Rothman (Phoenix: The Oryx Press, 1993), 29-30.

34. The one exception was another birth narrative, the birth of Jabez (1 Chr 4:9). Interestingly, John Paul II wrote extensively on the concept of work vs. toil in what is one of his most creative encyclicals, *Laborem Exercens* (see especially #27). But he does not tackle the issue of toil as an aspect of childbirth. (He does speak of the toil of a mother rearing a family, but childbirth is never mentioned as part of that.) Basically, John Paul II argues we consider work as part of the calling of what it means to be a thriving human being, and toil as the difficulty of work after the Fall. There can be a blessing buried within some natural toil, but the destructive difficulty of it is part of the fallen condition.

35. The Septuagint is accurate; Meyer argues persuasively that *eseb* does not refer to physical pain but to emotional challenge. Her preferred translation of the word is "travail." Meyer, 106-8.

36. Helen Wessel, Natural Childbirth and the Christian Family (New York: Harper and Row, 1963), 57-9.

37. All these relationships are held within the original call to humanity in Gn 1:28-30: "…Be fruitful and multiply, and fill the earth and subdue it…."

38. *Catechism of the Catholic Church* #399-406.

39. Fear, in this case, refers to being afraid. As the Oxford English Dictionary defines it, "The emotion of pain or uneasiness caused by the sense of impending danger, or by the prospect of some possible evil." The "fear of the Lord" that refers to wonder and awe may be etymologically similar in Hebrew but evokes a substantially different experience.

40. The commonality between holy fear and fear as peril is the sensation that what is before the person is much bigger than he/she is. The difference is that fear as peril sees the enormity of the one perceived as an immediate threat. See Rudolf Otto, *The Idea of the Holy: An Inquiry Into The Non-Rational Factor In The Idea Of The Divine And Its Relation To The Rational* (New York: Oxford University Press, 1958), especially chap. 4.

41. John Paul's discussion of shame is, in my estimation, the most confused section of the audiences: not because he doesn't have good points, but they are complicated by his use of multiple Italian words that denote different senses of shame, and these shades of meaning are not indicated in the English text except in the index. He also uses the terms for shame in a way that is quite different from most psychological understandings of the term, which makes the reader feel like he/she ought to understand what is being said, but inexplicably is not understanding it. A good article that summarizes John Paul II on shame: Mark Latkovic, "John Paul II On The Phenomenon Of Sexual Shame," *National Catholic Bioethics Quarterly* 3, no. 1 (Spring 2003): 45-51.

42. *Man and Woman*, 28:2.

43. *Man and Woman*, 28:3.

44. *Love and Responsibility*, 181.

45. Mark S. Latkovic, "John Paul II On The Phenomenon Of Sexual Shame," *National Catholic Bioethics Quarterly* 3, no. 1 (Spring 2003):48. Latkovic is summarizing insights from the May 14, 1980, audience found in *Man and Woman* #27.

46. Helen Merrell Lynd, *On Shame and the Search for Identity* (New York: Routledge,

1958).

47. H.A. Williams, *True Resurrection* (Springfield, IL: Templegate Publishers, 1972), 21.

48. *Semi-public* is a deliberately chosen phrase here: until recently, childbirth was an experienced part of community life that occurred in the home. Although not everyone was privy to the birthing room, people knew what was happening and could hear it, at minimum. I do not think most women are going to be happy with a fully public childbirth for prudent reasons, and there is often a desire to keep the event close to family and friends. The current wave of reality TV shows on live childbirth distort as much as show, highlight the medical technology more than the mother and child, and give credence to placing the phrase "Reality TV" in scare quotes.

49. There have been two dissertations written recently on a theology of childbirth: Dawn Alitz's "The spiritual formation of adults in the advent and event of parenting," diss., (Saint Paul, MN: Luther Seminary, 2009), and Rachel Rasmussen's "Crown of Creation: Toward a Theology of Birth," diss., (Harvard Divinity School, 1997). There are micro-publishing house books by two evangelical Christian women working as doulas, Jennifer Vanderlaan's meaty devotional *The Lord of Birth: Devotional Bible Study for Pregnancy* (Colonie, NY: Birthing Naturally, 2005), and Kelly Townsend's *Christ Centered Childbirth* (Gilbert, AZ: Four Winds Publications, 2005). There are occasional articles in perinatal education on the spirituality of childbirth (for example, Wendy Budin's "Birth and Death: Opportunities for Self-Transcendence," *The Journal of Perinatal Education* 10, No. 2 (2001): 28-42, and Trudelle Thomas's "Becoming a Mother: Matrescence as Spiritual Formation," *Religious Education* 96, No. 1 (2001):86-105. Sarah Smith Bartel wrote a fine article on natural childbirth as an extension of John Paul II's personalism: "Welcoming The Child At Birth," *National Catholic Bioethics Quarterly* 6, No. 2 (Summer 2006):273-294. I have written on the subject twice myself in *America* and *Sojourners*. But it is telling that a thoroughly secular article—*New York Times Magazine*'s "Unnatural Selection" on the phenomenon of selective reduction—elicited enormous outcry across the board in Catholic circles, saying the article described perfectly what pregnancy and childbirth is NOT supposed to be. See Ruth Padawer, "Unnatural Selection," *New York Times Magazine*, August 14, 2011, 22 on Academic Search Premier, EBSCOhost (accessed October 11, 2012).

50. Jean-Pierre de Caussade, *The Sacrament of the Present Moment*, ed. Kitty Muggeridge (San Francisco: HarperSan Francisco, 1989). As the text is a collection of presentations, published posthumously, and has been variously named, it is often titled *Abandonment to Divine Providence* or *The Joy of Full Surrender*.

51. Stephen Rossetti, *When the Lion Roars: A Primer for the Unsuspecting Mystic* (Notre Dame, Indiana: Ave Maria Press, 2003), 60-4.

52. To my mind, this does not mean God wants us in pain. Pain is a consequence of original sin, part of our walk toward death, but not something directly created by God. (See Colleen Carpenter Cullinan's "In Pain and Sorrow: Childbirth, Incarnation, and the Suffering of Women.") Yet even in pain, God can bring all things to good for those who love Him, as Rom 8:28 says. First and foremost, God wants to draw us near to him in the process of giving birth. And the best way to cooperate with that is to recognize that God is the Lord of fertility and birth and to cooperate with God's work in you by clearing distractions and allowing it to happen.

53. The following article cites a significant survey of American women who had re-

cently given birth, and almost 50 percent had artificially induced labor. The article goes on to argue why that number is far higher than it should be. Judith A. Lothian, "Saying 'No' To Induction," *The Journal of Perinatal Education* 15, no. 2 (2006):43-5.

54. De Caussade, *The Joy of Full Surrender*, trans. Hal McElwaine Helm (New York: Paraclete Press, 1986), 125-6.

55. John Paul II, *Crossing the Threshold of Hope* (London: J. Cape, 1994), 35-6.

56. McCown, 12.

57. Janet Ruffing has an excellent second chapter on forms of resistance in spiritual direction. One memorable piece in it recalls a comment from Paul Tillich: "If you've never run away from God, I wonder who your God is." Janet Ruffing, *Spiritual Direction: Beyond the Beginnings* (New York: Paulist Press, 2000), 33-55.

58. Ignatius of Loyola, *The Spiritual Exercises*, trans. David Fleming, par.315, 249.

59. The classic challenge to women's primary sin being pride is found in Valerie Saiving's article, "The Human Situation: A Feminine View," *Journal of Religion*, 40, no. 2 (April 2, 1960):100-12.

60. Emilie Griffin, *Clinging: The Experience of Prayer* (San Francisco: Harper and Row, 1984), 20.

61. "How Many Contractions Are There?" *PHDoula*, blog, November 1, 2010, http://dynamicdoula.blogspot.com/2010/11/how-many-contractions-are-there.html.

62. Jn 14:16.

63. Jim Forest, (lecture, Saint Mary's University of Minnesota, Winona, MN, March 2002). Forest's most recent biography of Dorothy Day is *All Is Grace: A Biography Of Dorothy Day* (Maryknoll, NY: Orbis Books, 2011).

64. Rupert Shepherd, "New Blood Test for Down Syndrome – During Early Pregnancy," *Medical News Today*, Oct 19, 2011, http://www.medicalnewstoday.com/articles/236256.php. At the time of this text's publication, this blood test has been made public, but it is not as low-cost as anticipated.

65. The abortion rate of women whose unborn children test positive for DS through amniocentesis and CVS is more than 90 percent. See Amy Harmon, "Prenatal Test Puts Down Syndrome in Hard Focus," *The New York Times*, May 9, 2007, http://www.nytimes.com/2007/05/09/us/09down.html and "Termination Rates After Prenatal Diagnosis of Down Syndrome, Spina Bifida, Anencephaly, and Turner and Klinefelter Syndromes: A Systematic Literature Review. European Concerted Action: DADA" at http://www.ncbi.nlm.nih.gov/pubmed/10521836?dopt=Abstract Plus, Sept. 1999.

66. Robert Watson and Michael Mangis, "The Contribution of the Desert Tradition to a Contemporary Understanding of Community and Spiritual Intersubjectivity," *Journal of Psychology and Christianity* 20, no. 4 (2001):315.

67. Kelle Hampton, "Nella Cordelia: A Birth Story," *Enjoying the Small Things*, January 29, 2010, http://www.kellehampton.com/2010/01/nella-cordelia-birth-story.html.

68. For example: "A lot of people who find out ahead of time, they have that period where they don't have a baby to hold, but when your baby is there, and you're bonding—it just changes everything." Kelle Hampton interview, BYUTV.org, http://www.byutv.org/watch/8303febf-8c13-4a43-a645-99439d54f350/fresh-take-inspiring-stories-2#ooid=p1cW9qMjriHZyhonSK0Ed5nG06IlB4eH

69. Matthew Lickona, *Swimming with Scapulars*, (Chicago: Loyola Press, 2005), 4.

70. About Kids Health, "States of Alertness," http://www.aboutkidshealth.ca/en/resourcecentres/pregnancybabies/newbornbabies/newbornbabybehaviour/pages/

states-of-alertness.aspx , (accessed 11/14/13).

71. In William and Martha Sears, *The Attachment Parenting Book* (Hachette Digital, 2001): "Within minutes after birth, the newborn enters the state of quiet alertness, the state in which, researchers have discovered, a baby is most able to interact with her environment. It is almost as if she is so enthralled by what she sees, hears, and feels that she doesn't want to waste any energy squirming....Within minutes the infant begins to sense to whom she belongs."

72. There is much more accumulated research on the phenomenon of quiet alertness in infants after birth in Klaus and Kennell's *Bonding: Building the Foundations of Secure Attachment and Independence* (Perseus Publishing, 1995), chaps. 3-4. For a psychologist's point of view influenced by phenomenological philosopher Maurice Merleau-Ponty, see Eva Simms on the experience of mother and newborn as dyad, *The Child in the World: Embodiment, Time and Language in Early Childhood* (Detroit: Wayne State University Press, 2008), especially 22-23.

73. Jn 16:21-22: When a woman is in labor, she has pain, because her hour has come. But when her child is born, she no longer remembers the anguish because of the joy of having brought a human being into the world. So you have pain now; but I will see you again, and your hearts will rejoice, and no one will take your joy from you.

74. *Love and Responsibility*, 204. I will discuss more the spiritual destructiveness of sentimentality in chap. 3.

75. *Love and Responsibility*, 201.

76. Ibid.

77. Ibid.

78. Ibid., 207.

79. See Phyllis Trible, *God and the Rhetoric of Sexuality* (Philadelphia: Fortress, 1978), chap. 2, for an extended treatment.

80. Lorenzo Albacete, "Younger Than Sin," *Communio* 22 (Winter, 1995):594, especially n. 4: "...she was subject to aging, pain, sadness, and death. She shared this dimension with all, including her divine Son. At this level she had to await the effects of the Lord's redeeming death. In a human being, the spiritual exists through the psychological and physical. Because the latter for Mary was not in the original state, we can say with Bernanos that she experienced physically and psychologically the pressure of sin in the world, but did so in "wondering sadness"...."

81. CCC #499: "The deepening of faith in the virginal motherhood led the Church to confess Mary's real and perpetual virginity even in the act of giving birth to the Son of God made man. In fact, Christ's birth "did not diminish his mother's virginal integrity but sanctified it." And so the liturgy of the Church celebrates Mary as Aeiparthenos, the "Ever-virgin.""

82. There is an entire book of academic essays dedicated to these issues (and more): Donald H. Calloway, MIC, ed., *The Virgin Mary and Theology of the Body* (West Chester, PA: Ascension Press, 2005).

83. It is typical in the Orthodox tradition to say that icons are not painted, but written. Those called to the vocation of creating icons are called iconographers.

84. One of the most thorough recent treatments is in Fr. Thomas Dubay's *And You Are Christ's: The Charism of Virginity and the Celibate Life* (San Francisco: Ignatius Press, 1987), especially 43-8. The teaching is affirmed in the Catechism of the Catholic Church #916: "The state of consecrated life is thus one way of experiencing a "more intimate" consecration, rooted in Baptism and dedicated totally to

God. In the consecrated life, Christ's faithful, moved by the Holy Spirit, propose to follow Christ more nearly, to give themselves to God who is loved above all and, pursuing the perfection of charity in the service of the Kingdom, to signify and proclaim in the Church the glory of the world to come."

85. E-mail communication between author and Heidi Hess Sexton, October 2011.
86. Cassidy, 199.
87. Cassidy, 198.
88. The story of Dr. Virginia Apgar is a good case in point. She was refused entry into specializing in obstetrics at Columbia University's medical school in the 1930s (women don't do that) and specialized in anesthesiology instead, focusing on childbirth anesthesia. Noticing that newborns came out in all kinds of conditions, she devised a quick way to "grade" the newborn's medical state, at birth and five minutes after birth, through numbers that have become the famous and enormously helpful "Apgar score." See Gawande, 169-200.
89. A couple who gives birth in this way, I must say from experience, is a witness. I have given birth four times, once by Cesarean, and three times a natural childbirth, all four times using The Bradley Method® to some degree. Every time, nurses, midwives, and doctors have commented with amazement on how well my husband and I worked together and supported each other; how well we moved through the contractions. (This earned us some extra visits from student nurses, midwives, and OBs who had never seen an unmedicated childbirth before.) This is not because we had uncomplicated births or because I was an athletic wunderkind. First, we were prepared for what natural childbirth looks like and entails. Second, we had help in the form of a doula, who aided us both. Third, we saw journeying through childbirth as a way of living out our marriage covenant. No matter how difficult the intensity was, I had none of the much-joked-about desire to hit my husband and scream, "This is all your fault!" Instead, supporting each other in our vocations is what marriage looks like.
90. Edith Stein, *Essays on Woman*, vol. 2 of *The Collected Works of Edith Stein, Saint Teresa Benedicta of the Cross, Discalced Carmelite*, trans. Freda Mary Oben (Washington, DC: ICS Publications, 1987), chap. 2 (especially 57-9).
91. *Man and Woman*, #104.
92. *Lumen Gentium* 1.1, cited in *Ecclesia in Africa*, #63.
93. *Ecclesia in Africa*, #63
94. *Man and Woman*, 79:5.

CHAPTER 3
The Gift Of The Impaired Body

The Vocation To Brotherhood And Sisterhood

 KEY CONCEPTS

> **This chapter** expands to the primordial experience of impairment, or limitation. Human beings, by definition, are limited. But we have misspent ages trying to define what is acceptable and unacceptable limitation within a human being—through illness, disability, injury, and more. This chapter is in deep conversation with contemporary theologies of disability (especially Vanier, Reynolds and Yong) but ultimately finds its inspiration in the concept of *kenosis*, or self-emptying. The chapter rejects humanly created boundaries of what it means to be human, seeing how they have been used for discrimination and judgment. But much of Jesus Christ's incarnation and death—his unique meeting with limitation and impairment—points to the ecstatic reality of his life and identity coming from and returning to God the Father. We who are impaired are called to do no less, to recognize life and identity as coming constantly from God, and to recognize that we are called to offer it back to God. The chapter ends with case studies of three different types of impairment, and how those experiences may differ from each other: genetic, psychological, and physical. We are all called to some form of spiritual brotherhood or sisterhood, and facing the experience of impairment lends meaning to what it means to be a spiritual brother or sister to Jesus Christ.

We do not get to make our lives up. We get to receive our lives as gifts. —Stanley Hauerwas, *Living Gently in a Violent World: The Prophetic Witness of Weakness*

L'Arche is a sign rather than a solution. —Jean Vanier, *An Ark for the Poor: The Story of L'Arche*

...[B]ut he said to me, "My grace is sufficient for you, for power is made perfect in weakness." So, I will boast all the more gladly of my weaknesses, so that the power of Christ may dwell in me. Therefore I am content with weaknesses, insults, hardships, persecutions, and calamities for the sake of Christ; for whenever I am weak, then I am strong.
—2 Corinthians 12:9-10

We know that all things work together for good for those who love God, who are called according to his purpose. For those whom he foreknew he also predestined to be conformed to the image of his Son, in order that he might be the firstborn within a large family. And those whom he predestined he also called; and those whom he called he also justified; and those whom he justified he also glorified. —Romans 8:28-30

One could say, a person who is bound for dismay
May not just be in dismay,
But might, perhaps, be able to pray.
...
...in my mind,
A spider spins a web so complex that, if God
Could possibly give birth to new life,
Maybe I could spin my disabilities, in time,
Into the prayer of a lifetime....
My disabilities are only a step toward new life.
—Chris Reynolds, quoted in *Vulnerable Communion: A Theology of Disability and Hospitality*

An article I held before me while writing the chapter on childbirth as spiritual sign was Colleen Carpenter Cullinan's somber "In Pain and Sorrow: Childbirth, Incarnation, and the Suffering of Women."[1] While I offer that childbirth was created by God as a spiritual sign, part of "the pre-given language of self-giving and fruitfulness" that points to our call to union with God through receptivity to the Holy Spirit, one has to acknowledge how deeply original sin has tarnished this sign: between 350,000-500,000 women a year die in childbirth. Many more are injured grievously in the process, suffering internal injuries and pain, lifelong incontinence, and partial paralysis. (This describes the injury of fistulae, an obstructed labor injury most common in extremely young mothers, and Carpenter's rendition is not for the faint of heart.[2]) Carpenter is outraged, rightly, that there are regions of the world where the lifetime maternal mortality rate is 1 in 67[3], and asks: *Where is the Church* in this resolvable crisis of poverty, denigration of women, and medical access? When will all birthing women receive the value and care they deserve, to take childbirth and its dangers seriously?[4] I credit her article for raising many challenges: the ethical call to respect the lives of the laboring mother and child, the need to avoid a blithe romanticism about motherhood, the need to recognize that the medical system of the Western world (the good and bad) is not the medical system of the rest of the world, the need for families and cultures to value each woman as "a person for her own sake"[5] beyond the cultural expectation to arrange marriage for familial and cultural profit while girls are barely in puberty. But raising the reality that some women cannot give birth naturally without injury or intervention also serves as a move to address the embodied reality of **impairment**: that is, when human beings experience their bodies as unexpectedly limited.

To say that we experience our bodies as limited should be obvious; in fact, it is much of what defines embodiment. I flap my arms, but I can't fly. I can't be in two places at the same time. I can strive to beat a two-minute mile running for my entire life, and it isn't going to happen. It may frustrate, but there is much to say about the gift of knowing one's limits. However, this chapter is going to focus on impairment, which has found particular focus in the past 20 years within an emerging "theology of disability."[6] What happens when human beings *seem* to be prevented—due to atypical genetic coding, mental illness, physical illness, or injury—from being a pre-given sign of self-giving and fruitfulness? Is that even true—is it possible for a natural sign to be *prevented*? Could a sign be present through the impairment? Could an impairment ever be a sign in itself?

One significant difference between this chapter and the previous one is that I argued that childbirth was created by God as a natural sign. The basic limitedness that is the human body is also created by God, a natural sign as well. But impairment—at least most of the time—is arguably *not* the direct will of God, but a consequence of our fallen world. Although impairment may be redeemed, and tapped for God's ultimate will in bringing all to Himself,[7] illness, injury, and death are understood traditionally as a result of original sin. Impairment is often, although not always, a result of illness or injury. Impairment is also a huge experiential category: to talk about persons impaired or disabled covers a wide swath of reactions. Some find their disabilities to be neutral and simply part of who they are; others, a trial; still others, a blessing. And when we break various impairments down, it seems obvious that the experience of being blind is going to be different from the experience of being unable to walk, and both different from losing one's memory. The experiential differences are simply wider than the differences we find in the lived experience of childbirth.

God desires us to be whole, to be healed of the illnesses and injuries that are part of the inheritance of original sin, in this world or the next. But how and when that healing happens does not prevent the human person from embodying the natural sign that points to union with God. The natural sign of limit is *underscored* by the lived experience of impairment. This underscoring of the ensouled body living with impairments often serves as both call and witness: a witness to the work of the Holy Spirit, a witness to the passion of Christ, and a witness to our vocation to union with God, where weakness and vulnerability are the subversive way to life in God (1 Cor 1:27-28). As we shall explore, these witnesses are held within a vocation to brotherhood and sisterhood with the one who suffered impairment for the salvation of the world, Jesus Christ.

Living In Reality? How We See Impairment

Beginning with a description of lived reality for impaired people is no simple task. Impairments in and of themselves are different, and much of how people experience impairment is shaped by their social contexts. Sometimes the impairment removes people from engagement with community (being in a coma, for example, or hearing loss, or amnesia). Sometimes the impairment is rejected by the community. (See the commentary below on "severity" and on mental delays, explanations for aborting children with special needs.) Sometimes the impairment is actually seen as a social good, as in the case of a Hmong family in California interpreting a child's epilepsy as a gift, a sign to be a shaman for others.[8] Or as one hears anecdotally—there are people who appreciate their impairments as having good effect: a blindness that enables a person to "see without prejudice," an illness that forces a person to slow down and de-stress, etc. Before we can address the lived experiences of people with impairments, we need to pay attention to impairment's various manifestations and consequences.

Impairment refers to a loss of physiological form or function. It is a limit, although a particular kind of limit: a limit that indicates less than expected wholeness. While a healthy person with two legs is usually able to walk, a person with one leg has a loss of function. This may be remedied through a prosthetic leg or crutches or a wheelchair, but without accommodations the impairment results in a loss of the expected function of walking. The consequences of the impairment are referred to as *disability*: an inability to walk, see, hear, etc. Finally, *handicap* refers to the societal disadvantage resulting from impairment. If you can't walk, you can't access certain buildings without accommodation, for example.[9] Although inevitably I will be speaking about disability, the issue here is whether the impaired body can be an underscored sign: that is, is there a theology of the impaired body? Without saying that God directly wills impairment—but *does* will limits—can we say that the impaired body holds a "pre-given language of self-giving and fruitfulness"?

Deborah Creamer, a Protestant theologian who lives with a disability, argues convincingly for attention to the *reality of limitation*, and seeing bodily limitedness as a model for discussing disability. Within disability studies, there are two prominent models of disability: the medical/functional-limitation model and the social/minority group model. The medical model sees disability as a limitation of physical and/or mental function that can be measured against a norm. Most people see impairment and disability through this lens: this understanding of disability occurs when the body is broken, or perhaps undeveloped. It assumes (rightly, I would say) there is a discernible difference between health and injury, a human body typically developing and a human body impeded (for whatever reason).

The second common model is the social model, whose advocates have argued that impairments are disabling only to the extent that society makes no place at the table for people bearing them. In significant part, this model has risen in reaction to the medical model and was fueled by the civil rights movements in the United States in the 1960s and '70s. For example: blindness is a disability only insofar as the world expects sight. In the dark, the impairment of blindness is irrelevant. Indeed, those who are blind may have an advantage over the rest of us: they have learned to navigate "in the dark," whereas sighted people will stumble and fall. The group that has most embraced the social model of disability is Deaf culture. (As opposed to the physical condition of deafness, the capitalized D in Deaf culture signifies any group of people who uses American Sign Language, or ASL, as a primary means of communication.) Many invested in Deaf culture argue there is no impairment (loss of hearing) defining them; indeed, hearing children born to Deaf and deaf parents may define themselves as Deaf because ASL is their first language.[10] They are no more disabled than Spanish speakers are disabled in a predominantly English-speaking culture. Some who embrace Deaf culture define themselves as a "linguistic minority,"[11] and this social group is anchored and nurtured by residential schools for the deaf and the influence of Gallaudet University (a university in Washington, D.C. established to teach the deaf and hard of hearing). Beyond the distinctive example of Deaf culture, many of the disabled and other advocates, especially parents of children with disabilities, have come to define themselves as participants in a civil rights movement, marked by mottos such as "Nothing About Us Without Us" and political accomplishments such as the congressional passage of the 1990 Americans with Disabilities Act, which improved issues of access and education for the disabled across the United States.

Each model has its advantages. But neither of them, in and of itself, covers the range of experience of impairment and disability. Beyond each one's confines, there are also internal problems with these prevailing models. The social model is a primarily socially constructed model, and as such has its challenges: What happens when one person sees a lived reality as impairment and another, not? What happens when society does not agree? The medical model attends to the physical reality of impairment, but who defines what is medically "normal"? And is living with a medical disability always, by definition, "a deficit"? The abuses regarding defining who is disabled, and what that means for treatment and inclusion in community, are legion.

The "limits model" that Creamer proposes—"limits are normal...intrinsic to human existence...limits are good, or at the very least, not evil"[12]—could predefine impairment and disability, and recognize that the reality is larger and more pervasive than the medical or social models allow: disability, after all, is an "open minority,"[13] one we will all join someday if we are not there already, because human beings are limited, and those limits will be felt. If nothing else, we age into limitations of expected function. Most people experience illness and some form of impairment, at least temporarily. Working through these theologies of disability is no esoteric theological interest, but essential to expressing an honest theological anthropology. The witness that human beings are limited is as old as the book of Genesis. The very creation of human beings makes it clear that human beings are creatures of time and space, as opposed to God, who is Creator (or "Uncreate," that is, not created). We have a span: we are conceived, and we die. The soul is immortal, and the body destined for Resurrection and transformation. But we are creaturely. That means we have limits. Human beings are, by definition, limited.

A Reality Defined By Others: Resisting Sentimentality And Fear

Acknowledging limitation indicates we "live in reality." But how we define reality—and how we define who is disabled and who is not—is where things become difficult, and the fallen nature of the world crashes in.

Many people have written that the label of disability has evoked two images: the angelic sufferer, which plays into sentimentality; or the misbegotten monster, which plays into fear. While the first category's sentimental untruthfulness causes squirming, the second category is where we see the worst of how human beings can treat each other. We do not have to scratch deeply to see how people with disabilities have been judged to miss the mark of "normal," with disastrous consequences. Beyond the daily access accommodations that could make possible participation within society, there are many who assume that disability is incompatible with community, even with life. For example, in Eastern Europe, there are orphanages and institutions that house abandoned children with special needs.[14] Although some are severely disabled from birth and need 24-hour medical care, most are not: children (and later, adults) with Down syndrome, cerebral palsy, fetal alcohol syndrome, and more. Although many are deeply disabled, much of the impairment comes from the inadequacy of institutional life, which can range from well-intentioned basic care to neglect and abuse. Just a couple of examples: A woman adopted a child with DS in one of those countries, and once the adoption was final, went to the store with her new son before flying home. A group of teenaged boys, after noticing the boy's DS characteristics, came over and spit in his face—in the direct presence of his new adoptive mother—before she knew what was happening.[15] Another adopted a child with DS, who was in very poor medical condition, and had to bribe a hospital in the country to provide emergency medical care for her child. It took four tries before she could find a doctor who would accept the bribe and provide any treatment for a child with Down syndrome.[16]

Before we muster American patriotic outrage, let's remember that the expected American response, if the disability is known before birth, is to abort the child. In terms of accepting people with disabilities, we are arguably no better. Additionally, many of these countries are dealing with political upheaval, poverty, and the legacy of Stalin. (These institutions are an inheritance of communist ideology driven by a person's use to the state.) In the midst of this, there are some people trying to treat these children and adults with compassion, and others trying to challenge the assumption that institutional life is the best care for most disabled children and adults. But they work against a cultural model of disregard for those with disabilities.

To speak of the "norm" or "normal" is to use a modern word.[17] Lennard Davis's *Enforcing Normalcy* links the word normal and the concept of normalcy to the rise of statistical method: "a use of data for promotion of 'sound, well-informed state policy.'"[18] Prior to the 19th century, human beings were understood next to an ideal prototype: a method that ensured everyone fell short. But with the rise in statistics, especially the bell curve, people began to think of the "normal" human being as falling within the mean. Hence the popular use of the statistical term "deviant" to refer to human beings who "don't fit within the norm." (It is rarely used in a neutral, much less positive sense: the positive would most likely be termed "exceptional"—i.e., the exception to the norm.) At the same time, the theory of evolution was transforming Western biological sciences. Although evolutionary theory opened people's eyes to a fascinating view of how the Earth and its life forms came to be, many took the theory out of the natural sciences and applied a version of it to the social sciences,[19] as a way to explain—and perhaps proactively shape and influence—the way of society. The "survival of the fittest" became a leading light and justification to isolate and starve out the deviant. The worst example of this was the rise of eugenics.

The widespread influence of eugenics in the late 1800s and early 1900s is not widely known. Most people are familiar with the Nazi eugenic program, where the combination of educated couples getting married and having children later in life reduced the German birth rate, while the less educated married younger and continued to reproduce at the same birth rate. Some Nazis were concerned that the population was genetically shifting to lesser intelligence and moral fortitude, which many eugenicists held was an inherited trait, working from a reference from Darwin's *The Descent of Man*.[20] It is no accident that the concentration camps immediately killed those who were suspected to be disabled, mentally or physically, and especially targeted racial groups who were "scientifically" deemed to be mentally or morally unfit: Jews and the Romany. (This explains why it did not matter whether Jews living in Nazi-occupied countries were practicing Judaism or not. For the Nazis, the Holocaust was an efficient form of eugenic racism, what we now call "ethnic cleansing.") What most people do not realize is how widespread eugenic thought and practices were throughout the world. Just to focus on the United States:

- One of the first American public health initiatives was a hospital run by the new Public Health Service, built on Ellis Island, the entry point of the great wave of European immigrants. Often this hospital simply took in sick immigrants to the United States and gave them free and needed medical treatment before release. But the hospital's doctors and the U.S. surgeon general were also influenced by eugenic science and tested immigrants against the statistical intellectual norm by stripped-bare physicals, facial photography, and administering the newly created IQ tests (in English), categorizing those who failed the test as feebleminded, morons, idiots, and imbeciles. These immigrants were removed from their immigrating families and sent back, alone, to their home country. Most, following the lead of eugenics' partiality for linking facial characteristics with intelligence, were Southern European and Eastern European, people considered to be of inferior racial stock.[21] The congressional Chinese Exclusion Act of 1882 (repealed in 1943), which disallowed all immigrants who were ethnic Chinese, also was supported with eugenic language.

- Margaret Sanger (1879-1966), the founder of Planned Parenthood, edited the *Birth Control Review* journal from 1917-1929, which more than once bore the motto: "Birth control: to create a race of thoroughbreds." Her arguments for the promotion of birth control, and later abortion, were shot through with eugenic language. The problem for society, argued Sanger repeatedly, was that misplaced sympathy and care had extended the lives of weak and ill people, allowing them to procreate weak and ill children, further creating a burden on society and degeneracy: "...the most urgent problem to-day is how to limit and discourage the over-fertility of the mentally and physically defective." Therefore, "possibly drastic and Spartan methods may be forced upon American society it if continues complacently to encourage the chance and chaotic breeding that has resulted from our stupid, cruel sentimentality."[22]Birth control and abortion were touted as the liberation of women from unwanted pregnancies, yes, but also consistently as a way to weed the human race of "undesirables," as defined by Sanger and other eugenic lights.[23]

- Between 1907-74 more than 60,000 Americans were forcibly sterilized because they had "unfit human traits" (usually rubber stamped by a state eugenics board upon a single report by an employer, family member, neighbor, or teacher).[24] An especially well-documented case—now politically relevant as the state governor has formally apologized for previous state action, and restitution is debated—is the state of North Carolina, which enforced sterilizations longer than most states. (Other states curtailed their programs after the negative publicity of the Nazi program became known following World War II.) Because of the span of the North Carolina eugenic sterilization program, what is particularly revealing is how the categories demanding sterilization (feeblemindedness, mentally diseased, epilepsy, etc.) began to be applied with increasing frequency to young African-American women starting in 1958, coinciding with the rise of the civil rights movement. Although motive is impossible to prove, the parallelism raises uncomfortable questions of a passive-aggressive vengeance.[25]

Although this crass application of eugenics has been recognized in most circles as the evil that it is, eugenics is by no means gone: genetic testing awakens all these moral possibilities again. Who is in the norm, outside the norm, and is it in everyone's interest to allow those outside the norm to live? The ugly modern history gives evidence for the need to make a place at society's table for everyone, and allow those living with disability a large measure of self-definition.

But the stereotyping and dismissal of the humanity of people with disabilities has deeper roots than the eugenic movement, one that theologians Thomas Reynolds and Stanley Hauerwas take to task in what Reynolds calls "the cult of normalcy." In 1972, Wolf Wolfensberger wrote a now modern classic, *The Principle of Normalization in Human Services*,[26] making an argument for securing the rights of the disabled in American society through the "normalization" of the environment of people with disabilities (i.e., more cultural access and participation, less institutionalization). The book spurred a wave of improvements for many with disabilities, with a call for increased physical access resulting in wheelchair ramps and elevators, Braille labels, ASL signing at public events, mainstreaming education when possible, etc. For decades, "normalization" has been the preferred practice in educational and social service settings. But for all the necessary and valued improvements that book promotes, there is a shadow side to "normalizing," especially if "normalizing" gets applied to people rather than environments. Hauerwas cautions that to approach people via the measure of "normalcy" effectively destroys genuine difference.[27] Reynolds expands that insight to caution reading reality through what he calls *the cult of normalcy*:

> It is clear that a vigorous inclusion of differences remains one of the more important tasks of Christian communities today....But we must tread with great caution. Inclusion is a risky business. Too often it is servant to the status quo, championing the interests of convention rather than attending to the particular uniqueness of persons.

Reynolds offers pointed analysis on the touted benevolence of tolerance and assimilation, which can "[grant] differences a share of the public space only so long as they do not disrupt or cause inconveniences to a dominant group's way of life."[29] That doesn't mean all tolerance is bad. But it does mean that when tolerance becomes the prime ethical law, there is an inevitable consequence: toleration is granted by those in power, that is, those who set the identity of the group. Reynolds doesn't hold back: "Normalcy operates as a cultural system of social control. On one account, it is simply a way of ordering and bringing meaning to the everyday world shared by a group. It is unavoidable and itself good. There is, however, an insidious undertow that accompanies it, working to draw all into a certain caste or type....To state it plainly, the 'normal' is relative to a group's values and aspirations, and conversely so, what is attributed 'abnormal' (disease, disability, etc.)."[30]

The cult of normalcy is a real challenge, because we human beings are by nature social beings: *we want to belong.* The Theology of the Body audiences are structured on the very idea that "it is not good for man to be alone." As such, we are created with a powerful desire to belong to another. But this natural desire to belong to God, and to belong to another person, becomes warped when a God-absent and fickle normalcy becomes the price of belonging. To go back to the orphanage example:

when children are separated from consistent caregivers at a young age, when their belonging is thwarted, the evidence is overwhelming: they do not learn to attach, and they do not thrive. Basically, they die a slow death less because of lack of food or shelter, and more because they do not belong—the cult of normalcy has made no room for them. They grow in an environment that is not trustworthy, and they respond by withering and dying.[31] In a (sometimes) less dramatic example, we see the incredible formative influence of peer pressure—and not just in junior high school. We see the giddy rush to identify ourselves through social networking's circles, friends, and followers.[32] We must belong, and crave to find our identity through a social group.

There is a way to avoid the social temptation to define reality through normative groupings and the extension of tolerance, a way given to us in Scripture and revelation: we can look to how God defines what it means to be human through the revealed humanity of Jesus Christ. And if one thinks that to speak of impairment and disability makes no sense given the life of Christ, one needs to look more closely at both his ministry and the reality of the Incarnation and Crucifixion—allowing those realities to inform how we learn to see the present. It is only then that we can release the impulse to belong from the bondage of the cult of normalcy, and place it where it was meant to be: a belonging to Christ.

The Life Of Christ And His Disciples: In Weakness, Strength

The Kenosis Of Jesus Christ

There is no lack of Scripture on the human being as limited, as we shall see. But the first Scripture I wish to reflect on is almost more an icon of Christ than a Scripture: the *ecce homo* passage, often translated "behold, the man":[33]

> Then Pilate took Jesus and had him flogged. And the soldiers wove a crown of thorns and put it on his head, and they dressed him in a purple robe. They kept coming up to him, saying, "Hail, King of the Jews!" and striking him on the face. Pilate went out again and said to them,

"Look, I am bringing him out to you to let you know that I find no case against him." So Jesus came out, wearing the crown of thorns and the purple robe. Pilate said to them, "Here is the man!" When the chief priests and the police saw him, they shouted, "Crucify him! Crucify him!" Pilate said to them, "Take him yourselves and crucify him; I find no case against him" (Jn 19:1-6).

The terse passage in John teems with barely controlled chaos and violence, and sentences that bear more than the words can hold. Minutes after Pilate asks Jesus "what is truth?" he accepts the hysterical crowd's pardon of a murderer, and sends Jesus to be whipped by Roman soldiers. Soldiers mock him with violence in the melee, grinding sharp thorns on his head in the shape of a crown, draping an expensive cloak on a bloodied body. And at this point in the reading, there seems to be a snapshot pause, a sudden silence, as Pilate announces to the crowd: "Here, behold: the man."

Once again we have the phenomenologically weighted word for *seeing with attention*: behold. Instead of Mary's "behold, all generations will call me blessed, for the Almighty has done great things for me," we have behold: the Son of God, bound and bloodied, improbably allowing himself to be controlled by the occupier's army. The Messiah has consented to a way of limitation, of embodiment that can be bound, injured, and killed, as the way to define "the man."

This imagery of divine self-limitation is not new with the Passion: the very shock that the omnipotent, omnipresent, and omniscient God would incarnate Himself in a newborn, born in a cow's stall to a woman of humble birth within another melee (the census of Caesar Augustus) is a shock that we miss in our romanticization of the birth narrative. Despite all attempts, it is difficult to romanticize the *ecce homo* moment. Most see the image as one of humble suffering. But before the suffering, there is the divine self-limitation that is embodiment. And in the image, there is ironic tension: the Son of God, present at the creation of the world, willingly bound by his creatures.[34]

An even more exacting reality is the Eucharist as the chosen self-limitation of God. As modern desert father Carlo Carretto said, "Either

Christ is a raving madman, or He is truly omnipotent and merciful Love, who has found the most direct road to our hearts, a road that will not frighten or scare us, a road that is as simple as could be."[35] Sharing His very life—body and soul, humanity and divinity—through the humble, sustaining consumption of transubstantiated bread and wine is as divinely self-limiting as one can possibly imagine. But do imagine, as Carlo Carretto does, what that tells us about God:

> Why do you find it strange that I should have wanted to become bread through love?
>
> Have you no experience of love?
>
> When you have loved, really loved, have you not wanted to become bread for your beloved? …
>
> You can argue about the Eucharist as much as you like, but on the day love really takes hold of you, perhaps you will understand that Jesus is not a fool or a madman.
>
> To be able to become bread!
>
> To be able to nourish the whole world with his flesh and blood!
>
> I am terribly selfish and fearful when faced with suffering, but if I could become bread to save all humanity, I would do it.
>
> If I could become bread to feed all the poor, I would throw myself into the fire at once.
>
> No, the Eucharist is not something strange: It is the most logical thing in the world, it is the story of the greatest love ever lived in the world, by a man named Jesus.[36]

If we cannot understand the Eucharist through the strange logic of love, we cannot understand the Incarnation. The Eucharist is a natural extension of the incarnation of God. It is also a divine extension of the law of love: "You shall not … stand by idly when your neighbor's life is at stake" (Lv 19:16).[37]

The "Behold, the man" moment—whether we are referring to Pilate's statement, the passion itself, or the Eucharist—should be understood as part of the mystery of divine self-emptying and self-limitation, *keno-sis*.[38] This mystery, and what it has to say about a theology of the impaired body, is explored later in this chapter.

Stanley Hauerwas, in some acerbic truth-telling, says: "Christian humanism is determined by the Father's sending of the Son to be one of us. So humanism must always begin with Jesus' humanity. When that isn't the case…compassion becomes a way to say certain people would be better off dead."[39] Jesus Christ allows through His life and death that this weakness, in this case limitation, is a natural sign of being human. The passion is the underscored sign of limitation, an intentional sign where the Son of God chose to yield His life to the Father for the good of His brothers and sisters. The sign of limitation that is the Incarnation points to what it means to be human: when we see or experience limitation, even impairment, we should not think, "behold, the monster," but rather "behold, the man." The incarnation of Christ and His passion is the "norm," not anything defined by the cult of normalcy.

Jesus Christ's Ministry Of Healing

But it would be wrong to look only at the person of Jesus Christ without some attention to His prodigious ministry to the sick and disabled. Through the Gospels, Jesus is healing people brought to Him of physical and spiritual illnesses. He typically does not seek them out; others bring the sick to Him (or the sick will go to Him themselves). Jesus is seen as a source of healing, and importantly, healing is seen as a *good*: a sign, a call to discipleship, and a restoration to community. John 9 (the healing of the man born blind) forthrightly looks at some of the challenges found around physical healing.

The chapter is an extended healing narrative of a man's blindness and its consequences for the healed man, his family, and his community. While the chapter contains many subthemes—a dynamic interplay between the synagogue leaders who rejected Jesus's disciples after the year 85 AD, John's ongoing theme of spiritual sight and darkness, and Jesus's sinlessness—it also treats long-standing biblical understandings of sin and impairment. The healing itself is presented rather simply: Jesus encounters a man born blind and has an exchange with His disciples: His disciples ask Him, "'Rabbi, who sinned, this man or his parents, that he was born blind?' Jesus answers, 'Neither this man nor his parents sinned; he was born blind so that God's works might be revealed in him.'"[40] Jesus then breaks the Sabbath laws by mixing spittle with mud and proceeds to heal the man of his blindness.

As the chapter continues, we see a certain amount of bedlam: this healing brought not rejoicing but a flurry of questions and not a little outrage, with people questioning the healed man, and synagogue officials questioning the man's parents, then the man himself. Finally, Jesus asks the healed man His own question:

> Jesus heard that they had driven him out, and when he found him, he said, "Do you believe in the Son of Man?" He answered, "And who is he, sir? Tell me, so that I may believe in him." Jesus said to him, "You have seen him, and the one speaking with you is he." He said, "Lord, I believe." And he worshiped him. Jesus said, "I came into this world for judgment so that those who do not see may see, and those who do see may become blind."[41]

Looking simply at the attitudes toward his impairment and disability of blindness, we see three things:

1. There was an assumption of a fairly direct connection between the man's blindness and his actual sin, or since he was blind from birth, the actual sin of his parents. This assumption is promptly denied by Jesus, who says the man's blindness exists to help make visible the works of God. Jesus' answer is person-specific, but the principle that the actual sin is not a cause of disability is found in other places as well.[42]

2. The healed man seems to have been treated as outside the cult of normalcy. When his parents are questioned by the synagogue officials, they turn the questions back to the officials, telling them "He is of age, ask him." While that is often interpreted as an indication of fear of the officials, it could also be seen as a way for his parents to demand that the officials take into account their son's humanity and full participation in the Jewish faith. He had the experience and was of age, so why didn't they ask him? Was he taboo? Was he

seen as an appendage of his parents? Did physical blindness, even healed, make him "deviant" to the point of not speaking to him?

3. The healing is given freely, but culminates in a call to follow Christ. First, the healed man spars creatively and truthfully with the synagogue officials, leading to naming Jesus as one "from God": "Here is an astonishing thing! You do not know where he comes from, and yet he opened my eyes. …. If this man were not from God, he could do nothing" (v. 30,33). Later, when Jesus asks the healed man if he believes in the Son of Man, with minimal clarification, the healed man eagerly makes a public profession of faith. He is called through the healing to bring the truth of God to others. Every healing in the Gospel has embedded within it a call to discipleship, and a call to witness.

It is also worth noting two things in the extensive treatment of Jesus' healing ministry throughout the Gospels: according to Gospel witness, Jesus never turned down healing a person—although the healing didn't always occur in the manner expected.[43] Indeed, He seemed to delight in the other's healing. If it were a matter of creating miracles to encourage belief, there were other things He could have done. (Maybe flashing lightning from the sky? Earthquakes beginning and ceasing at whim?) He often encourages the healings be kept quiet, which doesn't make the case that the healing was entirely for witness. But the power of God, prior to the Resurrection, is predominantly seen through healing. The other point: to our knowledge, Jesus never heals a person with what we call now an intellectual disability. He heals the blind, the deaf, the lame, the mortally ill, those possessed by evil spirits, and even the dead: but not those who are intellectually disabled. According to the Gospels, he was never asked to do so. This is a point worth discussion later.

Finally, the healing ministry of Christ was clearly not restricted to Jesus Christ's earthly ministry. The Book of Acts refers repeatedly to the healing work passed down to the apostles,[44] and the letter of James tells "the sick among you" to ask the presbyters of the Church to pray over them for healing.[45]

Paul's "Thorn In The Flesh"

The last scriptural touchstone for most theologies of disability is the famously enigmatic reference by Paul, in the Second Letter to the Corinthians 12:2-10:

> I know a person in Christ who fourteen years ago was caught up to the third heaven—whether in the body or out of the body I do not know; God knows. And I know that such a person—whether in the body or out of the body I do not know; God knows— was caught up into Paradise and heard things that are not to be told, that no mortal is permitted to repeat. On behalf of such a one I will boast, but on my own behalf I will not boast, except of my weaknesses. But if I wish to boast, I will not be a fool, for I will be speaking the truth. But I refrain from it, so that no one may think better of me than what is seen in me or heard from me, even considering the exceptional character of the revelations. Therefore, to keep me from being too elated, a thorn was given me in the flesh, a messenger of Satan to torment me, to keep me from being too elated. Three times I appealed to the Lord about this, that it would leave me, but he said to me, "My grace is sufficient for you, for power is made perfect in weakness." So, I will boast all the more gladly of my weaknesses, so that the power of Christ may dwell in me. Therefore I am content with weaknesses, insults, hardships, persecutions, and calamities for the sake of Christ; for whenever I am weak, then I am strong.

The "thorn ... in the flesh" of v. 7 has been interpreted through nearly every possible perspective: a physical disability, an ongoing temptation, an illness, even a person opposing Paul's ministry. The reality is, we do not know from the text what the "thorn" was. We do know from Paul's word that he found the reality debilitating, and he prayed without ceasing ("three times" refers to intensity of prayer) that the disabling reality be lifted. And we know that the disabling reality was not lifted, but Paul receives a word from the Lord: *My grace is sufficient for you, for power is made perfect in weakness.* Weakness, according to Paul, allows Christ the space to work within the human person, and the work of Christ makes the person spiritually strong in a way he or she could not have achieved himself or herself. Perfect healing may indeed take the route of living with a disabling reality through God's grace.

So there are three especially salient scriptural touchstones in reference to impairment: the divine self-limitation of *kenosis*, the undeniable mission of Christ to heal, and the allowance of debilitation to continue for a greater good: the work of the grace of Christ. All three together give a nuanced understanding of a humanism based in the person of Christ: His identity, His life, and His mission.

Theology Of The Impaired Body: Living In (Ecstatic) Reality

John Paul II, at a 2004 symposium on the "Dignity and Rights of the Mentally Disabled Person," stated that disabled people are God's privileged witnesses.[46] This was no facile, sentimental proclamation. The Theology of the Body provides real insights into the relationship we each have with those who are impaired in any way, and how the sign of the body impaired still points to our union with God. Once again, encountering the other, as well as encountering ourselves, as limited and impaired gives us opportunity to reflect on the broader *communio personarum*, or communion of persons. We move from the spousal imagery to imagery that John Paul himself argued was more original: the imagery of being the children of a loving Father, and brothers and sisters belonging to each other through our relationship to the Father. Through the hermeneutic of the gift, we are going to "behold" what it means to say the ensouled body is a created, fallen, and redeemed sign of the radical, healing love of God, seen and experienced through the bodily experiences of impairment.

It may be good here to remember what was covered in our first chapter, that is, what informs John Paul II's audiences on the Theology of the Body:

1. the influence of the phenomenological attitude ("an attitude of spiritual seeing in which one can see or experience something which otherwise remains hidden"),

2. the importance of *disponibilité* as a posture of openness to God,

3. the personalist insight on the fundamental dimension of human co-existence,

4. human value discovered and discerned in the light of God through love,

5. the providence and initiative of a personal God who wills good for us,

6. the constant and fruitful activity of the Holy Spirit (especially given way through the prayer lives of believers),

7. the essential spiritual move of detachment from created things in order to receive them as gifts ordered to God, "making room" for God to work,

8. and the language of covenant, chosenness, spiritual betrothal, and spiritual marriage.

How does the Theology of the Body call us to spiritually see the fundamental value of people living with impairment, not despite their impairment, not entirely because of their impairment, but to see them (and us) as integrated wholes: ensouled bodies destined for healing, for union with God, for the family of God? Although the personal experiences of living with impairment run from embrace to nuisance to devastation, the insights above as well as the interpretive key of "the hermeneutic of the gift" can teach us how we may approach our own impairments and limitations, and walk with others living that reality. When lived well, we can see the work of God in the sign of limitation.

A Phenomenology Of Vulnerable Communion

"*The fundamental dimension of man's existence ... is always a co-existence,*"[47] said John Paul II. It is no accident that the overwhelming majority of texts on theologies of disability, despite many other differences, focus on the *relationship* of those disabled to the larger community: foci on friendship, fellowship, communion, and ecclesial community abound.[48] One of the greatest contemporary signs of this call to relationship is lived out in Jean Vanier's L'Arche communities.

L'Arche began in 1964, when Vanier, a philosophy professor at St. Michael's College in Toronto, took in two men who had been institutionalized to live in his home. It was, by Vanier's admission, not a fully deliberated move, although he had been visiting many institutionalized people with profound mental disabilities through the friendship and lead of his mentor, Fr. Thomas Philippe. Gradually Vanier's decision to take in two men for "a while" became an international movement of small communities of those disabled and those not, living in Christian community, in small homes. These communities are rooted in respect for the profoundly disabled and the small but real joys of family-style living: eating together, working together, praying together, living together. These communities gained further recognition when Henri Nouwen, a priest and well-known professor of spirituality at Harvard Divinity School, left his academic life to live in the L'Arche community in Toronto, and wrote movingly of his spiritual transformation by the experience.[49] Stanley Hauerwas further opened the public door on this small movement, identifying L'Arche as a "peace movement" for our time.[50] Vanier has been nominated for the Nobel Peace Prize as well.

Vanier (and others) exemplify the phenomenological attitude when they affirm that L'Arche is "a sign, not a solution." To name those who are profoundly disabled a "problem" says less about the disabled and more about the society in which we live: that the cult of normalcy exerts its supposedly benevolent power when we name certain people as problems to be solved rather than mysteries to be discovered and valued. Hauerwas goes further than Vanier, calling L'Arche a prime example of the theology of witness that the church so desperately needs, a sacrament in the world.[51] It is for this reason that Vanier bristles a bit when he says, "I get upset when people tell me, 'You're doing a good job.' I'm not interested in doing a good job. I'm interested in an ecclesial vision for community."[52]

The sign of L'Arche fleshes out the shared reality of limitation and weakness and the common reliance on the unlimited strength of God, and points to the divine call to love as God loves. The mission of L'Arche, as stated in its charter, is simultaneously ambitious yet humble: "Our mission is to create homes where faithful relationships based on forgiveness and celebration are nurtured. We want to reveal the unique value and vocation of each person, and to live relationships in community as a sign of hope and love."[53] The process of living in community involves acknowledging weakness and confronting fear with the concrete power of love. The end of the lived experience is celebration and joy: not that every moment is joyful, or a celebration, but that the lived experience is a real gift of life shared.

But Vanier also says that community is not achieved but received, not a goal but a gift. Living together, guided by the above mission, opens our hands to receive that gift. And in doing so, he undercuts what I think can be a subtle temptation: the purpose of welcoming people with disabilities into small community, into the church, into our families, is not first and foremost to witness. It is *a response to a call* from God to love as God loves. It requires a "spiritual seeing," as Scheler would say, that all human beings are our brothers and sisters, called in Christ to be adopted sons and daughters of God. In doing so, Vanier clarifies what seems to be a temptation among first readers of the Theology of the Body literature: as central as the doctrines of Incarnation and incarnation are, the audiences are not about seeing the body of oneself or another in isolation. It is about the visible lived experience of call to love and response to love, of relationship to God and others. It is about the divinely ordained witness to love. This is seen in a powerful way by the union of a man and woman in sacramental marriage, and as John Paul II argues, was given to us at the dawn of creation as a sign of how we are called to be in union with God. I argue this can be seen in a woman giving birth, yielding to the work of the Holy Spirit, living out the "pre-given language of self-giving and fruitfulness" through answering the call to motherhood. The relationship of those who are obviously impaired to those of us who are less obviously impaired gives us practice in loving one another without preconditions, in accepting our identity as beloved children of the Father, and in sensing how our mutually sensed limitation and weakness points to God as our fulfillment. The sign is fully manifest in the finite human being's relationship to the infinite God and each finite other.

The Rooting Insight: A Relational *Imago Dei*

One of the new magisterial developments offered to Catholic theology in the audiences is John Paul's presentation of the *imago Dei* as best manifest through relationship. While there are other 20th century theologians suggesting this insight,[54] this is a radical development in the *imago Dei* tradition, and the first proposal of such in magisterial literature. John Paul says:

> The account of the creation of man in Genesis 1 affirms from the beginning and directly that man was created in the image of God inasmuch as he is Man and Woman. The account in Genesis 2, by contrast, does not speak of the "image of God," but reveals, in the manner proper to it, that the complete and definitive creation of "man" (subject first to the experience of original solitude) expresses itself in giving life to the "*communio personarum*" that man and woman form. In this way, the Yahwist account agrees with the content of the first account. If, vice versa, we want to retrieve also from the account of the Yahwist text the concept of "image of God," we can deduce that *man became the image of God not only through his own humanity, but also through the communion of persons,* which man and woman form from the beginning. The function of the image is that of mirroring the one who is the model, of reproducing its own prototype. Man becomes an image of God not so much in the moment of solitude as in the moment of communion. He is, in fact, "from the beginning" not only an image in which the solitude of one Person, who rules the world, mirrors itself, but also and essentially the image of an inscrutable divine communion of Persons.[55]

This is important, because as Hans Reinders rightly brings up in *Receiving the Gift of Friendship: Profound Disability, Theological Anthropology, and Ethics*, the doctrine of creation to the image of God has not been a traditionally helpful doctrine in asserting the value of each and every human being. The *imago Dei* tradition received its formation in the careful merging of Neoplatonism and Hebrew thought, which located the creation to the image of God in the human mind. Rationality, as an eternal, reflects (as images do) the eternality of God, whereas the created body destined for aging and decay certainly is not the image. From the beginning, there were hints that this focus on rationality as the human reflection of God could cause problems: the Antiochene fathers did say that women, clearly not being rational, were not created in the image of God. Augustine, not usually cited as a feminist, pruned that bud in the *imago Dei* tradition by noting that Scripture clearly states that "He created them in the image of God, man and woman he created them," therefore women are rational, sharing that common marker of humanity.[56] Reinders' work (and Vanier's practice in L'Arche) focuses on those many would call arational: the profoundly intellectually disabled. Does the traditional emphasis on rationality put in doubt his friends' creation to the image of God? John Paul's presentation of the *imago Dei* not only erases Reinders' question, it places the doctrine of the *imago Dei* in the doctrine of universal redemption and sanctification: we are created in the image of God for *relationship* to God and one another, and through that relationship, grow in holiness. The creation to the image is no longer a static honorific, nor a nod to rationality, but a dynamic call.

The communion that John Paul refers to in his relational creation to the image is rooted in the spousal meaning of the body, and that initial gift of union is the original effective sign through which holiness (living wholly to God through our vocation) entered the world. This is a distinctive sign: a first word, an acknowledgment of the similarity and difference of men and women, a sign for creation for union, the primordial sacrament that points to the Trinitarian life of God. The fruitfulness of that union expands into the natural sign of giving birth, of family. And loving our sons, daughters, mothers, fathers, brothers, and sisters is a natural extension of that first sign. Through the redemption of Christ, we are all brothers and sisters to each other. "For whoever does the will of my Father in heaven is my brother and sister and mother" (Mt 12:50). To see it otherwise, to negate this natural extension, is both to isolate sexual union as a good unto itself (which can fall quickly into idolatry) and to deny the radical universality of Christ's redemption.

Vanier alludes to the power of family when he says "the first and primary belonging begins with the family."[57] And it intrigues me that one of the most powerful advocates for living the "vulnerable communion" is Tom Reynolds, who wrote his theology of disability as a father, raising two sons, one with multiple disabilities. I would like to spend some time looking specifically at Vanier's and Reynolds's phenomenological insights on *disponibilité*, fear, mutual vulnerability, and the healing gift of presence.

Disponibilité

Reynolds openly acknowledges his debt to Gabriel Marcel (recall, a philosophical influence on the Theology of the Body literature) when he speaks of *disponibilité*, or availability, but applies *disponibilité* in situations Marcel never did. In short, availability is the "moral fabric"[58] of love; and as such, it is the natural negation of the cult of normalcy. Love recognizes a common humanity, love heeds the call to love as God loves, that is, to see each person as a son and daughter of God and your brother or sister, and love embraces the person as he or she is. Reynolds continues to expand the practice of availability through the "interrelated postures" of respect (giving way for the other), fidelity (faithfulness to the other), and compassion (sympathy with the other, for his/her well-being).[59] If the cult of normalcy operates on systems of management and control to evaluate the value of any given person, availability "marks a morally charged willingness to participate in and undergo—that is, to suffer—the presence of another." This is not tolerance, he says: "Rather, it is an availing of oneself which risks vulnerable openness to another's vulnerability. It is disposing oneself to the other for its sake and on its terms. This is the fulcrum of being with the other, binding together a relation of mutuality."[60]

L'Arche is one concrete embodiment of that intentional availability, and as such, I am not surprised that Jean Vanier has less to say about the detailed challenges of the intellectually disabled and more to say about the brokenness and call to healing embedded in the human condition. People living with disabilities call all of us to acknowledge our human weaknesses and, in doing so, open us to receiving the grace of God.[61] When we enter a "binding relation of mutuality," when we make ourselves available to the other and solemnly promise to "suffer with and for" that person, it necessarily exposes our own vulnerabilities and weaknesses. It is the difference between a community and a social services agency. While the social service agency may indeed do good work, the intentional community of L'Arche is a home of welcome. Both may be necessary, but they are different: social services function for problem-solving, and L'Arche focuses on living out a sign.

Living the posture of *disponibilité*, through respect, fidelity, and compassion opens the door to recognizing the intrinsic limitedness of humanity and allows the work of God to break through.

Fear

In the previous chapter, I addressed the many similarities between the experience of fear and the experience of shame as described by the Theology of the Body audiences (see pages 61-65). Fear can prevent *disponibilité*. But the smallest bit of *disponibilité* practiced also brings hidden fears to light. Vanier is quick to meet this reality head on.

> Fear makes us push those with intellectual disabilities into far-off, dismal situations. Fear prevents all of us with the price of a meal in our pocket from sharing with the Lazaruses of the world. It is fear, ironically, that prevents us from being most human, that is, it prevents us from growing and changing.[62]

If you ask people who are more abled to speak of their hesitation to engage the disabled, the answer will almost always be, "I just don't know how to act, or what to say." There is a fear among those of us anchored in the cult of normalcy to risk the simplest conversation with those outside "the norm," to be exposed as incapable and uncharitable (and we see the experiential overlap between fear and shame easily here). Vanier suggests that we have all kinds of fears, fears especially made visible when we meet our impaired brothers and sisters: fear of dissidents, difference, failure, loss, and change.[63] But the sense of peril that is fear is rarely about physical danger. The fear is about a head-on encounter with our own limitations and impairments as human beings, and a frightening call to move beyond them and respond to this call to family, this call to love. It is about recognizing we have ordered our lives wrongly; we follow a cult rather than our faith, and we are called to change. Now.

Fear, as John Paul says, shares the boundary experience of shame, marking that the human being lives in a fallen world where trust in God is not a purely desired inclination. When we who are abled react in fear (or at least disquiet) as we encounter the profoundly disabled, it reveals where we are. It reveals, in fact, that we are Adam. Recall John Paul II's statement from the audiences:

> "I was afraid, because I am naked".... These words reveal a certain constitutive fracture in the human person's interior, *a break-up, as it were, of man's original spiritual and somatic unity.* He realizes for the first time his body has ceased drawing on the power of the spirit, which raised him to the level of the image of God. Its shame bears within itself the signs of a certain humiliation mediated by the body.[64]

In fear, we realize—perhaps in an unconscious way—that *we* are broken when we encounter a profoundly disabled person. Only instead of hiding ourselves from God, we take and hide the disabled Other: in an institution, in the back of the church, in abortion. And we then place ourselves before God saying nothing is amiss.

In the previous chapter, we explored fear in some depth, and there is no need to repeat it all here. But it is worth looking again at the "shape of fear," particularly, this fear:

> "the *shape* of fear is usually defined by its object. ...[A] fear of God's call is seen in shrinking away from the call, redefining the call's terms, or attempting to 'get ahead of God' and take control. It may mean change on your part, less being 'in charge.' This fear of God's call is usually manifest as *resistance*. And if entering into giving birth is an experience of God's call, the fear of the terms of the call often results in women resisting, which increases pain." (see page 66)

How is our participation in the cult of normalcy the modern person's way to "get ahead of God" and take control? How does this call to seeing those profoundly disabled as your brother or sister automatically make you less "in charge," and more likely to need to change?[65] Vanier recalls presenting the life of L'Arche to a Muslim community in the Middle East, and a Syrian mufti stood up and summarized, "If I have understood well, people with disabilities lead us to God."[66] If this bald state-

ment is true, how can this fear, and the avoidance and societal seques-
tering that often follows fear, be anything other than a classic example
of resistance? The challenge of resistance, we find in spiritual direction
literature, is that we avoid God even at the same time that we say we desire God. The shape of this particular fear, while following the shape of
fearing the terms of God's call, is a fear of truth. And the truth is that we
are called to be brothers and sisters to those people whom we may not
understand, those who remind us of humanity's weakness and fragility.
This is a truth that demands change.

But it is also a truth, a reflection of the Truth, that sets free. Although
Reynolds does not speak much of fear, in one of the most moving passages of the book, he alludes to it, and where recognition of fear leads:

> By honestly confronting and accepting my own
> vulnerability and limitations I have grown in the capacity
> to let go of my need for control and to risk moving beyond
> my own fears, affirming Chris for who he is. Chris is not
> pathetic. His genuine otherness breaks through pity and
> astonishes me as something surprisingly precious in its
> own right. His is a young life seeking creatively to affirm
> itself, thwarted by conditions that he did not ask for
> and for which he is not responsible. This vulnerability
> rouses me to attend to him in ways that lure me outward
> beyond self-preoccupation; and the first taste of this
> conjures something akin to repentance.[67]

Both Vanier and Reynolds approach availability and fear from the perspective of "affiliates," as they are sometimes called: those who are more
abled caring for a person or persons who are disabled. Fear, to them,
comes from a particular place. But they both allude to the call to quell
the fears of those they care for, as well. Reynolds' entire book is centered
upon the desire to communicate the world as home, as a generous gift
of God, and we are all called to affirm its goodness and live out an ethic
of hospitality to all. Concretely, he says, this can look like when he hugs
his son with multiple disabilities after a hard day at school and says, "It
will be alright; I am here with you." (He quickly adds this is not ego-
ism, but an attempted expression that his son is connected, is loved, and
the world has hope.)[68] For Vanier, the consummate storyteller, addressing the fear of those he cares for—a fear that is often sadly legitimate,

rooted in abuse and ill-treatment—occurs through story. Reason is no help here. Fear is banished and trust is earned through doing simple acts—washing, sharing food, listening, being together—with great tenderness.

> There is no fear in tenderness. Tenderness is not weakness, lack of strength, or sloppiness; tenderness is filled with strength, respect, and wisdom. In tenderness, we know how and when to touch someone to help them be and to be well…. Through my contact…I have in some small way learned to inhabit my body and to see it not just as a channel for therapy, but as a way of revealing my heart and of being in communion with others.[69]

Perhaps, as noted in John Paul II's analysis of shame, the experience of fear can be "swallowed up" in faithful love, when one lives one's limitations and vulnerability as part of our call to self-gift, open receiving, and union.[70]

Disponibilité and fear lead us to the third overlapping theme:

Mutual Vulnerability

Hauerwas (another "affiliate" to the disabled; he would prefer the word "friend") notes wryly, but aptly: "Academics are notoriously bad listeners…. To learn to listen well, it turns out, may require learning to be a gentle person."[71] Academics are trained in argument, and there is nothing inherently wrong with that. But the academic zeal for argument (not to mention our desire to "belong" to a peer-reviewed group) can trample authentic listening. Gentleness is not a virtue much upheld in our culture: it's nice, but not considered especially essential to being a virtuous human. Yet Hauerwas claims it is the way to peace, and the road of witness: to be gentle is the physical expression of humility, which yields to allowing God's spirit to work through us.

Vanier holds up the example of one of his friends in L'Arche, Antonio:

> Antonio came to our community in Trosly when he was twenty years old, after many years in the hospital. He could not walk, speak, or use his hands; he needed extra oxygen to breathe. He was a weak and fragile man in

many ways but he has an incredible smile and beautiful shining eyes. There was no anger or depression in him. That is not to say he didn't get annoyed from time to time, especially if his bathwater was too hot or too cold or if his assistants forgot about him! What is important is that he had accepted his limits and disabilities; he had accepted himself as he was. Antonio could not love by being generous, by giving things to people or by doing things for them....He lived a love of trust. In this way, he touched many people's hearts. When one loves with trust, one does not give things, one gives oneself and, so, calls forth a communion of hearts.

Antonio touched and awakened the hearts of many assistants who came to live in his house. He led them into the way of the heart. Often, they would tell me so, in words to this effect: "Antonio changed my life. He has led me out of a society of competition where one has to be strong and aggressive into a world of tenderness and mutuality, where each person, strong or weak, can exercise their gifts."[72]

One of the real difficulties in this field of study has always been how to allow people with profound mental disabilities to speak their piece. With Antonio, speech isn't even an option. But to tell his story, and the impact his life had on others, to focus on how he loved, is a start.

Other times, a person's verbal language may be limited. But an emotional language beyond speech can speak volumes to mutual vulnerability. Vanier also offers the story of Claudia:

We welcomed Claudia into our L'Arche community in Supaya, a slum area of Tegucigalpa, Honduras. She was seven years old and had spent practically her whole life in a dismal, overcrowded asylum. Claudia was blind, fearful of relationships, filled with inner pain and anguish. Technically speaking she was autistic.

...

Claudia lived a horrible form of madness which should not be idealized or seen as a gateway to another world. In L'Arche, we have learned from our own experience of healing, as well as through the help of psychiatrists and psychologists, that chaos, or "madness," has meaning; it comes from somewhere, it is comprehensible....

Twenty years after she first arrived in Supaya, I visited... and met Claudia again....She still liked being alone but she was clearly not a lonely person. She would often sing to herself and there was a constant smile on her face.

...One day, I was sitting opposite to her at lunch and said, "Claudia, can I ask you a question?" She replied, "Sí, Juan." "Claudia, why are you so happy?" Her answer was simple and direct: "Dios." God. I asked the community leader, Nadine, what the answer meant. Nadine said, "That is Claudia's secret."[73]

...

There was a secret moment, known only to Claudia, when she recognized that she was loved.

With that realization, Claudia entered into a relationship of belonging. The opening of Claudia's heart brought about a new opening in Nadine's heart, bringing her out of her own loneliness. ... [74]

What is typical of the stories Vanier tells is that they are stories of *mutual* transformation. Nadine grew through and in her community relationship to Claudia. Many grew in their relationship to Antonio. Vanier admits that through L'Arche, he has grown beyond his pet love for abstract conversation, and into a more "embodied life," a greater appreciation for the simple pleasures of celebration, laughter, and fun. Stepping into a covenantal community,[75] into a belonging to each other, requires living out a love that casts out fear, acknowledges vulnerability, and grows through the action of the Holy Spirit.

Although Vanier works with the profoundly disabled, we can raise examples of the influence of mutual vulnerability from people less profoundly disabled. One of the most moving quiet moments I have experienced was participating in a Mass regularly offered by a local priest, who has significant challenges walking (and is otherwise healthy). He manages walking with a cane, and some days seem to be better than others for him. One daily Mass, when he was carefully deliberating a short set of steps to the altar, a young woman near the front assessed the situation, jumped up, and quietly offered her arm to help him up, which he accepted with graciousness. Sitting in that Mass, thinking about how we believe we are at Calvary with every Mass, and every priest stands "in persona Christi" (in the person of Christ offering the sacrifice), that we all sit or stand or kneel and pray together as broken, limited people—I was overwhelmed with the beauty of our mutual vulnerability, and how we offer it to each other, and together, to God.

While Vanier excels at telling the story of mutual vulnerability, Reynolds excels at describing what this means to those of us immersed in the cult of normalcy. "Disability is not something less than normal, an inferior or broken nature. Disabled and non-disabled people do not count as two exclusive categories of human beings. All people are linked indissolubly, sharing a fundamental condition: vulnerable personhood." And acknowledging that our limitations as human beings create an inevitable vulnerability, he continues: "When privileged and brought from the margins to the center, disability deconstructs the cult of normalcy and opens up the possibility of a wider human solidarity. Our way of seeing things changes."[76]

Our way of *seeing* things changes. And as noted in the first chapter, sight calls to response. In relationships founded on *disponibilité* and rejecting fear, our response is shaped in manners closer to the sight of "original man." In fact, we glimpse the "redeemed man" at work when we see these relationships that honor that humanity comes from God, the Father, that are defined by Jesus Christ, and are enlivened by the Holy Spirit. Mutual vulnerability is a humility that makes room: not only for the other, but for the Other, the work of the Holy Spirit. This leads us to the healing gift of presence.

The Healing Gift Of Presence

Mutual vulnerability makes room for the work of the Holy Spirit. It is the door to love, and wherever love and charity are found, there is God. It is right that Hauerwas notes that the L'Arche communities are characterized by gentleness. Gentleness is a fruit of the Holy Spirit (Gal 5:23). That is, gentleness exists not through some personality trait nor as a side effect of any "disability," but it is the promised consequence of a life that makes room for the healing that is the work of the Holy Spirit.

The gift of gentleness often elicits space for acknowledging wounded-ness and healing. Another L'Arche story comes from Kevin Reimer, who interviewed a long-time caregiver in a L'Arche community. The woman asked to remain anonymous:

> I was raped in high school. Even though my family moved around a lot and there was a lot of suffering and isolation, as a people person I was able to fit in and make friends quickly—even when I was dying inside. After the rape I gained 30 pounds; I probably became severely depressed, severely dissociated. This was an insane time. I never told anybody.
>
> …
>
> [On how this background relates to living at L'Arche, talking about the disabled residents]…[W]hat more rejected group is there? What group wears its pain in such a manner?…I used to think, I'll never get married. No man could ever love me. I've dwelt in the shadow lands. But I think it [L'Arche] impacted receptivity in my heart. …It's impacted my ability to be more forgiving. I think the community allows people to be free. …it's a movement toward more freedom, more joy, more peace, more tolerance for other people. I get less worried about things now. I feel like, I've always said God will provide, but now I am living it….[77]

This is a remarkable transformation and witness. But as Reimer points out: "This is hardly a linear process."[78] Finding healing through mutual vulnerability recognizes that our relationship to each other, marked by limits, impairments, and wounds, is a privileged place where the Holy Spirit can break in. But there is no real formula to this. The Holy Spirit works with our free will, our openness to healing and growth, and presents healing—His very presence—as we are able to handle it. When we are open to the work of the Spirit, the more room we can make for it, the more we bear the fruits of joy, peace, and gentleness. In such fruits our authentic humanity is no longer cloaked, but present for all to see.

Recognizing that we are all limited, impaired, and broken in spirit is the first step, a clearing of vision, in realizing that the vision of the autonomous, self-made man is wrong. Again: "*The fundamental dimension of man's existence ... is always a co-existence.*" And communion and fellowship are part of the healing sustenance of the Holy Spirit's work.

This phenomenology, or "spiritual seeing," bears within it a very immanent understanding of God: we meet God in relationship to the embodied care of the vulnerable other, recognizing our own vulnerability and need for healing. And there is a need for this horizontal presentation: in the Western world, we simply do not believe that people with profound impairments are icons of God. We say we believe it, but our actions prove that we do not. Vanier tells these stories over and over to break through our preconceptions and encourage us to risk otherwise. And when people do, they sense that God is at work, and they are changed. The lavishness of God rushes in where people live together in fidelity, *disponibilité*, vulnerability, and without fear—illumining the value of each human being, and giving witness to the Giver of Life who brings forth all good gifts in gentleness. As Ignatius famously says in his rules of discernment, the work of the good spirit in a soul disposed to God is sensed "gently, lightly, and sweetly, like a drop of water going into a sponge," and then the good angels "come in quietly, as one would enter one's own house by an open door."[79] Not only a phenomenological but a contemplative attitude is needed to recognize the Holy Spirit in this abiding immanence.

But it is important to move beyond this "horizontal" sign and embed it within the transcendent sign of God's love for all of us. Only then can we affirm that the call to brotherhood and sisterhood is a universal call, neither particular nor individual, rooted in the humanity defined by the life, death, and Resurrection of Jesus Christ.

The *Kenosis* Of God And "Ecstatic Identity"

The phenomenological attitude also can be brought to bear on an examination of the Passion, the visual high point of the *kenosis* of the Son of God. I argue here that the hermeneutic of the gift is embodied in the phenomenon of "ecstatic identity": the received but non-possessed identity of Jesus Christ as the only Son of God.[80] The ecstatic identity of Christ as Son of God is real and certain, but it is not "grasped" by Christ: the Sonship is a perpetual gift of the Father, an aspect of his eternal begottenness. The Son open-handedly receives his Sonship, but he remains open-handed, not clutching at his identity as Son. In this way, Jesus's life and death is self-emptying, the temporal expression of His eternally receiving from (and offering back to) the Father the primordial gift of His identity as Son.[81] The second person of the Trinity lives in uninterrupted perfect trust and love—that is, He lives as gift, in perfect relationship to the Father and the Holy Spirit. The ecstatic identity is a phenomenological description of the classic Trinitarian doctrine of perichoresis.

The idea of "ecstatic identity" comes from another contemporary theologian, Arthur McGill (1926-80),[82] and helps us to see John Paul's hermeneutic of the gift in the life, death, and Resurrection of Jesus Christ. *Kenosis*, usually translated the "self-emptying" of God and associated with the Christic hymn in Philippians 2, has long been a flash point for poets and mystics and a migraine headache for ontologists. McGill makes a wholly phenomenological move when he brackets questions of being and explores the visuality of the death of Jesus Christ as revealing Christ's perpetual receptivity of his identity as Son of God from the Father.[83] From the witness of Scripture, Christ's self-emptying is constant. Jesus of Nazareth affirmed his Sonship but never strove to "possess" it, meaning that He constantly received His identity as Son of God from the Father, and through his identity as Son pointed to the Father.[84] And in death, he did not release a possessed life, nor have it "taken away." But Christ's life was, moment by moment and beyond all moments, a gift of the Father to the Son, and His passion and death a return (self-emptying) of that gift of Sonship to the Father on a cross. In making visible this glorious exchange, we can move to receive Christ's gift to the whole of sinful humanity: the substitutionary sacrifice of his life for the sins of the world.[85]

Although McGill does not directly address the role of the Spirit in the Crucifixion, it is easy to see the fullness of the Trinitarian relationship there as well: in the Gospel of John, the Spirit moves with the Son uttering "it is finished" and "he bowed his head and gave up his" (19:30). Arguably the piercing of Jesus' side in v. 34, issuing forth blood and water, would be seen by practicing Jews through Ezekiel's vision of the Spirit of God flowing like water from the side of the Temple and giving new life,[86] and the spontaneous tearing of the veil segregating the Spirit of God's dwelling place in the Holy of Holies in the Temple certainly indicates a release of the Spirit of God to the whole world (Mk 15:38, Mt 27:51, Lk 23:45). The hermeneutic of the gift continues through time, in the giving of the Advocate at the Pentecost, and continues in the vigorous sacramental life of the church.[87] The Crucifixion is a profoundly dynamic moment of gift and giving, a singular visualization of the life of the economic Trinity as well as the immanent Trinity. It is the most visible moment of this divine dynamic, the most obvious moment of the law of the gift. The limitation that is inherent in the Incarnation reveals the purely ecstatic, that is, non-possessed, identity of the Son of God through death. And in this unveiled event, we learn who God is, and hear our own call.[88]

What does this have to do with impairment? If limitation is part of the design of our ensouled bodies—and obviously it is—then limitation has meaning. Limitation was created as a natural sign to point us to our own call to depend on God. And impairment—that term we use when we are more limited than we or others expect to be—is given model in Jesus Christ's own Crucifixion. Like Christ on the cross, we are called to live an ecstatic identity, an identity that is not our own but comes continually from God, and be prepared to engage that gifted identity and offer all we are to the Father in trust. We are created to receive and give: not just at special mystical moments in our lives, not just when we are healthy and well, but always.

McGill is worth quoting in full on this point:

> Too often in our churches we hear the gospel of love without the gospel of need. Too often we hear the lie that to love is to help others without this help having any effect upon ourselves. But too often we also hear another lie: that to love our neighbors is so to give to them that they are free from need ... It is another lie of Christianity

> today, this gospel of love, this gospel which says, not that Jesus Christ enables us to be needy, but that he enables us to be loving, and by loving to remove all neediness....
>
> The gospel of Jesus Christ, however, is very different. Nowhere does Jesus promise the removal of need. On the contrary, he promises to each of his followers the *intensification of need*. He calls them to take up his cross; he warns them that it is only insofar as they are willing to be poor and sick and needy that he can help them... A love that is afraid of need ... - that love does not belong to those who have put on Jesus Christ.
>
> The reason is obvious. The condition to which we are led by Jesus is a condition of *utter dependence* on God and *relative dependence* on one another... Love can thrive *only within* need; a love that fears need, that wants to overcome and remove need, is a lie and therefore irrelevant. And Christian ministers that are motivated by a fear of need, by the will to remove need, and by the assumption that the minister should have no needs - such ministries can only be a torment and a shock for persons who go to them for help....[89]

The *kenosis* of Christ—the swaddling clothes, the scraped knees, the felt hunger and need to eat, the bound and tortured man before Pilate's crowd, and most especially, the man who suffered death on a cross—is *made visible* by the spatial reality of self-limitation that is the Incarnation. Within the immanent Trinity, the doctrine of perichoresis expresses the unseen perpetual dynamic of giving and receiving within the Godhead.[90] But the Crucifixion is, along with being the sacrifice that redeems the world, the ultimate *sign* of giving and receiving. The *kenosis* is both natural sign and intentional sign: the limitation of the Incarnation is a natural sign, the Crucifixion is an intentional sign.[91] This is one departure I make from some theologians of disability,[92] who argue that we do well to remember we worship a disabled Christ on the cross. In fact, we do not. The torture, binding, and execution of Jesus does not prevent what he intended to do, did not prevent him from accepting his identity as Son of God in an ecstatic manner. The perpetual acceptance of his Sonship facilitated the self-emptying. The *kenosis* is what He intended to do. In fact, it expresses exactly who He is: the Incarnation, as part of the divine mystery of love, limited. But it did not disable.

In a similar way, sharing Christ's human nature, no one is ultimately disabled in the spiritual life, except through sin. And our limitedness makes witness to us and others that we are called to rely on the unlimited sustaining power of God.

If we take the ecstatic identity of the Son of God seriously, *kenosis* speaks secondarily to the "self-emptying" of God. To speak of *kenosis* is first to speak of the providence of God. *Kenosis* reveals first of all not the poverty of Christ, but the fecundity of the Father. McGill points out this is no new insight at all; it was Athanasius's position in the hotly debated ontological argument that embroiled the Council of Nicaea:

> For Athanasius the simple unitarian notion of Arius is too crude a notion for God. God is one, yes, but in a very special sense. The content of his reality is one, because the being of the Son is derived from the Father and therefore possesses no new content. But more important, God's unity is a unity of love, a unity in which the identity of each partner is not swallowed up and annihilated but established. Arius' notion of unity is devoid of the richness—and the mystery—of God's unity. It is devoid of the unity of love.
>
> …Athanasius points out that any god with the kind of monadic unity and self-sufficient absoluteness that Arius celebrates must be, within Himself, an *agonos theos*, a sterile God. …
>
> …Athanasius identifies the dynamic giving between the Father and the Son as the inner life of God, as the life that vitalizes God, not only in all his dealings with his creatures, but also eternally within himself…. Throughout all eternity the Father is communicating his reality to the Son; and throughout all eternity the Son is giving glory to the Father. These are not acts which cause changes in God; they are eternal processes which make up God's essential aliveness…. [93]

We didn't take an odd turn into the details of perichoresis and conciliar history for casual interest. These doctrines directly express the hermeneutic of the gift offered in the Theology of the Body audiences, anchored in John of the Cross's gift-based spiritual theology. This is a natural extension of the Theology of the Body—or perhaps the Theology of the Body is an extension of *kenosis*. To look at John of the Cross: one of his present-day interpreters, Iain Matthew,[94] is especially good at recognizing that John of the Cross had a profound experience (several, actually) of the mystical presence of God and allowed that "impact" on his soul to drive away his desire for other goods in place of God. It spurred the *nada* doctrine for which John is well known, and much misunderstood: a simple and daily affirmed desire to put God first, above all things, nothing (*nada*) but God.[95] When, with the help of God, you are able to do that, the order of creation falls into place: all mutable goods rightly point to God, and the Immutable Good is honored as the source of mutable goods. Matthew is a helpful interpreter of John because he communicates well that this process of sanctification and spiritual growth is initiated by God. He also communicates John of the Cross's spiritual theology in spatial terms—impact, make room, give shape, entering caverns—that communicate that this is a spiritual and physical experience, that the experience of God is (once again) a sign to read and behold. You can see it, and others can see it, if we know what to look for. It is a seeing that demands response.

What John assumed—and what John Paul II assumes as well—is that God is abundantly lavish in his graces. God wants to share himself with us much more than we, in our sinful state, want to receive. And the lavishness of God, a God who wants relationship with us, presumes that we were created to be "receivers" of God. Many through the ages have found language for the indwelling of God: the human being as a Temple of the Holy Spirit, saints desiring to be a "living tabernacle." John of the Cross expresses supreme confidence that a God who cares for the sparrow and has numbered the hairs on your head is constantly seeking ways to persuade you to accept His life. As Reimer said above, there is no linearity to transformative, healing relationship. But it is a relationship that has its own logic. And that logic is based on the Theology of the Body principle that God is a giver of good gifts. While accepting the gifts will require making a gift of ourselves to God, which will involve attention, darkness, and suffering, the gifts are real. In fact, the gift is

God.

When John Paul II speaks of a spousal meaning of the body and offers marriage as a primordial sign of self-giving and fruitfulness, he is calling us to imitate the *kenosis* of Christ. Yes, it involves dying. But most importantly, it involves trust in a God who nourishes us through the tunnel of constricting limitation to promised new life. It perhaps comes as no surprise that John Paul II named *kenosis* as the primary challenge to theologians today: "From this vantage-point, the prime commitment of theology is seen to be the understanding of God's *kenosis*, a grand and mysterious truth for the human mind, which finds it inconceivable that suffering and death can express a love which gives itself and seeks nothing in return."[96]

If we take *kenosis* seriously, the ecstatic identity of Jesus Christ as the Son of God gives us sign, hope, and guidance toward where we find our own identity as human beings: not in the cult of normalcy, but in the Fatherhood of God as His adopted sons and daughters. We are brothers and sisters to Jesus Christ, and our identity comes from that relationship. Our limitations, borne in our bodies, point us (as natural sign) to the call to rely on the Father for everything: our identity, our life, our existence. To be human is to be limited, in relative dependence on each other and utter dependence on God. It is not what abilities we have or do not have, physically speaking: we are not our own, we *are* a gift of God. We do not *have* anything.

And the healing mission of Christ, culminating in His Resurrection, is the visible reason for our hope. Our God is abundantly extravagant with His grace, constantly lures us, and is trustworthy. The abundance of God's love and willingness to nourish humanity open to His love is eloquently prayed by St. Catherine of Siena, to the Trinity:

> How, then, did you create, O Eternal Father, this your creature? [...] Fire constrained you. O ineffable love, even though in your light you saw all the iniquities, which your creature would commit against your infinite goodness, you looked as if you did not see, but rested your sight on the beauty of your creature, whom you, as mad and drunk with love, fell in love with and out of

love you drew her to yourself giving her being in your image and likeness. You, eternal truth, have declared to me your truth, that is, that love constrained you to create her.[97]

The Holy Spirit And The Modern Search For Providence

Kenosis, then, is a doctrine that first points to the lavish providence of God. Frankly, we don't hear much in current theological circles about providence, at least not directly.[98] Traditionally, providence is a doctrine that springs out of the doctrine of creation and is defined as theological reflection upon divine preservation or sustenance, divine cooperation with the work of the world through inspiration and initiative, and the divine governance that fulfills God's will through His guidance.

We hear little about providence as a doctrine—yet classic Christian spirituality is completely bereft without a vigorous assertion of God's providence. To begin with the Carmelites, John of the Cross assumes that every person is called by God to union with God, and his letters of spiritual direction reveal that he believes that God works through the very particular specifics of our lives. The reality of the call to holiness is universal, but the particulars of the call are very specific to the individual, and assume the providence of God. Beyond the Carmelites, Ignatius of Loyola and the classic Jesuit spiritual directors assume that God "speaks" to each and every one of us. It is the basis of Ignatian spiritual direction: that God's work in the world is constantly luring us to Him in a created order made of communications and signs. These communications require prudent interpretation, but are meant to lead us to God. When Jean-Pierre de Caussade (another Jesuit) used the phrase "abandonment to divine providence," it is impossible to read his influential work in spiritual direction as abandonment to fate, or simple presence. The presence of God can be arresting, certainly, but it is not a *simple* presence. There is always a call that comes with presence. This is part and parcel of the dynamism that is part of the economic Trinity and embraces humanity through the immanent Trinity. The providence of God—His work in the world in concert with the free will of human beings—is based in the very nature of the Trinitarian God. It is seen in the extraordinary dynamism of the Crucifixion and Resurrection. And it is inscribed in the spousal meaning of the body, created for self-gift, union, and fecundity. I cannot think of any saint who did not see and embrace God in the details of daily life.

I would say there are two primary challenges to upholding a theology of providence in a limited, impaired world, often under the sway of the cult of normalcy. One is the modern surge of theodicy. The other is the historic weakness and modern decline of a theology of the Holy Spirit.

Theodicy, which reflects on the dual characteristics of God as just and good in the light of experienced evil, is a needed subdiscipline within theology. Even though it was introduced as a modern study with Leibniz's 1710 *Theodicy*, there are multiple historical references to the issue, biblically and magisterially. The experience of evil clearly leads us to lean on "faith seeking understanding." But modern theodicy seems to have grown a life of its own, as a set of considerations in the modern age. I suspect there is a reason, and it is found in the most revealing commentary within an autobiographical section of Cynthia Crysdale's *Embracing Travail*, where Crysdale is musing at a conference discussion of the (then) new book edited by Emilie Townes: *A Troubling in My Soul: Womanist Perspectives on Evil and Suffering*[99]:

> …I enjoyed the articles and the wonderful retrieval of resources from African-American slavery: songs, stories, narratives, autobiographies. I could not help but feel, however, that the issue of theodicy—how can we get God 'off the hook' when so much suffering surrounds us?—was not really addressed. When I dared to express such misgivings at Breakfast with an Author at the annual meeting of the Society of Christian Ethics, at which the editor and several contributing authors were present, the revealing response I received was, "We've always known *God* was good; it's *people* we have trouble with." This generated a new insight for me, which was that theodicy questions, as I have known them, may be questions arising from privilege: when we are raised to expect the natural order to serve our needs, we are indignant when our expectations are thwarted, and call God to account. Theodicy from the underside may be quite a different set of questions; given the reality of lives suffering, how can we find hope and make sense of our

experience, especially in light of our faith in God?[100]

Crysdale is absolutely right. Although the questions are absolutely legitimate, the *preoccupation* with theodicy is a preoccupation born of privilege. Theodicy fails as honest seeking when presented in any of these ways: as a rather desperate need for everything to "make rational sense," when invoked at the behest of the cult of normalcy, and when the questions begin as accusations aimed at God. At minimum, there needs to be a real first attention to questions such as: "Where was God in this event? And how did human beings fail God and neighbor?" There should be a focus on the providence of God before we move to the theodicy questions, and not let the "tail" of theodicy "wag the dog" of providence.

The second reason we don't speak of providence is that we do not consciously live out a doctrine of the Holy Spirit. The lack of theological attention to the Holy Spirit is a common self-criticism within Western Christianity; indeed, the Nicene Creed codified it with its single sentence on the Holy Spirit before the "further development" of the creed at the first Council of Constantinople. But the lack of attention has persisted as a challenge to theologians and believers of all kinds, so much so that we can (almost) say with the Ephesians: "No, we have not even heard that there is a Holy Spirit" (Acts 19:2). As many know, when the Catholic charismatic renewal swept the United States in the 1970s, many were first introduced to a devotion to the Holy Spirit through our Protestant brothers and sisters. And some of those charismatics have been marginalized by other Christians—sometimes for excesses, which could certainly happen, but sometimes because charismatic prayer and worship directly challenge the cult of normalcy. (And let's be honest— if speaking in tongues doesn't challenge the cult of normalcy, nothing will.)

Amos Yong, who writes from the Pentecostal tradition to an ecumenical audience, helps us a great deal with his concept of a "pneumatological imagination."[101] Yong argues that if we take the Pentecost seriously, we will see that event as one where the Father gives the Holy Spirit to as diverse a number of people as can be described by the writer of Acts: And they all spoke under the influence of the Spirit, in their own languages, and all understood each other. He is more careful than most interpreters here: Acts 2 does not tell of speaking in a language unknown to the speaker, but of a hearing and *understanding* of different tongues influenced by the Spirit. The descent of the Holy Spirit has two-fold implications: first, the Holy Spirit is given to all. Second, each person received that Spirit and "translated" it, proclaimed it, in his or her own tongue: and all understood. Yong sees the Pentecost as the archetypal event of understanding the impact of God through different people and languages. The Pentecost gives witness to the Spirit-led call to speak, but also to listen.

The other receiving of the Holy Spirit mentioned in Scripture is the Resurrection appearance in the Gospel of John (20:22-3), when the resurrected Christ breathed on the assembled apostles in the Upper Room, saying: "Receive the Holy Spirit. If you forgive the sins of any, they are forgiven them; if you retain the sins of any, they are retained." There is a *receptiveness* in both descents of the Spirit that reminds us that the Spirit of God is introduced into our lives as unmerited gift. And the Spirit is given, in both instances, for relationship (specifically, healing relationship: communicating, listening, understanding, forgiving) and for a call to discipleship. The Holy Spirit is the gift that enables living out a call. Any reading of the sign of limit—even impairment—through the lens of Christ's *kenosis* must be held together with a full-throated faith statement that affirms and seeks the providence of God. Increased attention to the receptivity witnessed within our doctrine of the Holy Spirit affirms this lavish fecundity of God. And when our limited selves practice *disponibilité* through receiving the Holy Spirit, we say yes to God, a yes that gives us a call, an identity, and a relationship that draws us into the divine life of the Trinity and the Kingdom work for the world.[102]

In summary: the natural sign of limitation provides both immanent and transcendent signs pointing to our call to union with God, interpreted through the hermeneutic of the gift. Impairment, as underscored sign, does the same. If the cult of normalcy gives each of us a false identity, and as Christians we are called to model what it means to be human in the Incarnate God-Man, Jesus Christ, what *is* our identity? Our identity as adopted sons and daughters is one persistently given to us by the Father, and seen through the ecstatic identity of the crucified Son, and our call is to accept that identity open-handedly, without possession, and constantly make a return of it as gift to God. When we do this, relying on the providence of the Holy Spirit, our "spiritual seeing" is opened to the reality that we all live as limited brothers and sisters, relying on the life of God. We are named and identified at our conception into God's marvelous, harrowing, stunning story of sanctifying union with God against all odds and powers and principalities: as Hauerwas often says, "We don't get to make our lives up. We get to receive our lives as gifts. The story that says we should have no story except the story we chose when we had no story is a lie."[103] And we participate in the story of God's family when we make ourselves available to the Holy Spirit, to allow the Spirit to twist and turn and shape what is limited into a witness to the Glory of God. It means we are called to kenotic identities: to define ourselves by receiving our identity from God, and offer it to God and others. That may involve self-abjection, suffering, and pain. But it also promises ultimate happiness and joy: regardless of limitation, or better, *through* limitation, we are invited to deepest intimacy with the God of all goodness and justice.

Imitating Christ through living an ecstatic identity—life as gift—will be a call with a specific shape for each individual, and a specific response. This last section will explore in more detail what the specifics may look like through looking at three case studies of disabilities. These case studies offer commentary on the challenges of specific kinds of impairing conditions, but they will also bear the character of witness. The witness of God's call and response in individual persons, even persons with the same impairment, will not be identical. But some of the challenges will be the same, and I hope these sketches provide some breadth to what imitating the Son's ecstatic identity and accepting our identity as adopted sons and daughters of the Father looks like.

Case Studies

This chapter is meant to be a simple "first pass" at what the Theology of the Body, extended, could contribute to the theological anthropology raised by theologies of disability. So far, we have focused on the natural sign of physical limitation, a gift that points to our relationship to God. Impairments, and their corresponding disabilities, can serve as an underscored sign of limitation, even as we say that illness and injury are not given by God. However brief this next section may be, I do think various impairments and disabilities need to be presented to get a grasp of the different experiential challenges in this broad category, and how the sign of limitation may be engaged as call and response. The following is necessarily sketchy: even when focusing on particular impairments, people may not share common experiences of it. When the person became disabled (at conception? at birth? in adulthood?), how (an accident? an occasion of violence? an illness? a genetic mutation?), and the social context in which the person lives (supported? alone? stigmatized? an "invisible" disability?) are key elements to shaping the experience of impairment and disability.

Yong speaks wisely when he says as Christians, we should never say that a disability is ordained by God.[104] This is too direct a connection to God, and if the disability is a result of illness or injury, then it is traditionally understood as a consequence of original sin, our first parents' act of rejecting God. But Yong also says that people with disabilities should be allowed to adopt such a self-understanding of their lives with a disability: that is, that the disability may be given by God. (I prefer the word "shaped" over "given," to honor the ambiguity of impairment.) The key is to permit each person involved, not outside observers, to name the details in how each person's relationship to God is wrought.[105] Some may honestly say that the disability is a gift of God. Others would not, but say that God has given them the grace to live with it. Yet others may be in despair. Some may desire the impairment gone, others not. If God's providence demands that God work with us in our particularity, the responses will certainly be different. What we can assume and practice as a constant is this: all are loved deeply by an all-powerful and good God, and God desires our healing, if not in this world, then in the next. That process of spiritual and physical healing—embracing what it means to be a brother or sister of Jesus Christ—is part of the road to union with God.

I want to reflect, briefly, on what considerations particular to living for God can look like in three different kinds of impairments: genetic impairment (within which I look specifically at Down syndrome), disorders that affect personality (depression and dementia), and physical impairment (deafness/hearing loss). This is not an attempt to posit meaning on the lives of people living with any of those impairments. To be a sister or brother in Christ is to seek their witness, not impose a meaning.

Genetic Impairment: Down Syndrome (Trisomy 21)

Down syndrome (DS) is the most common source of birth defects, and occurs when a child is conceived with 47 chromosomes rather than 46. The extra chromosome in DS is a copy of chromosome 21 and causes changes in the person's physical and mental development from conception onward. Down syndrome certainly has its advocates. Andrea Roberts, who is a mother of a son with Down syndrome and the director of Reece's Rainbow, a ministry that advocates for the international adoption of children with DS and other special needs, argues that "the extra chromosome is a divine mark." She means it in a wholly positive way, highlighting the joys these children and adults bring their families and friends. Within the modern Jewish tradition, especially in Israel, there is a habit of naming children with Down syndrome *tzaddikim* (righteous or holy ones).[106] One Jewish mother from New York City described the first three hours visiting Jerusalem with her young son:

> By now everybody reading this knows that our darling little Y has Down Syndrome. It is a disability that is pretty apparent, as you can see it on his cute little face. Everywhere we went today, we were met with comments about our son. Not the comments that make you cringe, good comments and compliments….
>
> We took several cabs today, trying to get around Jerusalem and keep the kids entertained. Our first cab driver was a real sweetheart who told me not to worry about M crying in his car. When I tried to quiet him, he said, "Let him scream here, I don't mind." As we were leaving the cab and Y tried to stay in the car as he usually tends to do, the cab driver asked him his name and told us that he was a *neshama*- a pure soul.

Our second cab driver had a fancy car and was concerned about his leather seats. When Y got in the car, he started yelling at him to get his shoes off the seats. When he turned around and saw that Y has Down Syndrome, his tone completely changed. He apologized and called him a *tzaddik*, loosely translated as a "righteous person." Later on when walking down the street, a stranger spotted Y and started showering him with blessings. He told us that G'd should bless Y and called him a *tzaddik* several times.

That was three times in the span of about three hours. I know it sounds all romantic and idealistic. I am sure we will not be showered with blessings everywhere we go but it is reflective of an attitude that seems to exist here. The attitude that children with disabilities are "special" not just because they have extraordinary needs but because they truly are special and unique.

G'd puts us all where we need to be at different times in our lives….So while the services such as OT, PT and Speech may be better in the US, Israel definitely seems to have a leg up on attitude.[107]

These beautiful images—underlining that people with Down syndrome are a gift to the world—are often reiterated by many parents, teachers, and assistants to people with DS. Although the images can be overstated (as it is indeed possible for a person with Down syndrome to have a temper, understand and do wrong, etc.), the gift language seems to be an understandable foil against a culture that assumes a DS diagnosis is an unmitigated tragedy.

As a hyper-cognitive society, the primary challenge many associate with DS is that people with DS are intellectually disabled.[108] There are other typical physical markers as well, some of which could be considered impairments and others not: congenital heart defects, low vision, short stature, low muscle tone, a small chin that may disable speaking clearly, almond-shaped eyes, etc.

The trisomy, argues Yong, is not something to be healed in and of itself. While there may be elements that require medical treatment (glasses improve vision, heart surgery may improve heart function, etc.), there is no "eliminating" the extra chromosome: to do so would eliminate the person.[109] As mentioned earlier, it is interesting that in the corpus on healing narratives in the New Testament, there is not a single example of healing a mentally disabled person, or even a *request* to heal a mentally disabled person. Perhaps intellectual disabilities, DS or not, were not seen as an impairment needing healing.

Yet there is no question that people with DS live medically challenged lives, outside of intellectual impairment. They are also more dependent on the care of others, especially early in life, although many can live in adulthood with a measure of independence. And of course, people with DS have a spiritual aspect as well that needs healing, as all humans do. How can we respond to the Christian understanding that we all—people with DS included—are called to be healed by Christ? What is healed, here, exactly? It is difficult to argue that DS characteristics are the result of illness or injury, as genetic trisomy: a provident God could presumably have created this person *with* the trisomy, a speculation that I think is best left to the mystery of God's design. But if the trisomy could have been intended by God, would a person with DS "lose" who he/she is with such a healing?

There is loss only if we understand healing within the cult of normalcy. Physically and mentally speaking, Paul argues that the Resurrection body is continuous with the earthly body, yet transformed.[110] Yong takes up Paul's insight, arguing that our eternal healing means that disabilities do not "disappear," but are redeemed.[111] Once again, we look to Jesus Christ as the guide: His Resurrection body bore the marks of the Crucifixion, yet was glorified. True, a cure (miraculous or medical) may erase an impairment or disability. But we are discussing the healing offered by God, which is a broader category than cure. God heals. God does not always cure.

The person's limitations, even impairments, are the home of his or her soul, unified with the body and inseparable unto death, Yong reminds us. The embodied soul is enticed into the life of God without limit. "... [W]hereas bodily appetites admit of limits, spiritual aspirations can deepen forever without limit given the infinite divine 'object' of the soul's desires."[112] We are all created for an everlasting progress in knowing and loving God, and we should never assume that the intellectual or physical disabilities of Down syndrome prevent a person from a life of holiness. To do so harms the person with DS, creates a cult of normalcy for the spiritual life, and dishonors God's love for each person.

Vanier prods us continually: do we really believe in the holiness of people with disabilities? If we want to see a "sign" of witness that usually holds deep meaning to Catholics, there is a small order of religious sisters in France called the Little Sisters Disciples of the Lamb. It is a small contemplative community of nuns who have Down Syndrome in community with other nuns who do not. From their own literature:

> Guided by the wisdom of St Benedict, we teach our little disabled sisters the manual labour necessary for their development. We live poverty in putting ourselves at their disposal. With them, we share the work of everyday life.
>
> The office, adoration and the praying of the rosary are adapted to their rhythm and their capacities. In a spirit of silence, our prayer feeds every day on the Eucharist and on the meditation of the Gospel. ....
>
> "We follow every day the 'little way' taught by Saint Therese; knowing that 'great actions are forbidden to us', we learn from her to receive everything from God, to 'love for the brothers who fight', to 'scatter flowers for Jesus', and to pray for the intentions entrusted to us."[113]

It is striking, and produces a smile, to see the pictures associated with this small group of consecrated women: one never sees women with DS in a full habit. The description of their life together reminds one a bit of L'Arche. But perhaps the most salient reactions I have had are when I share this group with other Catholic women who have children with DS, or love someone with the diagnosis: they sometimes break down crying, with comments such as: "I would wish this so much for my daughter/niece/friend. I know she is so close to God. Why don't other people see how holy these people can be?" Granted, a habit does not make one holy. And choosing the religious life needs to be a free choice, so I assume they practice ways of discernment that make certain that this calling is from God and a truly free choice for these women. But the habited nuns with DS stand as a stark visual reminder of the universal call to holiness. That indeed, regardless of any limitation, we are called to a spiritual infinite—we are called to union with God.

As a balance, I want to offer part of the story of Amos Yong's brother, Mark. Yong's *Theology and Down Syndrome* is especially well-presented, in part because he intersperses his prodigious research with personal narratives: his own experience living with a brother with DS, his parents' (and still primary caregivers') experience, and his brother's own experience through interview. One of these reflections describes the path of discipleship Mark walks with the rest of us. Yong describes at length how his mother sees Mark as compassionate, lovable and loving, pure of heart, and sensitive to God. But there is more. Yong's language reflects the Pentecostal practices of his family:

> Yet, Mark has fallen short of the glory of God like everyone else. A case in point is his aforementioned stubbornness, which sometimes leads to extended periods of sulking and serious face-frowning—and on more rare occasions, foot-stomping and door-slamming—all of this registering his frustration when he feels like he is being misunderstood….[Dad] has taught Mark to pray through these periods of resentment, to get angry not at Mom [Mark's primary caregiver] but at the powers and principalities against which we are engaged, and to say to the adversary and accuser of all humanity, "Get thee behind me!" Mark will retreat to his room…usually coming out after 5-10 minutes…saying "I told him!" This leaves him smiling and feeling much better and, oftentimes, includes him saying "I'm sorry," to those with whom he felt contentious. In these and many other ways, Mark is learning just like the rest of us about what it means to be conformed to the image of God in Christ.[114]

My thought upon first reading this was that I had something important to learn from Mark.

Yong's thesis throughout the book is that the Holy Spirit "creatively enables and empowers our full humanity in relationship to our embodied selves, to others, and to God, even in the most ambiguous and challenging of circumstances."[115] Although we should be careful not to beatify a person with DS sight unseen, it is clear that DS is no impairment for God, and we can learn how to live the spiritual life as well from them as from others. To assume otherwise is to take our own interpretation of limit and put it on God.

Disorders Affecting Personality: Depression And Dementia

It is incredible that the English book list on systematic theology and depression contains one, perhaps two, books. Once again, the complexity of depression—causes, manifestations, treatments—cannot begin to be broached in a few paragraphs. But more theological attention should be paid to people living with the disability of mental illness, especially depression, which affects 9 percent of the population of the United States at any given time. Some comments here would also apply to the challenges faced in diseases that cause dementia and amnesia. The core challenge here is: what happens when a disability affects the mind, and the person loses his or her understanding of God and self?[116]

Whether the cause of depression is genetic, situational, or a mixture of both, Greene-McCreight, in her remarkable theological reflection on depression titled *Darkness Is My Only Companion*, finds it important to name active depression first and foremost as a brain disorder with spiritual side effects.

> ...a PET (positron emission tomography) scan can tell you by the colors of the different parts of the brain whether or not a patient is depressed....[T]he fact that metabolically the depressed brain takes on different colors in a PET scan, even if the brain is anatomically healthy, is fascinating.... We can say, then, incorporating the medical model, that depression is a physical event with spiritual side effects.[117]

The physical impact and spiritual side effects of Greene-McCreight's own experience (remember, we are honoring witness here) were intensely challenging. Five different times, Greene-McCreight was hospitalized for severe depression—initially, a last resort that she resisted. But she came to appreciate the hospital as "God's castle to keep me safe."[118]

For her, it was a place to stop pretending that everything was all right—she had long known it was not. Her solitary goal while in the hospital was to pray the daily office: morning and evening prayer. Typically, this spiritual practice would take 25 minutes. In her deeply depressed state, unable to concentrate, it took all day to complete. Even being awake hurt. Her mind couldn't focus on the text, and she felt no connection to anyone, much less God. Her descriptions of attempting to pray every day strike me as a true portrait in courage.

The spiritual danger of depression, argues Greene-McCreight, is that "it can lock us in ourselves, convincing us that we are indeed our own, and completely on our own, isolated in our distress. ...Mental illness is a veil that shrouds our consecration to God, blocking out the glory of the Holy One....All is experienced as pain."[119] Sylvia Plath's famous image of the inverted bell jar is relevant: one sees a distorted world through a glass jar, and cannot interact with it, trapped, alone.[120]

Greene-McCreight argues that one of the things that saved her in that darkness was knowledge that the soul, her soul, was not a collection of functions in the human mind. She retrieves the Hebrew understanding of Adam as *nephesh hayah*, living being or living soul. The mind and the rest of the body can affect the soul, given their intertwined unity. But the mind/body cannot *destroy* the soul. "Mental illness can potentially damage the soul, since it preys on the brain and the mind, but it cannot destroy the soul, for God holds the soul in his hands."[121] Further in the book, she reflects on the Resurrection appearance of Jesus to Mary Magdalene in John 20:13: "'Woman, why are you weeping?' She said to them, 'They have taken away my Lord, and I do not know where they have laid him.'" Her response:

> I thought I knew who Jesus was. I thought I could sense his presence. But in mental illness, I weep like Mary.... My presuppositions about the love of the Lord have been turned upside down. My brain, my cognition and my memory, can't find Jesus. Only my soul is safe in the Lord, without my awareness.[122]

When cognition and the ability to feel anyone's presence fails to assist at the most basic level—her long-held love for God—Greene-McCreight admits she learned how to pray.

> I learned during these years to pray. It was not as if I
> had never prayed before. As with learning compassion,
> which I thought I already knew, I relearned how to pray.
> The Daily Office helped....However, it was more....
> Prayer from a mentally ill mind is exceedingly difficult.
> Not only is it hard to concentrate, which is necessary for
> prayer; it is also painful to give thanks. Which means one
> has to try all the harder, or not at all: to let the Holy Spirit
> pray through you is a form of prayerful surrender.[123]

I ask at this point, as I did in the Down syndrome section: do we believe in the holiness of the mentally ill? To put it bluntly, I rarely hear
prayers for the mentally ill on any parish's intercession list. I also know
many ministers who are rightly suspicious (not to mention feel out of
their depth) with the religiosity of some of the mentally ill they encounter, seeing it as psychosis, not spiritual health. Greene-McCreight's
narrative is damning against the multiple psychotherapists she had encountered who dismissed her faith as a potential problem and sign of
madness.[124] Do we Christians too quickly dismiss the religiosity of the
mentally ill as well? Do we believe that God can work to raise a person
to holiness through the slow process of living and healing in mental illness? Do we deny those who live with mental illness the most basic call
of God—to hear that God loves them, where they are? And hope is real,
because God is real?

The other insight that Greene-McCreight offers in her book is a reflection on personality. Personality can change, drastically, with depression:
a person with a bright outlook on life suddenly cannot see any meaning
to it. Anxiety often coincides with depression, affecting personality in
other ways. Many people who are depressed have lost much sense of
who they are. Greene-McCreight's conclusion? "[P]ersonality matters
little to our life before God."[125]

> ...[W]hen major depression gets really bad, it is indeed
> like madness. The personality dissolves. Tastes, desires,
> dispositions that formerly marked our personality
> vanish with mental illness. Will I ever be me again, and
> if so, what will me be on the other side of this madness?...

> What does this mean *coram Deo*...? I suppose it means that the personality is relatively unimportant vis a vis God. In God's eyes we are not how we feel, we are not what we think, we are not even what we do. We are what God does with us, and what God does with us is to save us from our best yet perverse efforts to separate ourselves from his presence, from his fellowship, communion, sharing.[126]

She continues to accuse Americans of an idolatrous love of "personality betterment"—eating habits, exercise, friendships—which assumes we will feel good about things as a consequence. We confuse personality betterments with the God of the Scriptures, and ignore that God demands our worship and obedience regardless of how we feel about it. We are told to choose life regardless of our emotional state, she says, and that is the hard part. While this truth is almost too bracing, I want to be clear that all she is saying is to put God first: not personality. After all, while God cares about your personality, He does not put your personality first. Your identity before God is not, first and foremost, your personality. Your identity is a beloved adopted son or daughter of God, and it is seated in your soul.

The insight that our identity before God is not rooted in personality has deep meaning beyond the "personality-dissolving" effect of major depression. One of the most frightening diseases of our time is Alzheimer's disease, as well as a constellation of similar diseases marked by progressive dementia. Many who treat patients with dementia observe that there are phrases, commonly used, which are simply demeaning. You cannot say "he really isn't there anymore" or "it's just a husk, my father has been long gone"—because as well as being degrading, it's simply not true. It is important, they say, to gently remind people with dementia of their identity (even if it seems not to be heard by the person): "Our task as moral agents is to remind persons with dementia of their continuing self-identity. We must serve as a prosthesis that fills in the gaps...our task is to preserve identity."[127] Usually, we see this in kind attempts to honor the person by using their name or title, to engage them in a past they can remember, to maintain known good habits, to root the person in small ways to the entire life he or she has lived.

As important and life-honoring as such efforts are, preserving a lived social identity is not the only identity we should bear in mind. We remember the *kenosis* we are called to imitate, the ecstatic identity of Christ: to receive and give back who we are to God the Father. This is safe, because there is no more secure place to live than to put your life in God's hands. People who live with Alzheimer's and other dementias find themselves in a situation where they need to cling to that crystal-sharp truth in a radical way. It may be helpful to recall that even Jesus seemed to question who He was at the height of His *kenosis*—"My God, my God, why have you abandoned me?" is a cry of disorientation. (There is a difference between Jesus truly not knowing who He was and disorientation, and I am not saying that Jesus did not know who He was.) Medically, disorientation would have been completely understandable under the circumstances of the Crucifixion—ongoing pain, blood loss, and lack of oxygen. Even within the likely disorientation, though, Jesus's prayer is mixed with trust in God the Father's plans—read the last line of Psalm 22: "future generations will be told about the Lord, and proclaim his deliverance to a people yet unborn...." This may be something worth remembering for those of us who live with family and friends affected by dementia: that in the person's apparent disorientation, there still may be something that knows who he or she is before God that we cannot perceive. This is a way of holding the person's holiness, despite disorientation and the sometimes violent response that comes with that: a willingness to allow that there is a mystery and communion based in the dynamic of *kenosis* that we cannot see as God sees.

Some writers have argued that people who live with progressive dementia of any sort are living out a dark night of the soul, and Greene-McCreight raises the language with regard to depression.[128] Technically, I would hold this is not quite right. John of the Cross offers the dark night of sense, and further within the spiritual life, the dark night of the soul, as periods when God restrains a felt presence of Himself in order to purify the human soul of any earthly desire but God. It is a providential discipline, a path to greater holiness: God is fully present, but the presence is not offered as felt presence to the person. It is a difficult segment of the spiritual journey, to put it mildly, and is usually given to people who are fairly advanced on the path. In contrast, the darkness that is part of depression or dementia is not given by God, but is a physical illness with possible spiritual effects. If treated successfully, the darkness lifts. The dark nights of John of the Cross would not lift until God removed them. This is not to say that a Christian desiring to grow in holiness could not approach either depression or dementia with an acceptance of the possibilities for purification, and recognize that many have weathered the darkness with God's help. McCreight-Greene went this route, and says she was indeed purified by the experience. But she is happy to be well, and lived through the depression striving to be well. It is natural and right with dementia and depression to seek healing first, since the illness in and of itself does not come directly from God. A purification found through living with these personality-altering diseases can and should be honored. But we also need to encourage people to seek healing, and to remind them: our God is not one who inflicts pain, but a God who heals.

So far, our case studies lift up certain elemental questions of an underscored sign of limitation, felt in specific ways but bearing relevance to all human beings:

- How can we respond to the Christian understanding that we all are called to be healed by Christ? What is "healed," exactly?

- Do we believe in the holiness of people with impairments and disabilities?

- How is impairment a physical event with spiritual side effects?

- How may impairments and disabilities "lock us in ourselves" and prevent relationship? How is this a spiritual danger?

- How can impairment be "disorienting"?

- What does it mean to say the soul can be affected by impairment, but it is not destroyed by it?

- What does it mean to say your identity as an adopted son or daughter of the Father is rooted in your soul?

With these questions in mind, I move to a personal experience.

Physical Impairment: Deafness/Hearing Loss

Up to this point in the chapter, I have been quiet about my perspective and place within this study. Some in disability studies require an honest admission of where the researcher finds him/herself within the spectrum of disabilities. It is understandable that a group of people who have been "spoken for" and defined without their consent or input would be especially sensitive to this. Creamer tackled this challenge directly when she asked whether she is "disabled enough" for the disability studies arena (she walks with a cane and is challenged by chronic pain).[129] Others get categorized as "affiliates" to someone disabled (family member, friend, patient, or client). Hauerwas, who had done significant volunteering with people with intellectual disabilities, has expressed deep hesitance about writing and speaking on the subject, since his connection is no longer as acute. Reynolds speaks as a father and is careful not to speak directly for those disabled. Vanier usually speaks for the L'Arche movement, for community, and not an individual. Henri Nouwen was yet another "affiliate": *Adam* is a memoir of a friend, a deeply disabled man for whom Nouwen was primary caregiver at L'Arche, a man Nouwen called his spiritual director.[130]

I am family and friends to many who would qualify as disabled: my husband has low vision to the point of needing a restricted driver's license and multiple work accommodations. My husband and I have adopted a son, who has cerebral palsy. My father-in-law was legally blind, and also died after years of mini-strokes, resulting in dementia and diminished balance and walking ability. I have a few relatives with learning disabilities. I have other relatives who have dealt with depression, and I had postpartum depression myself. This list is not exhaustive, and I don't think this family (and friends) tree is terribly unusual.

But it would be dishonest not to mention my unusual connection with disability. My fullest immersion in the world of disability occurred 15 years ago, when I was a healthy 29 year old, a research fellow at a small university. I woke up one morning feeling "off." I tried to get up and collapsed to the floor as the ground gave way: vertigo. I somehow managed to slither to the bathroom and stayed on the bathroom floor the rest of the day, throwing up with vertigo that wouldn't stop. It was only eight hours later, when the vertigo stopped enough that I felt somewhat alive again, that I realized that I couldn't hear in my left ear. That had been the case since morning; I was just so ill I didn't fully note it. After many doctor visits, ratcheting up the specialist route each time, I was told the hearing loss in my left ear was nearly total and permanent, the result of a viral infection.

I had never thought much about hearing, but physics began to play a more obvious role in my life than heretofore. Sounds waves don't curve, so on one side of my head, I was fully hearing, and on the other, functionally deaf. Also, the purpose of two functioning ears is to help you locate where sound is coming from. While teaching, a student would ask a question, and I would have literally no idea where to look for the source of the question. The first weeks I couldn't interpret sounds at all—rain on the car roof became an engine problem, a pot of water boiling over became an unnerving puzzle I couldn't figure out until it nearly boiled away. A hearing aid half-worked; music was a nightmare. My hearing loss was not less hearing, but less and very broken hearing.

The even bigger problem was that the vertigo attacks kept coming, knocking me flat for hours at a time, and leaving me woozy for days afterward. With the inner ear injured, I had shakier balance all the time, but the vertigo was something else entirely. If anything, these attacks were more disabling than the hearing loss: Could I drive today? What do I do if this happens in class? How many days can I "take off" in a new job without jeopardizing getting a contract for next year? Besides—the vertigo was miserable. Nothing stopped it: you just got flat and waited it out.

So: more trips to even more hyper-specialized specialists. Finally, a new diagnosis: Meniere's disease. For those who know of it, please recognize that I had an unusually severe onset and case of it; often Meniere's is less intrusive. In short, it is a collection of symptoms: inner ear pressure, vertigo attacks, tinnitus, and progressive hearing loss. A person could have Meniere's loss in one ear or two. The chances of developing Meniere's in the second ear, a doctor told me, were about 50/50. Treatment options were slim: Valium for the worst vertigo, surgeries that often didn't help and could make things worse. I was blessed to be seeing an internationally recognized expert on Meniere's. But I was not feeling especially blessed at that point.

Things changed again when I had a vertigo attack a couple of months later—and I recognized it was coming from my right ear, my "good ear." Now I had tinnitus, pressure, and vertigo in both ears. My right-side hearing appeared undamaged. But if it was anything like what happened in the left ear, I knew I could wake up one morning profoundly deaf. At this point, I began to panic.

I had thrown myself into researching accommodation options for the hard of hearing. I quickly got up to speed on ADA issues in the workplace. (What would the accommodations be in a college classroom? In a faculty meeting?) I quickly learned that Deaf culture was a model in bucking the victimization model, which was both inspiring and terrifying. (Could I fit in there?) I talked (well, e-mailed) with a very happy deaf man who was a drummer for a rock band. (He said the rest of the band was very, very loud, and he played through sensing vibration.) I was banking on the motto "knowledge is power," and sought as much knowledge as I could. I bought a couple of books on ASL and signed English, but every time I looked at them, my heart broke. I didn't know anyone who communicated with ASL. Would my family be willing to learn it? Any friends at all? I was frightened, and not without reason, that going deaf could be close to living in solitary confinement with a good view. One article that I cannot find now argued that people who go deaf in adulthood have much higher incidents of severe depression than people who go blind—simply because deafness can sever relationships in a way blindness does not. True or not, that article haunted me.

This period definitely fit in the list of questions raised in the other case studies: this physical event was spawning significant spiritual side effects, all of them challenging. The anxiety and fear definitely locked me inside myself, and this was spiritually dangerous. The experiences were profoundly disorienting in basic physical ways, but also spiritual ways— it was hard to know who God was and where He was in the midst of it. And I would go so far to say my soul sustained a kind of damage from the physical events, especially the panic they created. If I ever knew I was an adopted daughter of God the Father, I certainly forgot it then.

I was very much in "I'm managing this" mode, and had no idea where God was.

I managed to work around this reality with mounting terror and anxiety, getting up from the ongoing vertigo blows and continuing to teach my students and make revisions on my dissertation. An almost "normal" life. But when classes ended in May, the yawning space of freer time meant no more distractions from the reality: I needed to talk to someone, and fast. I asked a friend and priest[131] I worked with whether an offer he had made months ago—to pray with me about the hearing and vertigo issues—was still open. He said it was, and we met the next day.

Most of that conversation and prayer remains etched in my memory. I was nearly hysterical, and he spent a fair amount of the time in compassionate presence and "talking me down." Some of the conversation was practical (let's think through how you could still teach), some sociological (what do you think of disabled people?), and a lot spiritual (what do you really want in this situation?). Then he began to pray for me, hands hovering over my ears, for healing.

Somehow, I had not picked up on the fact that this priest was charismatic. It was a surprise. I thought the prayer was going to be for good, safe things like courage and strength, not physical and spiritual healing. But I liked and respected him, and thought…well, I could sit through this. At one point, I moved to thinking…maybe…maybe I could be healed. After some imaginative prayer (see chapter 1), he abruptly asked if I had received a sacramental anointing of the sick. I had not and agreed it was a good idea, so I received the sacrament. I had never seen the sacrament given nor had I ever received it, and was struck by the intense beauty of the words: "…may the Lord in his love and mercy help you, with the grace of the Holy Spirit. May the Lord who frees you from sin save you, and raise you up."

Immediately, viscerally, I realized: I was not panicked. I was calm. I was still somewhat sad, but intensely peaceful as well. God was there, indeed. My friend suggested a particular book on healing prayer, and offered to pray together again if I wished, suggesting it would be wise to continue the prayer. And I left.

For two days I walked and thought and prayed. I felt like I had been placed in a lifeboat of tranquility, and began thinking about accepting whatever lay ahead with an unusually quiet heart. I may go completely deaf, I may be unable to walk well, I may have a lot of vertigo, but it's OK, because God is here and will be there too. One walk took me to a bookstore, where I found the book my priest-friend recommended, bought it, and read it. It had a "light touch" on healing prayer, emphasizing that others have asked God for healing, and we should too; that healing (physical or spiritual or both) is part of God's plan for humanity. However God responds, you grow in relationship to God when you ask and are open to God's response. And so, book in hand, I settled down, and prayed.

There was no way I could be prepared for what happened next. Basically, God happened. It felt like a roaring wind, a shocking burst of energy, and a very deep heat in my ears. I had a sense of light, although my eyes were closed. I felt I had to stay still and let this happen, but beyond that, I could not think, other than recognize: this is God. Whatever is happening, this is beyond good. It was overwhelming, and I am positive I was being given the grace to endure it. (I remember sensing "breathe, stay calm" when I began hyperventilating and shaking, and suddenly could breathe calmly.) Then I was "told" to go to sleep, so, shakily, I did.

I woke up in the morning, got up, thought rather inadequately, "Wow," and after a minute of getting ready for the day's activities, heard and felt a loud "pop" in my left ear. It took perhaps a minute to sink in: almost all my hearing had returned. I ran around the house, testing what things sounded like with my healed ear. After about 20 minutes, finally convinced this was real, I sat down and cried.[132]

It seems obvious that many, even most, people who pray for physical healing are not healed. But as I shared this story with friends, I was amazed at how many quietly have said, "Let me tell you a story...." Physical healing may be the ultimate taboo in the Catholic Church.

I appreciate your indulgence in reading that too-long witness.[133] There are points I want to highlight in this story, points that connect with the themes of extending the Theology of the Body in this chapter focused on impairment. The main point, remarkably, is not the physical healing itself. The impairments as underscored sign made visible my need to rely on God, and taught me that God was good and provident—all this before my hearing was restored.

I learned a lot about vulnerability in those 16 months. The vulnerability—physical, emotional, spiritual—was always there, of course, but I was not living a life where I had to face it. I had my health, good work, plans, friendships, family, and all of it was placed over a pitch overnight. I had assumed health could be fixed. I had assumed that if I didn't teach, I had other talents—I could just do something else. I had assumed I could talk to people and hear what they said. Some in disability studies called the abled "temporarily abled," and I had to face that my life to that point was of the temporarily abled sort.

I learned that God is good. But I only learned that in a deep way when I was humble enough to ask for help, to admit I was limited and weak—more spiritually weak than physically weak—and could not handle this illness. I knew that God was good immediately after the sacrament of anointing, before the physical healing occurred. To my mind, that freedom from fear and abiding peace still remains the core healing. And the physical healing that followed—although incredible—placed a light on my life that exposed a lot of dark things (like my lack of belief that God could or would want to heal me in any way), and made life very difficult for a time. In essence, it forced me to recognize and expose more spiritual illness. That was a good—but not a simple good.

I also learned God is provident, that I was not being forgotten, and that God had a plan for my life. But I needed someone to tell me that directly; I needed the mutual vulnerability and the courage to witness, which I received in the conversation and prayer with the priest. In fact, I couldn't really pray, and that is often a challenge when people are ill. (Frankly, when people are well, too). He didn't just pray for me, he prayed with me, and in that prayer, God allowed me to "get atop" of my fear, and risk *disponibilité*, openness to God's will. This was no drive-by healing event, or a weak "that's too bad and I'll light a candle for you" response, both of which can be disastrous: they ignore John Paul's insight that all existence is a co-existence, and the necessity of relationship.

I learned that this was about God, not so much me; that is, I did nothing to merit this. Teresa of Ávila once suggested that the reason she received such remarkable mystical experiences was because she was so weak and thick-headed she needed them more than most to believe who God was, that it was no mark of merit whatsoever, but most can know and love God without these gifts. I sympathize with that insight. This healing—spiritual and physical—was gift, and I couldn't do a thing to make it happen. I also knew I hadn't really believed God could or would give me any gift. My openness to God's plans was barely there.

I also learned that these healings (spiritual and physical) were the beginning, not the end, of God calling me to discipleship. As in the Gospels, the healing narratives are not about getting a dose of "God's Tylenol," but virtually always an invitation to follow Christ in a more direct and full manner. And healing is a process that is lived through the call to discipleship, never full until we live with God in heaven. When vulnerability is exposed and God's light shines on things, you quickly realize there is more sin, more illness, more resistance: more healing needed. But, warts and all, the call is recognized because the relationship to God as God is recognized in a fresh way.

I raise this story, grateful I can point to God's goodness, squeamish I have spent many pages ostensibly about me. But it is not about me, it is about God. It is about God's call, our response; God's gift, our receptivity; what the call means to children of the Father and brothers and sisters to Jesus Christ, open to the life of the Spirit. Spiritual healing occurs when we ask, thanks to God's constant mercy and love. Physical healing can occur in this life, if God wills it as the best way to draw you to Himself. Physical healing will occur in some sense in the life to come, in the transformed body, because God desires our healing. But the point I am trying to make is that all the themes of this chapter do not *demand* immediate physical healing as a result. Living these themes opens you to God and how *God* best chooses to draw you to union with Himself. The crystal exchange in the initial encounter with my priest-friend was when I was asked if I wanted to live for God, more than anything else.

After I paused (it's a huge question!) and said yes, my friend kindly replied, "Then God will help you do just that, through healing your disease or giving you the grace to live with it." When you offer to join your will with God's, He leads you in the way best suited to your redemption. I am and will always be deeply humbled by the physical healing, but honestly, I am even more humbled by the salvation God has offered us individually and collectively as a deeply fallen, broken, shot-through-with-evil world. Our limited lives point in various ways chosen by God to that remarkable reality.

I do not hold that this experience directly taught me about faith. I would say faith (and not that much of it; I was bolstered by my community of faith) taught me and led me through that experience. As Waldstein interprets Wojtyla, "The superiority of faith over all experience does not imply that the whole order of experience is irrelevant. On the contrary, it is relevant inasmuch as a living faith deeply transforms human experience by introducing the person to a path of union with God."[134] *And the possibility of that transformation is embedded and witnessed in the limitedness of the human person.*

Spiritual Brotherhood And Sisterhood: A Call To Relationship And Witness

At this point, we recall John Paul's model of church in *Ecclesia in Africa* as a possible extension of Theology of the Body themes: the call for the church to the Family of God:

> Not only did the Synod speak of inculturation, but it also made use of it, taking the *Church* as *God's Family* as its guiding idea for the evangelization of Africa. The Synod Fathers acknowledged it as an expression of the Church's nature particularly appropriate for Africa. For this image emphasizes care for others, solidarity, warmth in human relationships, acceptance, dialogue and trust. The new evangelization will thus aim at *building up the Church as Family*, avoiding all ethnocentrism and excessive particularism, trying instead to encourage reconciliation and true communion....[135]

While motherhood and fatherhood, spiritual and physical, are certainly calls, they are also lived realities. In this chapter, having focused on our inherent limitedness, I suggest we pay attention to the call and lived reality of our brotherhood and sisterhood, rooted in the Brotherhood of Jesus Christ.

To call Jesus our brother is to point again to the theological key of this chapter, the self-emptying of God, or *kenosis*. Jesus lived out an ecstatic identity, receiving eternally from God the Father His Sonship, and offering the return of it in His dying. Beyond Colossians 2 and the Crucifixion narratives themselves, the other major *kenosis* text in the New Testament is Hebrews 2:5-18, quoted here in part, starting at verse 10:

> It was fitting that God, for whom and through whom all things exist, in bringing many children to glory, should make the pioneer of their salvation perfect through sufferings. *For the one who sanctifies [hagiazó] and those who are sanctified all have one Father. For this reason Jesus is not ashamed to call them brothers and sisters*, saying, "I will proclaim your name to my brothers and sisters, in the midst of the congregation I will praise you." And again, "I will put my trust in him." And again, "Here am I and the children whom God has given me."
>
> Since, therefore, the children share flesh and blood, he himself likewise shared the same things, so that through death he might destroy the one who has the power of death, that is, the devil, and free those who all their lives were held in slavery by the fear of death. For it is clear that he did not come to help angels, but the descendants of Abraham. Therefore he had to become like his brothers and sisters in every respect, so that he might be a merciful and faithful high priest in the service of God, to make a sacrifice of atonement for the sins of the people. Because he himself was tested by what he suffered, he is able to help those who are being tested. [Italics added.]

He who sanctifies—Christ—and those who are being sanctified—us— "all have one Father": the origin here is ambiguous, but context points to Adam or the patriarch Abraham. Therefore, he is "not ashamed to call them brothers and sisters." The passage goes on to affirm that Jesus Christ shared the fullness of humanity ("he had to become like his brothers and sisters in every respect") in order to die, destroying the power of death and freeing those in fear of death. Hebrews as a letter is extraordinarily focused on the salvific nature of Jesus's death (the Resurrection is assumed but not part of its argument). Only a brother— even the One who can consecrate as the God-Man, the One for whom and through whom all things exist, states Hebrews—could call those being consecrated, set aside for God the Father, brothers and sisters. Only a brother, who shares our humanity through Adam, could die in sacrifice for us to destroy the power of death forever. The kenotic Son of God establishes the reality of the brotherhood of Christ. Not a metaphor or a generous word play, but a reality: Christ, our brother, saves and consecrates all of his brothers and sisters.

If the *kenosis* of Christ makes visible the brotherhood of Christ, our relationship to both Him and each other is cast in high relief through the boundary that is the Crucifixion. We are God's family through Christ's incarnation and death. We are called to love each other and support each other on the road to union with God as family. Quite a few of the theologies of disability encourage seeing those abled and disabled through the lens of a call to friendship.[136] It is a worthy move, but I argue that the call to live out brotherhood and sisterhood is better. First, it roots what it means to be human (abled or disabled) in the incarnation of Jesus Christ, our brother and Son of the Father. Second, it names the universal vocation (child of God) and gendered vocation (son or daughter of God) of all human beings.[137] Third, friendship is generally understood to be a choice. But we do not choose our brothers and sisters, yet are called to love them and recognize the common bond (our parents) regardless. It is a more primal connection, and brotherhood and sisterhood speak better to the universal nature of God's family and His love and providence.

As mentioned in the last chapter, language of family can clang like a wooden bell for some in Western cultures. The ideal of a household headed by a father and mother, with sisters and brothers, is not within everyone's direct experience.[138] But…if the body is a pre-given language of self-giving and fruitfulness, then family serves as a natural extension of that sign. And as Vanier said, the first and primary belonging is in the family. This is where we learn—where we were created to learn—*disponibilité*, trust, mutual vulnerability, the healing gift of presence (or not). This is where we were created to know and live in the Holy Spirit, to know we "belong" to each other and belong to God: "The condition to which we are led by Jesus is a condition of *utter dependence* on God and *relative dependence* on one another."[139] As John Paul II said, all existence is a co-existence. As in the sign of childbirth, the sign of brotherhood and sisterhood as currently experienced bears the mark of the Fall. Some families may work mightily to serve as counter-sign. But the sign was created by God as a natural first word, as a reality that points to our invitation to complete union with God.[140]

The limitation that is the reality of incarnation is the natural sign that marks us as family, as brothers and sisters of Christ. We are not angels, we are certainly not God. We are created in time and space for a reality beyond time and space. Our embodiment—whether named as limitedness, weakness, impairment, or disability—is a sign that points to the call to live ecstatic identities as sons and daughters of God, brothers and sisters of Christ. That identity is sure, because God the Father is trustworthy. In trusting God to nourish us beyond our given limitations and eventual death, we imitate our Brother in returning our life, our identity, to the Father. And in our spiritual brotherhood and sisterhood with each other—especially witnessed through relationships of mutual vulnerability and *disponibilité*—we allow the work of the Holy Spirit to heal us, and heal the other, strengthening the sign and witness as we live together as the family of God.

There is a long tradition of people in the consecrated life of the Catholic Church taking the name of "brother" or "sister." The wisdom of this may be unseen in the pervasiveness of the language. But working at a college run by the De La Salle Brothers of the Christian Schools (more commonly known as the Christian Brothers) gives me insight into the language of brotherhood. The impoverished young boys who were without options in 18th century France, the ones who were recognized by John Baptist de La Salle as needing help and education, did not need a father or mother—they often had them. They needed a brother, an older brother, to guide them and help them. They needed someone willing to work at their level and be with them, be one of them. De La Salle gave up his comfortable position as a cathedral rector and his family inheritance to live with the Brothers, the consecrated laypersons serving the boys as teachers. The order decided after de La Salle's death to remain an order of brothers, not priests. The brotherhood was essential to the charism. My campus's main chapel is dedicated to St. Thomas More: an odd choice. Wouldn't it make more sense to dedicate it to St. John Baptiste de La Salle? But Thomas More is the patron saint of the laity, the people the brothers serve. It strikes me as a good example of the self-effacing nature of this call to brotherhood, a call that is often ignored and misunderstood (mirroring Jesus' "brotherhood" to us in that way). It makes me wonder, as an associate of the Christian Brothers,[141] if I strive to teach as an "older sister" to my students, and what that means.

My last comment in this long chapter: John Paul II *did* speak directly to the language of brotherhood and sisterhood, albeit not in the Theology of the Body audiences. In 1987, John Paul II is known for introducing a new virtue into the Catholic lexicon: solidarity.

> Solidarity is undoubtedly a Christian virtue. In what has been said so far it has been possible to identify many points of contact between solidarity and charity, which is the distinguishing mark of Christ's disciples (cf. Jn 13:35). In the light of faith, solidarity seeks to go beyond itself, to take on the specifically Christian dimension of total gratuity, forgiveness and reconciliation. One's neighbor is then not only a human being with his or her own rights and a fundamental equality with everyone else, but becomes the living image of God the Father, redeemed by the blood of Jesus Christ and placed under the permanent action of the Holy Spirit. One's neighbor must therefore be loved, even if an enemy, with the same love with which the Lord loves him or her; and for that person's sake one must be ready for sacrifice, even the ultimate one: to lay down one's life for the brethren (cf. 1 Jn 3:16).
>
> *At that point, awareness of the common fatherhood of God, of the brotherhood of all in Christ - "children in the Son" - and of the presence and life-giving action of the*

Holy Spirit will bring to our vision of the world a new criterion for interpreting it. Beyond human and natural bonds, already so close and strong, there is discerned in the light of faith a new model of the unity of the human race, which must ultimately inspire our solidarity. This supreme model of unity, which is a reflection of the intimate life of God, one God in three Persons, is what we Christians mean by the word "communion." This specifically Christian communion, jealously preserved, extended and enriched with the Lord's help, is the soul of the Church's vocation to be a "sacrament," in the sense already indicated.[142]

That is, when we are able to see the sign of all humanity as *family*, we will interpret our call to self-gift rightly. We will model the life of giving and receiving seen in the kenosis of the Son of God, our brother, and upheld in the primordial sacrament of union, marriage. Another virtue within Catholic social teaching that John Paul upheld was the preferential love for the poor and vulnerable: preferential not in that the poor deserve more love through any merit, but that their situation calls for those who can serve to love them, help them, be a brother and sister to them. The preferential love for the poor demands that we listen to our brothers and sisters, and calls us to provide for their needs—which as all families know, may be more than material, but does not dismiss the material needs, either. Brotherhood and sisterhood should demand no other justification for acting this way than the call of the relationship itself. It is a call to be the sacrament of unity, to reflect "the intimate life of God."

The next chapter is in many ways a re-application of the Theology of the Body insights in these last two chapters: how does the Theology of the Body, when extended, inform our understanding of dying not as something to endure, but a sign?

ENDNOTES

1. Colleen Carpenter Cullinan, "In Pain and Sorrow: Childbirth, Incarnation, and the Suffering of Women," *Crosscurrents*, Spring 2008, 95-107.

2. Ibid., 95-96.

3. According to UNICEF, the current lifetime maternal death rate in Ethiopia is 1 in 67, in the United States, it is 1 in 2400 (and that U.S. number is a sharp increase from the 1980s). Ethiopia: http://www.unicef.org/infobycountry/ethiopia_statistics.html, USA: http://www.unicef.org/infobycountry/usa_statistics.html, and the reporting on the sharp increase in maternal deaths in the 1990s and 2000s: Stephanie Smith, "Doubling of Maternal Deaths in U.S. 'Scandalous', rights group says" http://www.cnn.com/2010/HEALTH/03/12/maternal.mortality/index.html?iref=allsearch. I would be cautious in reading those numbers as examples that all third-world women have a much higher chance of dying in childbirth: the evidence is clear that quite a few third-world countries have comparable or better maternal death rates than the USA (which, for all its wealth, is also not the best in the world). Money and health access is one issue, but perhaps not the primary issue. Please see my next note.

4. Some could say that this question undercuts my valuation of natural childbirth as a sign, but I don't think so: the reality is, if women are not valued in the society, both the spiritual aspects of childbirth *and* the medical challenges of childbirth are dismissed. Some of the countries with the worst maternal death rates are indeed desperately poor and lack access to emergency care in childbirth. But there are countries that are poor that have a much better maternal death rate—comparable to the "first world" States or better. The key seems to be the root valuation of both women's lives and the act of childbirth: although all maternal deaths cannot be prevented, many can without expensive medical help. And although I don't entirely agree with Carpenter's theological argument, she is absolutely correct that valuing women to the extent that they are not marked as property to be married off and bearing children at age 14 is a basic and effective way to prevent much of the disabling and killing scourge of fistulae. Securing more medical help for very young mothers (and all medically at-risk mothers) is another.

5. John Paul II, *Mulieris Dignitatem*, #11.

6. The following list is not exhaustive, but includes the constructive texts that I consider to be some of the formative works in this field: Stanley Hauerwas, *Suffering Presence: Theological Reflections On Medicine, The Mentally Handicapped, and The Church* (Indiana: University of Notre Dame Press, 1986); Nancy Eiesland, *The Disabled God: Toward a Liberatory Theology of Disability* (Nashville: Abingdon Press, 1996); Jennie Weiss Block, *Copious Hosting: A Theology of Access for People with Disabilities* (New York: Continuum, 2002); David A. Pailin, *A Gentle Touch: From A Theology of Handicap to a Theology of Human Being* (London: SPCK, 1992); John Swinton, ed., *Critical Reflections on Stanley Hauerwas' Theology of Disability: Disabling Society, Enabling Theology* (Binghamton, NY: Haworth Pastoral Press, 2004); Amos Yong, *Theology and Down Syndrome: Reimagining Disability in Late Modernity* (Waco, TX: Baylor University Press, 2007); Stanley Hauerwas and Jean Vanier, *Living Gently in a Violent World: The Prophetic Witness of Weakness* (Downers Grove, IL: IVP Books, 2008); Hans S. Reinders, *Receiving the Gift of Friendship: Profound Disability, Theological Anthropology, and Ethics* (Grand Rapids, MI: William B. Eerdmans Publishing, 2008); Thomas

E. Reynolds, *Vulnerable Communion: A Theology of Disability and Hospitality* (Grand Rapids, MI: Brazos Press, 2008); Deborah Beth Creamer, *Disability and Christian Theology: Embodied Limits and Constructive Possibilities* (New York: Oxford University Press, 2009). Finally, I warmly recommend an excellent book that does not address school of the theology of disability in itself but certainly treats some of its concerns within the written corpus of John Paul II: Jeffrey Tranzillo's *John Paul II on the Vulnerable* (Washington, DC: Catholic University of America Press, 2013).

7. This perspective is most succinctly communicated through Paul in Rom 8:28-30 (see chapter frontispiece).

8. Anne Fadiman, *The Spirit Catches You and You Fall Down: A Hmong Child, Her American Doctors, and the Collision of Two Cultures* (New York: Farrar, Straus and Giroux, 1997).

9. Deborah Creamer's first chapter in *Disability and Christian Theology*, "Understanding Disability," is the best brief but thorough treatment of the various definitions that come from disability studies. Although I don't agree with some of her constructive argument later in her book, I respect the first chapter as the best single treatment on the topic available in English. See pp. 13-14 for a treatment of the above terms.

10. American Sign Language, or ASL, is not English being translated into sign. ASL has its own grammar, idioms, and dialects. It cannot be transliterated into English. Although there is signed English, and the signed alphabet for various English words, ASL and English are different languages. People who communicate with ASL and are able to read English are in every sense bilingual.

11. Creamer, 28-9.

12. Creamer, 93. The "we are all limited" insight is also raised by Jürgen Moltmann, another theologian who has embraced a theology of disability: "In actual fact the distinction between the healthy and the handicapped does not exist, for every human being is limited, vulnerable, and weak....It is only the ideal of health set up by the society of the capable which condemns a certain group of people to be 'handicapped'...." Moltmann quoted in William Gaventa, "Learning from People with Disabilities," in Hans Reinders, ed., *The Paradox of Disability: Responses to Jean Vanier and L'Arche Communities from Theology and the Sciences* (Grand Rapids, MI: William B. Eerdmans Pub, 2010), 105.

13. Lennard J. Davis, *Enforcing Normalcy: Disability, Deafness, and the Body* (London: Verso, 1995), 1.

14. Many may remember the outrage in America when a news story in 1990 (first covered by ABC News, and then by the *Washington Post*) documented the deplorable conditions in overcrowded Romanian orphanages. This was before the fall of the Ceaușescu regime, and a probable result of Ceaușescu demanding that women bear more children for a Romanian workforce—only to recognize later that the children could not be raised by the parents living in extreme poverty, who released them to just-as-poor mega-orphanages. The hue and cry of those reports and images resulted in many changes within Romania, and orphanages years later were better (although not without human rights abuses). However, the positive changes didn't trickle down to the disabled children in state care, who were neglected and often tied in cribs all day and night. See *ABC News*, "Disabled Children Confined and Abused in Romania," May 10, 2006, http://abcnews.go.com/GMA/story?id=1941485&page=1#.TymRW4HGDTo.   Romania's

examples of neglect or abuse may be extreme (or not), but the orphanage and institutionalization system in many Eastern European countries reflects an inheritance of the Soviet Union's condemnation of people with disabilities. To see a 1998 report from Human Rights Watch on abuse and neglect in Russian special needs orphanages, see *Human Rights Watch*, "Abandoned to the State: Cruelty and Neglect in Russian Orphanages," December 1998, http://www.hrw.org/legacy/reports/reports98/russia2/.

15. Leah Spring, "Reality Check," *Finding Spring*, blog, December 6, 2010, http://myianna.blogspot.com/2010/12/reality-check.html.

16. Julia Nalle, "Kori's Story," *Micah 6:8*, blog, January 31, 2012, http://covenantbuilders.blogspot.com/2012/01/koris-story.html.

17. Lennard Davis, *Enforcing Normalcy: Disability, Deafness and the Body* (New York: Verso, 1995), 24.

18. Ibid., 26, quoting Theodore Porter's 1986 text *The Rise of Statistical Thinking, 1820-1900* (Princeton, NJ: Princeton University Press, 1986), 18.

19. Arguably, Darwin himself took it out of the natural sciences with his *The Descent of Man*. See following note.

20. Charles Darwin, *The Descent of Man, and Selection in Relation to Sex* (Princeton, NJ: Princeton University Press, 1981) 1.3, 92.

21. Lorie Conway and Elliott Gould, *Forgotten Ellis Island: The Extraordinary Story of America's Immigrant Hospital*, DVD, (Alexandria, VA: PBS Home Video, 2009).

22. Margaret Sanger, *The Pivot of Civilization* (Elmsford, NY: Maxwell Reprint Co., 1969), 25.

23. For a thorough and well-documented Christian critique of Sanger, see Benjamin Wiker's *Moral Darwinism: How We Became Hedonists* (Downers Grove, IL: Intervarsity Press Academic, 2002), 264-72.

24. Paul A. Lombardo, *A Century of Eugenics in America: From the Indiana Experiment to the Human Genome Era* (Bloomington, IN: Indiana University Press, 2011), 96.

25. There is an excellent series of investigative reports on the era, including interviews with those sterilized, doctors, members of the state board, and deep historical background into eugenics as embraced by the state. *The Winston Salem Journal*, "Against Their Will: North Carolina's Sterilization Program," http://www.journalnow.com/specialreports/againsttheirwill/ (accessed November 17, 2013).

26. Wolf Wolfensberger, *The Principle of Normalization in Human Services* (Toronto: National Institute on Mental Retardation, 1972).

27. See especially *Suffering Presence*, 211-17. Hauerwas does clarify in later works that he is all in favor of more humane and typical living environments, and is a good friend to L'Arche movement for that reason, but maintains that to use the word normal and normalization inevitably has a shadow side.

28. Reynolds, *Vulnerable Communion*, 46. In my opinion, the entire chapter in Reynolds on this topic should be required reading for Christian theologians.

29. Ibid.

30. Ibid., 48.

31. There is a persistent urban legend about a mid-20th century Russian experiment that involved institutionalized infants being raised without any human touch or interaction, and half of the group dying as a result. The 1998 Human Rights Watch report "Abandoned to the State: Cruelty and Neglect in Russian Orphanages" indicates the fabled "experiment" is uncomfortably close to the ongoing truth for

special needs children in institutions: children (and later adults, should they live that long), left in cribs all 24 hours of the day, only fed and changed. However, the story of the experiment likely came from Harry Harlow's experiments in social isolation of rhesus monkeys, in which isolation left the young monkeys severely disturbed. The 1960s studies, which would be considered unethical science today, are used to help understand the experience and behavior of children who have been abused or have suffered neglect. H.F. Harlow, R.O. Dodsworth, and M.K. Harlow, "Total Social Isolation in Monkeys," *U.S. National Library of Medicine, National Institutes of Health Database* http://www.ncbi.nlm.nih.gov/pmc/articles/PMC285801/pdf/pnas00159-0105.pdf (accessed Sept 25, 2013).

32. Google plus, Facebook, and Twitter language for "belonging," respectively.

33. The Greek term used is *ho anthropos*, which is the human rather than the man (*aner*). "Ecce homo" comes from the Latin translation.

34. It is exactly this tension that appealed to Nancy Eiesland in writing *The Disabled God: Toward a Liberatory Theology of Disability*. In page 89 of that text, she mentions dreaming of the resurrected Christ in a sip-puff wheelchair and finding the "survivor" image that it expresses meaningful. (A sip-puff is a shorthand term for a type of wheelchair that is operated by a person who is paraplegic puffing or sipping on a blowhole.) While I basically agree with many who question this image as one that illumines the resurrected Christ—there is no question it is arresting. Especially if it is considered as a teaching moment on the nature of the incarnate God: was the binding limitation of the Incarnation different from the daily binding of paraplegia, and if so, how? Did Christ's interaction with the world as fully divine and fully human, omnipresent yet self-limiting, feel like being constrained to the sip-puff chair? If not, why not? A paraplegic likely would see the sip-puff chair as a kind of liberation from an isolated life, an instrument that enabled full communion. Could Jesus have seen the cross as his instrument, liberating for communion in a similar way? The imaginative symbol underlines, in any case, the exacting reality of limitation.

35. Carlo Carretto, *The God Who Comes* (Maryknoll, NY: Orbis Books, 1974), 113.

36. Ibid., 115-16. Also, as my colleague Jeff Tranzillo noted, Carretto's insight could be extended fruitfully to the "confinement" of the Eucharistic Jesus in the tabernacle, waiting for union with us.

37. The Leviticus passage is from the New English Translation. In his first post-synodal apostolic exhortation, Pope Benedict offers a beautiful reflection on how the self-giving of the Eucharist, understood as Carretto describes, draws humanity into Jesus's gift of self to the Father, altering the very dynamic of the world. "The remembrance of his perfect gift consists not in the mere repetition of the Last Supper, but in the Eucharist itself, that is, in the radical newness of Christian worship. In this way, Jesus left us the task of entering into his 'hour.' The Eucharist draws us into Jesus' act of self-oblation. More than just statically receiving the incarnate *Logos*, we enter into the very dynamic of his self-giving. (21) Jesus 'draws us into himself.' (22) The substantial conversion of bread and wine into his body and blood introduces within creation the principle of a radical change, a sort of 'nuclear fission,' to use an image familiar to us today, which penetrates to the heart of all being, a change meant to set off a process which transforms reality, a process leading ultimately to the transfiguration of the entire world, to the point where God will be all in all (cf. 1 Cor 15:28)." *Sacramentum Caritatis*, #11.

38. John Paul II called for theologians to renew their focus on *kenosis* in *Fides Et*

Ratio #93: "From this vantage point, the prime commitment of theology is seen to be the understanding of God's *kenosis*, a grand and mysterious truth for the human mind, which finds it inconceivable that suffering and death can express a love which gives itself and seeks nothing in return." More on this in the last section of this chapter.

39. Hauerwas and Vanier, *Living Gently in a Violent World: The Prophetic Witness of Weakness*, 53.

40. Jn 9:2-3.

41. Jn 9:35-39.

42. See Jesus's question about the sinfulness of those who died at the tower at Siloam in Lk 13:4, or Job's entire counter-argument against his "friends" in the Book of Job.

43. For the best example of this, see Mk 2:1-11, the healing of the paralytic whose sins are forgiven first and the physical healing only after a vigorous debate on blasphemy breaks out.

44. Acts 3:10 ff.

45. Jas 5:14.

46. Quoted from Jean Vanier's "What Have People With Learning Disabilities Taught Me?" in *The Paradox of Disability*, ed. Hans Reinders, 22.

47. John Paul II, *Crossing the Threshold of Hope* (London: J. Cape, 1994), 35-6.

48. In order, these are the primary categories of Reinders and Hauerwas (friendship), Moltmann (fellowship), Reynolds (communion), and Block and Vanier (ecclesial community). Hauerwas is also a prominent advocate for a Church-based framework. I am particularly fond of Reynolds's term "vulnerable communion."

49. Henri Nouwen, *The Road to Daybreak: A Spiritual Journey* (New York: Doubleday,1988). Also *Adam: God's Beloved* (Maryknoll, NY: Orbis Books, 1997).

50. Among numerous examples, see Hauerwas's "Seeing Peace: L'Arche as a Peace Movement," in *The Paradox of Disability*, 113-126.

51. A good summary of this notion is provided by John Swinton in the preface of *Living Gently in a Violent World*, 17.

52. *Living Gently in a Violent World*, 34.

53. *The Paradox of Disability*, 60.

54. Karl Barth is the most prominent, in emphasizing that our creation to the image should be understood as an *analogia relationis*, based on a reflection of the Trinitarian relationship. Barth may have received this understanding in part from Dietrich Bonhoeffer, who directly says that the divine image is "not a substantial or logical similarity but only a similarity in intra-divine relationship." In 1985, Orthodox theologian John Zizioulas recovered the Cappadocian fathers' understanding of being as understood only through relationship. But the audiences provide the first modern magisterial teaching in the Catholic Church of a relational imago. A good summary may be found in Peter Oh's, *Karl Barth's Trinitarian Theology: A Study in Karl Barth's Analogical Use of the Trinitarian Relation* (New York: Continuum, 2007) in chapter 3, esp. 44-45. I also try to make a similar argument in my dissertation, *The Redeemed Image of God: Embodied Relations to the Unknown Divine* (Lanham, NY: University Press of America, 2002).

55. *Man and Woman*, 9.3.

56. See Augustine's *De Trinitate* XII. Augustine is not without many detractors in his particular argument, but everyone admits it is a better argument than that of many of his contemporaries, who simply said that women obviously were not created

in the Image.
57. Jean Vanier, *Becoming Human* (New York: Paulist Press, 1998), 67. Vanier has no rosy picture of the reality of family in our current world. "Among humankind, the family represents the basic social unit. However, everywhere we look, this basic place of belonging is breaking down" (50). L'Arche, as we will see, tries to create a family-like atmosphere in its small communities, and lives out a covenantal relationship with the residents. But it is true that some of the mentally disabled members of the community are there because their family units broke down or rejected them. Vanier's point is more basic: the family is the original social unit throughout the world.
58. Reynolds, 123.
59. Reynolds, 124-6.
60. Reynolds, 124.
61. *Becoming Human*, 39-41.
62. *Becoming Human*, 73.
63. *Becoming Human*, 74-9.
64. *Man and Woman*, 28:2.
65. Reading John 9 in this light is helpful. The tangible fear in that passage found after the healing of the blind man is suffused through a mad scramble of others "controlling the situation" and what it meant.
66. Swinton, Introduction of *Living Gently in a Violent World*, 64.
67. Reynolds, 116.
68. Reynolds, 50.
69. *Becoming Human*, 98.
70. The sentence is a twist from a statement on shame swallowed up in covenantal love, in *Love and Responsibility*, 181.
71. Swinton, Introduction to *Living Gently in a Violent World*, 79.
72. *Becoming Human*, 91.
73. *Becoming Human*, 21-2.
74. *Becoming Human*, 28. Much of this extended story, which is hard to excerpt and deserves to be read in its entirety, is how people learned to listen to Claudia's "madness" and respond to it in ways that were concrete, loving, and practical, but also assumed that all of us are broken and needing to be led to the unconditional love of God. In a sense, we are all Claudia.
75. *Becoming Human*, 30. Vanier and L'Arche create their small communities as communities of fidelity, where the abled members of the community embrace a "covenantal relationship" with the disabled members. "As we live and work and play together, we build a new form of family."
76. Reynolds, 105.
77. Kevin S. Reimer, "Moral Transformation in L'Arche Communities for People with Developmental Disabilities" in *The Paradox of Disability*, 61-2.
78. Ibid.
79. From the *Spiritual Exercises*, #335. This translation is from Michael Ivens, SJ, *The Spiritual Exercises of Saint Ignatius of Loyola* (Surrey: Gracewing, 2004). "The good spirit" comes from Ignatius's understanding of spiritual warfare present in the world.
80. This term comes from Arthur McGill, see below. Within theologies of disability, there are two contemporary theologians working in the theology of disability who address the relationship of God to those persons disabled (and vice versa) es-

pecially forthrightly: Hans Reinders (*Receiving the Gift of Friendship*) and Amos Yong (*Theology and Down Syndrome* and *The Bible, Disability, and the Church*). Reinders suggests that a theology more widely influenced by John Zizioulas's dynamic Trinitarianism in his ground-breaking *Being as Communion* would be a fruitful way to engage and embrace the insights raised by the relationships between the disabled and those more abled. [See John Zizioulas, *Being As Communion: Studies in Personhood and the Church* (Crestwood, NY: St. Vladimir's Seminary Press, 1985).] I am in sympathy with Reinders on this point. But in the interest of connecting these concerns with an extension of the themes specific to the Theology of the Body, I'd like to pay attention here to the phenomenology of Sonship as an ecstatic identity, and connect it to John of the Cross's dynamic Trinitarianism.

81. See notes 88 and 90.

82. McGill was a professor of theology at Princeton and then Harvard for many years, his legacy felt more in his influence on students (of which Hauerwas was one) than his relatively slim, although powerful, publication list. He was, by all accounts, a disarming Christian provocateur. One book, *Death and Life: An American Theology*, deserves a wider readership than it has received. It is from there that I introduce the notion of Jesus Christ's "ecstatic identity." Arthur Chute McGill, with Charles A. Wilson, and Per M. Anderson, eds., *Death and Life: An American Theology* (Eugene, OR: Wipf and Stock Publishers, 2003).

83. This focus on phenomenology in no way disagrees with the ontological affirmation of the consubstantiality of the Father and the Son. Indeed, I would hold that McGill's analysis complements that core doctrine. It is a difference between the shared being of the persons of the Trinitarian God and the lived experience of the economic and immanent Trinity. It is a matter of approach, and as John Paul II says, phenomenology must complement revelation to be in service to theology. This exploration is a case in point: holding the consubstantiality as a central assumption but examining how the gift of identity illumines this revealed teaching. See *Fides et Ratio*, #83.

84. This is frankly all over the Gospel of John, but a good place to start would be a close reading of Jn 17 (sometimes called "The priestly prayer of Christ").

85. This is similar to the classic "moral influence" theory of atonement—that the Crucifixion of Christ, the death of our best friend for us, moves the person to conversion and acceptance of Christ as Son of God. While I would hold moral influence theory is untenable as a "stand-alone" atonement theory, it is an absolutely necessary element in the world of the sign and revelation. David Power speaks movingly of this theological *vox populi* doctrine, seen in the para-liturgical devotions to the death of Christ in multiple cultures, in his excellent *Love Without Calculation: A Reflection on Divine Kenosis* (New York: Crossroad, 2005), chap. 1.

86. Ezekiel 47:1-12.

87. Of course, the Holy Spirit proceeds as the Person-Gift through whom God exists in the mode of gift. See John Paul II's *Dominum et Vivicantem*, #10.

88. The theological key here is to use the language of identity as a way of living in the world of sign that makes up the Theology of the Body literature. Any sign we express, and the sign Jesus Christ as Incarnate God expresses, comes from the dynamic giving and receiving that is the Trinitarian life of the Godhead, immanent and economic. But in the case of Jesus Christ, that is only what is seen and (perhaps) experienced. It is important to affirm simultaneously the revealed

metaphysical truth: Jesus holds fully the divine nature, and His relation of filiation in the Holy Trinity, like the relations of the Father and the Holy Spirit, is subsistent in that nature, and hence fully held.

89. McGill, 90.

90. See David Power's *Love Without Calculation*, especially the full paragraph on 175, quoted here in part: "Self-emptying and self-giving are key to divine gift and divine naming, as well as to the world's participation in the divine, to its deification....When we see this communion of the divine persons made known as gift and invitation in the economy of salvation, we behold the dance of perichoresis, a constant interaction between the Word and Spirit that draws humankind and creation into the communion of the divine life-force poured out as a communion of love, ever coming forth from its unique source, ever moving toward consummation in God....."

91. See Chap. 1, pg. 30.

92. To wit, Reynolds: "At the cross, Jesus *subjects himself* to disability, and his resurrected body continues to bear his scars as a sign of God's solidarity with humanity," (emphasis added) 207. Eiesland also uses the language extensively in *The Disabled God*, and Amos Yong (*Theology and Down Syndrome*) has some measured sympathy for the language. Yong is also a good source of theological critique against the "disabled God" image (175-6).

93. McGill, *Suffering: A Test of Theological Method* (Philadelphia: Westminster Press, 1982), 77-8.

94. Iain Matthew, *The Impact of God* (London: Hodder and Stoughton, 1995). Interestingly, there is a glowing foreword from none other than Jean Vanier.

95. This *nada* doctrine is illustrated in a well-known sketch by John of the Ascent of Mt. Carmel, which can be seen here in English translation: http://www.icspublications.org/images/Drawings1.html.

96. From *Fides et Ratio*, #93. The fuller citation within the encyclical helps place this call in context: "The chief purpose of theology is to *provide an understanding of Revelation and the content of faith*. The very heart of theological enquiry will thus be the contemplation of the mystery of the Triune God. The approach to this mystery begins with reflection upon the mystery of the Incarnation of the Son of God: his coming as man, his going to his Passion and Death, a mystery issuing into his glorious Resurrection and Ascension to the right hand of the Father, whence he would send the Spirit of truth to bring his Church to birth and give her growth. From this vantage-point, the prime commitment of theology is seen to be the understanding of God's *kenosis*, a grand and mysterious truth for the human mind, which finds it inconceivable that suffering and death can express a love which gives itself and seeks nothing in return. In this light, a careful analysis of texts emerges as a basic and urgent need: first the texts of Scripture, and then those which express the Church's living Tradition. On this score, some problems have emerged in recent times, problems which are only partially new; and a coherent solution to them will not be found without philosophy's contribution."

97. Quoted in papal household preacher Fr. Raniero Cantalamessa's 2011 homily for the second Sunday of Lent: "Father Cantalamessa's Second Lenten Homily: God Is Love," *Zenit*, April 1, 2011, http://www.zenit.org/article-32192?l=english.

98. The exception, and it is a rather significant one, is found in process theology. These theologians, influenced by Alfred North Whitehead, do address all of the traditional themes within providence. However, they do so by taking God's om-

nipotence off the table—a move that I would hold makes no sense within the inheritance of the tradition. Regardless of its insights, I would say that process theology offers a God who is not provident. The classic introduction to process theology may be found here: John B. Cobb and David Ray Griffin, *Process Theology: An Introductory Exposition* (Philadelphia: Westminster Press, 1976). Another emerging theological school is Open Theism, which works with the interaction of omniscience and omnipotence through new understandings of time and space. While this school (made of mostly less conservative Evangelicals and Calvinists, with a few exceptions) posits some very interesting ideas, it seems young to name as having definitive marks within its school. The modern texts grounding Open Theism discussion are Richard Rice's *The Openness of God: The Relationship of Divine Foreknowledge and Human Free Will* (Nashville, TN: Review and Herald Pub. Association, 1980), and Clark H. Pinnock, et al., *The Openness of God: A Biblical Challenge to the Traditional Understanding of God* (Downers Grove, IL: InterVarsity Press, 1994).

99. Emilie Townes, *A Troubling in my Soul: Womanist Perspectives on Evil and Suffering* (Maryknoll, NY: Orbis Books, 1993).

100. Cynthia Crysdale, *Embracing Travail* (New York: Continuum, 2001), 32.

101. Yong, 10-14.

102. There is a remarkable poem that articulates the Holy Spirit as a fiery gift and a call to yes in the Pentecost segment of Kate Bluett's "Triptych," in the online version of the journal *Dappled Things*, Easter 2008, http://archive.dappledthings.org/east08/poem11.php.

103. *Living Gently*, 92.

104. Yong, 162.

105. Ibid., 244ff.

106. A sample narrative, relayed by Sara Esther Crispe: "As I walked I was reminded of a beautiful story. It is a story of how a *tzaddik*, a holy man, was sitting with his disciples when a child with down syndrome passed by. As the child passed, the tzaddik stood up and greeted him with 'Baruch Habbah.'" His students couldn't understand why, as this was a greeting generally reserved for other tzaddikim. One student finally had the courage to ask the tzaddik why he would address a child with such an honored greeting. The tzaddik explained that we are all brought into this world because we have a mission to complete. Many of us need to come back into this world many times until we fulfill our duties through our Torah study and mitzvot. However, the souls of tzaddikim, of the purely righteous, come into this world with no benefit to themselves, only for the sake of others. They have already completed their mission in this world. … The only reason for him to be here is to help others achieve their purpose. 'So this is why I stood up for the boy,' the tzaddik explained. 'He was a complete tzaddik who is only in this world to help those around him.'" Sara Esther Crispe, "The End of the World," Chabad, http://m.chabad.org/m/article_cdo/aid/691459, (accessed September 27, 2013). What is most appealing about this notion of the tzaddik is that his mission is to help others achieve their purpose, that their mission is simply "to be." There are also Jews who criticize the too-easy connection of children with DS with tzaddikim, saying it objectifies them and places them "out of social engagement" in a harmful way that does not encourage growth. See William Kolbrener, "Please Don't Call My Son A Tzadik," *Open Minded Torah*, blog, June 22, 2011, http://openmindedtorah.com/uncategorized/please-dont-call-my-son-a-tzadik/.

107. "My little tzaddik," *Frum Doula*, blog, July 26, 2010, http://frumdoula.blogspot.com/2010/07/my-little-tzaddik.html.
108. The exception is when the person is diagnosed with Mosaic Down Syndrome, in which the trisomy disorder—an extra chromosome on the 21st chromosome—incompletely adheres to the DNA, so people with Mosaic DS may have some characteristics of DS but not others. Also, it is worth noting that in the grand scheme of biology on earth, the intellectual capabilities of those people with DS are close to identical with "cognitively typical" human beings.
109. Although not talking specifically about DS or genetic impairment, I think Hauerwas is entirely right when he says, "You cannot cure the mentally handicapped without eliminating the patient." *Living Gently*, 52.
110. 1 Cor 15:35-44.
111. Yong, *Theology and Down Syndrome*, 279.
112. Ibid., 277. The next chapter assumes Gregory of Nyssa's theology of epektasis, which interprets eternal life as an infinite growing in relationship with God, and this will have bearing on how we can understand the ongoing maturity of people with DS (indeed all people) in the Kingdom of God. Yong develops this idea with impressive potential in *Theology and Down Syndrome*, 271-82.
113. "Little Sisters of the Lamb," *Laodicea*, Jan 11 2010, http://exlaodicea.wordpress.com/2010/01/11/little-sisters-disciples-of-the-lamb/. The order was established in 1985.
114. Yong, *Theology and Down Syndrome*, 156-7.
115. Yong, *Theology and Down Syndrome*, 191.
116. My discussion is informed primarily by Kathryn Greene-McCreight's *Darkness Is My Only Companion: A Christian Response to Mental Illness* (Grand Rapids, MI: Brazos Press, 2006). Greene-McCreight, an Episcopal minister who lives with bipolar disorder, has written a remarkable book that details (courageously, given the stigma of mental illness) much of her personal history with severe depression and mania, a theological response to some of the issues raised by depression, and a pastoral guide for Christians working with depressed individuals. Other resources are portions of Marva Dawn's *Being Well When You Are Ill*, and Vanier's *Seeing Beyond Depression*. Rosemary Radford and David Ruether have also written a searing book on the experience of being the parents of a son who lives with schizophrenia, asking the scathing question "what would we as a society do if we really cared?" There are a few articles on mental illness written from a theological point of view as well. But the literature is stunningly slim. Marva J. Dawn, *Being Well When We're Ill: Wholeness and Hope in Spite of Infirmity* (Minneapolis, MN: Augsburg Books, 2008); Jean Vanier, *Seeing Beyond Depression* (New York: Paulist Press, 2001); and Rosemary Radford Ruether and David Ruether, *Many Forms of Madness: A Family's Struggle with Mental Illness and the Mental Health System* (Minneapolis: Fortress Press, 2010).
117. Greene-McCreight, 96.
118. Ibid, 79. She pulls the castle imagery from Ps 71:3.
119. Ibid., 116.
120. Sylvia Plath, *The Bell Jar* (New York: Harper & Row, 1971).
121. Greene-McCreight, 97. Greene-McCreight offers a nuanced understanding of t relationship between sin and health, leaving the door open that sinful actions can have natural effects that can damage health, physical or mental. However, most mental illness is not a result of anyone's sin, and its reality as a physical

disease among diseases, an inheritance of the Fall, should be the default position of Christians.

122. Ibid., 111.

123. Ibid., 158-9.

124. To be fair, she also mentioned some who helpfully accepted faith as part of her life, even though they were not religious themselves.

125. Ibid., 160.

126. Ibid., 89.

127. Stephen Post, "Preserving Love in the Face of Hyper-Cognitive Values," in *The Paradox of Disability*, 34. Incidentally, note the disability language—where the caregiver becomes a "prosthesis."

128. *Paradox of Disability*, 47-8 and Greene-McCreight, chap. 10.

129. Deborah Creamer, "Am I Disabled [Enough]? Disability, Diversity, and Identity Hermeneutics" (paper presented at the AAR/SBL National Meeting, San Antonio, TX, November 2004).

130. Although Nouwen approaches this book primarily as a testament to Adam's witness, Nouwen also admits that the safety and gentleness of L'Arche opened up for him his own woundedness and impairment, which came in the form of a significant depression.

131. Fr. David W. Smith, of the archdiocese of St. Paul and Minneapolis and former Director of the Justice and Peace Studies program at the University of St. Thomas.

132. The next week, I saw the ear specialist for a scheduled appointment, which included a hearing check. My hearing was much better in my left ear: there remained some very mild hearing loss (10-15 decibel range), as compared to the previous severe hearing loss (60-100 decibels across different tones). My right ear was completely fine. My vertigo attacks, much milder, now occur about one to two times a year, as opposed to severe attacks one to two times a week. For the record, hearing loss occurs because the inner ear cells die, so I cannot explain the recovery through any medical reason.

133. I would like to be clear: I raise this in part to be honest about my perspective in coming to these questions in the chapter with an unusual experience: I had been disabled, and expected to be my entire life, but was healed. I found the experience harrowing, but still consider the spiritual healing more extraordinary than the physical (although they both were astounding to me). I know discussing physical healing is a red flag for many—as Reynolds shared, a friend of his warned him to be careful discussing theology and disability: "You are venturing into a troubling area." And there was a part of me that was disoriented when this happened: not that I wasn't happy to hear again, without constant vertigo. I was beyond happy and grateful. But I was also disturbed that I received this kind of healing and others apparently do not, and working through that required more prayer.

134. Waldstein, 83. Waldstein is summarizing Wojtyla's dissertation on faith and John of the Cross, but this is an insight that John Paul II carries into his audiences.

135. *Ecclesia in Africa*, #63.

136. Reinders's book *Receiving the Gift of Friendship* is the most obvious example, and he cites the current trajectory as well. Additionally, there is a philosophical tradition to be honored there, and in current times, the Quakers (or Society of Friends) witness to a beautiful tradition of honoring church members with the title "friend."

137. Edith Stein, *The Collected Works of Edith Stein, Vol II, Saint Teresa Benedicta of*

the Cross, Discalced Carmelite, trans. Freda Mary Oben (Washington, DC: ICS Publications, 1987), chap. 2 (especially 57-9).

138. However, having the perfect experience is by no means necessary to embracing the language. John Paul II and his older brother were raised mostly by his father; his mother died when he was quite young. As a young adult, his older brother died as well. Part of the point of this reflection on the church as God's family is that we do not need the experience to recognize the call: it is embedded in our bodies, part of the extended spousal meaning of the body.

139. McGill, *Death and Life*, 90.

140. Consider in Gn 4, the killing of Abel by his brother Cain (a Scripture with which John Paul II opens one of his most important encyclicals, *Evangelium Vitae*): most people cite the passage as the first murder, the quick bitter fruit of the Fall in chapter 3. It is certainly murder, but in the sign of the family, it is also the destruction of the first family. We are descendants of a broken family, of grieving ancestors.

141. The Christian Brothers do not have a third order, but speak of the partnering with laypeople in their educational endeavors as a joining "by association."

142. *Sollicitudo rei socialis*, #40. Emphasis added.

CHAPTER 4
The Gift of the Dying Body

The Vocation To Elderhood

 KEY CONCEPTS

This final chapter focuses on the experience of dying and asks the question the Theology of the Body insights would naturally pose: how is the dying body given in love? There are similarities to the second chapter's focus on the experience of birthing, with a focus on being overwhelmed, availability to God, self-abjection, hospitality, and tenderness. There are also shared insights with the previous chapter on impairment, because death is the most visual and experienced limitation that human beings can perceive. The presentation of death in the third chapter of Genesis is examined as a way that God shapes human limitation to draw humanity to himself, even after the Fall. In conversation with the *ars moriendi* tradition and the hospice movement, we take a contemplative look at how we die and how it may point us to a God eager to nourish us beyond this limit and into a union with His life. This sign reveals in all of us a call to the vocation to elderhood— that is, we all exist in order to teach others how to die, or specifically, how to give one's dying ensouled body in love.

Then the Lord God said, "See, the man has become like one of us, knowing good and evil; and now, he might reach out his hand and take also from the tree of life, and eat, and live forever"— therefore the Lord God sent him forth from the garden of Eden, to till the ground from which he was taken. He drove out the man; and at the east of the garden of Eden he placed the cherubim, and a sword flaming and turning to guard the way to the tree of life.
—Genesis 3:22-24

When this perishable body puts on imperishability, and this mortal body puts on immortality, then the saying that is written will be fulfilled: "Death has been swallowed up in victory." "Where, O death, is your victory? Where, O death, is your sting?" The sting of death is sin, and the power of sin is the law. But thanks be to God, who gives us the victory through our Lord Jesus Christ. —1 Corinthians 15:54-57

Since, therefore, the children share flesh and blood, he himself likewise shared the same things, so that through death he might destroy the one who has the power of death, that is, the devil, and free those who all their lives were held in slavery by the fear of death. —Hebrews 2:14-15

"And if I go and prepare a place for you, I will come again and will take you to myself, so that where I am, there you may be also. And you know the way to the place where I am going." —John 14:3-4

I'm not afraid of death, but the dying part is still a little troublesome. —Jim, ALS patient, in Rob Moll's *The Art of Dying*

I think I was meant to come here, so that at last, I could experience joy. —Lillian Preston, hospice patient, in Sandol Stoddard's *The Hospice Movement*

When someone is critically ill, I don't tell him to prepare for death, for such an approach would hardly allay his fears. Rather, I insist that we are all in God's Hands, that God is the best Father we could possibly wish for; ever watching over us, ever knowing what is best for us. I urge the patient to abandon himself to Him, just as a child does with his father, and to be tranquil. This allays the patient's fear of death. He is delighted by the thought that his fate is in God's hands and he peacefully waits for God to do as He wills in His infinite goodness. —attributed to St. John Bosco

As I mentioned earlier, my father-in-law died a very long and disabling death, suffering mini-strokes that affected his balance, strength, and memory. After years of peaks and valleys, he moved into his last days at home, with the help of hospice and his family. My husband broke away from our family travels to fly home and be with his parents and siblings for the last five days. Then began long days of prayer, waiting, brief talking, observation, prayer, sacramental anointing, more prayer, more waiting, steps away to take a brief walk, and more prayer. Finally, his father died, and hours later, I asked my husband how he was. He smiled wanly and shook his head in wonder, saying: "That was the most intense retreat I have been on in my entire life."

In a less intense manner for most of us, there was a kind of long, observed dying of John Paul II as well. John Paul was diagnosed with Parkinson's disease years before his death in 2005. Over the years, many commented on how he seemed to be dying in a very emphatically public fashion: traveling until near the end, meeting people, giving audiences, allowing the world to see him grow increasingly frail and shaky, a rather active pope until close to the very end. There were people who questioned that choice, commenting that he should step aside and allow a healthier man to serve in such a crucial leadership role. But there seemed to be something very deliberate in this prayerful living out of his final days, a bodily *ars moriendi* for the world. When he died in his apartment, many thousands were holding candles and praying in a multi-day vigil in Saint Peter's Square—and I wouldn't be surprised if many of them named it one of the more intense retreats of their lives.

This chapter will specifically examine dying as a bodily and spiritual sign that points to God. Currently, there is a lot of public discussion of dying from a medical ethics perspective. But there is a great deal *less* discussion of the experience of dying, and seeing one we love die. How does dying teach us? What does it teach us? If the limitedness of the human body is a natural sign, then the approach of that particular physical limitation called death should *signify* something: both in the individual's experience of dying, and in others' experience of being with the dying person.

Sustained examination of the experience of death is difficult in many ways. First, dying can be very hard. Some people have very hard deaths (just as some people have very hard lives), and I do not want to say that these people undergo unusually challenging suffering just to teach others something. There is a way in which that imposes a meaning that cloaks the integrity of their experience, and does not acknowledge the tragedy of the suffering: in fact, it can sanitize it beyond recognition. It is also difficult to reflect on the experience of a young person's death. There is a sense of injustice to it, of greater loss and sadness because of his or her potential, and a profound echo in the room where parents are meant to watch children grow, not wither. Examining a sudden and unexpected death, and its effects on family and friends, can be excruciating. But while the *harshness* of death—that is, when dying is sudden, out of season, or with incredible pain—is not a sign from God, I will argue that the *process* of dying in itself can yield its own wisdom. In that way, even the youngest who die can serve as our elders, the ones who bear the wisdom of God to us. Like the ensouled body itself, dying is never meaningless.

Dying is also not solitary. Even when people do not have the company of other human beings, they are not alone, as we will discuss. But it has long been a work of mercy to be with the sick and dying, to provide comfort, care, and friendship. The process of dying yields a kind of spiritual housecleaning. It is work that is rarely done alone. When we talk (if we talk) about a "good death," we talk about a death where the person is ready to meet God. And whether a person is ready to meet God depends much on how the person lives. This last leg on this side of the veil is shaped, I would say, to stretch and test the strength of our spiritual family ties. When we "farm out" being with the sick and dying to "professionals," we all lose an important insight into being the fullness of the image of God.

Death as sign is veiled in ambiguity. But as sign, it was meant to be clearer than it is currently perceived in our fallen vision. Jesus grieved death, did not look forward to it, and found it painful. Yet Good Friday is, in some way, truly good: the embrace of the cross is a witness of love and trust in the most difficult of circumstances, an act of love that redeemed humanity. Death can be the door to unfettered life in God.

Living In Reality? How We See Dying

What Dying Used To Be

This text is not meant to be a medical text, and cannot be. Although I want to pay attention to the body in the dying process, most of what follows is a viewing of death through the ensouled body within its prism of relationships: person to God, person to medical staff, person to family and friends. Dying is not something we do alone, and this focus is not to take the eye off the body, but to recognize dying's impact in the structure of relationships. Not breathing looks like not breathing, across cultures and times. But how we interpret that dying process within relationships is very different from what it used to be.

The majority of Americans want to die at home, and one assumes that means more than a familiar bed; it means in the known presence of family and friends and familiar patterns of life. Although this was typical for generations past, it is anything but typical today. A British study states that 54 percent die in acute care hospitals, 13 percent in nursing homes, and the rest at home (sometimes with the help of home-based hospice).[1] Why is this? Dying at home seems like a fairly simple wish to grant—at least in many cases.

Phillipe Ariès, a historian who has written extensively on dying across Western culture, argues that we have lost the historically typical experience of death, what he calls a "tame death." This "tame death" is not meant to be a romantic sense of slipping quietly and painlessly into the deepest sleep, but is defined as "a death that was tolerable and familiar, affirmative of bonds of community and social solidarity, expected with certainty and accepted without crippling fear."[2] He contrasts this tame death, "the oldest death there is,"[3] with the current "wild death" of technological medicine, marked by "undue fear and uncertainty, by the presence of medical powers not quite within our mastery, [and] by a course of decline that may leave us isolated and degraded." Others who had read Ariès admit that the first reaction to his research is that Ariès must be overstating things: surely the process of dying has become somewhat more comfortable, and with the alleviation of pain, there is less fear. But they also admit that Ariès makes a strong case:

by all evidence, people behaved differently, more calmly, around dying then as opposed to dying now. Our experience of the process of dying is different, and in many ways, it is worse than what our ancestors lived through.

One of the reasons for the change is a byproduct of improved health care: people in the modern Western world die of different diseases. Christopher Vogt points out that in the 17th century, the average life expectancy was 35 (if this seems low, remember the average was pulled down due to the significant childhood mortality rate). In large part, this was because the majority of people died of infectious diseases. Death was relatively sudden and usually "unexpected." (Although living with the possibility of death throughout life made it expected in a more concrete sense than today.) The average length of time from onset of infectious illness to death was eight weeks. Of course, people died at home: there were no other options. Today, with the discovery of antibiotics and the success of childhood vaccinations, the life expectancy in the Western world is around age 72. More significantly, two-thirds of all people die of three diseases: cancer, stroke, and heart disease. A person who dies of cancer has an average illness decline of three years. A stroke can be fast, but can also disable people for years. Heart disease can be treated for literally decades. People die more often in hospitals—as a result of a crisis event within a chronic illness—or nursing homes than in their family home.[4] We "live with dying" in a new and very different way. It is a good question as to whether our ancestors would recognize our way of dying.

Another change is the change in the goal of medical care. All care prior to the 18th century was palliative care, which treated symptoms and attempted to provide comfort. The concept that doctors had a duty to attempt to cure is a modern reality borne of the possibilities revealed by better science. Care had shifted to attacking diseases at their root. While this was and is a boon and created a healthier population overall, the focus on attacking disease obscured the classic role of physician as a caregiver. A very young Daniel Tobin, who would later write a book called *Peaceful Dying*, experienced what Ariès would call a tame death, the death of his grandfather: he died at home, as family life continued to be reasonably busy with his grandfather "taking it in" from his bed, and the doctor made house calls to see how he and the family were doing. This was very different from an elderly man who begged the young adult Tobin, as a new medical resident on call, to just let him die in the nursing home and stop running tests. When the man went into cardiac arrest, the other doctors ignored the patient's homemade "do not resuscitate" note, and performed energetic CPR on him for 10 minutes. When the CPR did not resuscitate him and he died, the medical team walked away, dejected, clearly assuming they had failed. Although different diseases often result in different ways of dying, Tobin's point was that medical doctors in a short time became trained to attack rather than to care.[5] Through little fault of their own, they do not know when to say "enough." The very fact that palliative care is considered to be a "new discipline" gives evidence of the fact that medical professionals are not trained and do not know how to handle dying as a process. As Callahan says, this is not to demonize doctors. In many ways this situation has arisen out of the *success* of their dogged work—the extension of life into the realm where people die of complications from chronic diseases. Modern medicine "finds it harder and harder to locate the line between living and dying and thus to know when to stop treatment."[6] Combine this with what Callahan calls the practice of "technological brinkmanship," using medical technology "up to the line" of death. This sounds reasonable, but in practice, people are being aggressively and often painfully treated for disease until days or hours before their deaths. There does seem to be a new driving ethic in contemporary science—that death is the enemy—which ancient physicians simply didn't hold. Then, death was not embraced as a good, but it was recognized as inevitable and natural.

Another reason we live in a new world of "wild deaths" is the reverence of control. To be clear, autonomy in balance with other goods is something to preserve when at all possible. As dying persons, we should be able to make decisions as we are able about preferences in the dying process: staying at home or being in a hospital; the use of drugs that may dull pain but also dull the mind, or rejecting drugs; the use of extraordinary means or not. Indeed, this is the impulse behind the move to living wills and advance directives, and is honored by the hospice movement (which I will discuss later). These choices are not problems. The problem is when individual autonomy is revered and replaces the actual meaning of life and death. Callahan argues that we are under an illusion that we (patients and doctors) can master our medical choices: we live by "a naive belief that the most watchful self, aided by the right laws and medical practices, can master the body by means of carefully controlled medical technology…. [and] we will understand ourselves well enough to know when to give up the struggle to stay alive."[7] For example: advance directives are a good thing, but if the doctor cannot determine that the actual process of dying has begun, most of the direction given by the patient cannot be honored. Without clarity, the medical default mode is attack the disease. Also, we assume medical science has advanced to the point where we know what will happen next in the dying process. That isn't always true. Even the simple question "how long do I have to live?" is hard for doctors to answer with precision. There is a great deal we do not know. Callahan notes that we can see how we revere autonomy in the very ethical situations now presenting themselves: for example, doctors resisting turning off respirators on irreversibly dying patients because they say they would "bear responsibility" for the person's death, or research organizations arguing that a loss of funding to find cures results in blood on the funder's hands. "Allowing" a person to die by stopping treatment is seen by some as a discrete way of intentionally killing the patient. With examples like these, is it not clear that many medical professionals cannot see the rule of nature over the rule of human control? That killing and allowing to die are two different things? That, indeed, we "allow" little: death will always occur, because it is the *destiny* of the ensouled body?

Many physicians believe that a patient is dying not because of what is happening to his body but because there are no further medical or technological strategies available to keep the patient alive. Death is not construed as an inevitable biological denouement but as a medical failure. "The patient," an important study found, "is not even defined as dying until the clinicians determine there are no further interventions they can make that will improve the patient's condition." Death has been moved out of nature into the realm of human responsibility.[8]

In short, Callahan argues that these various changes in medical science and care have created longer lives and worse health, longer illness, and slower deaths, longer aging and increased dementia.[9] Without offering judgment, it is clear that this is simply a different experience than earlier deaths by infectious disease used to be. Having moved from what the experience of dying used to be, let's move into what the contemporary experience of dying is.

A Phenomenology Of Dying

A phenomenology of dying is somewhat difficult to offer for two reasons: One is the shift in focus among medical professionals. (Descriptions of dying patients are simply rare in contemporary medical textbooks.)[10] The other is an important but somewhat odd question: when does dying begin?

American Resistance To Dying

Arthur McGill, in *Death and Life: An American Theology*, helpfully argues there is a difference between medical death, the observations of bodily functions shutting down, and continuous death, recognizing that in real ways, we die a bit every day. (His best line: "Every day the enamel wears a bit thinner.") His book begins with a cultural analysis of continuous death. American culture, he argues, has a perverse relationship with death: on the one hand, it is ignored and denied in every conceivable way. Aging is "corrected" through a multibillion-dollar industry; exercise becomes status within glass entombed workout spaces that scream "conspicuous consumption"; those unable to exercise are sequestered in hospitals and nursing homes; and the young are so venerated that high school and college are widely spoken of as "the best years of your life." In a culture that embraces the pursuit of happiness as living the physically full life, death has taken on the character of abnormal, an accident of nature: it always seems to "come out of nowhere." But this cultural work of death avoidance takes enormous effort, energy, and cost: as a process, exposed aging and dying equal failure in American culture.[11]

The result of not "seeing" death—resisting its natural reality—is that we understand Americans as "the bronze people." McGill uses the term in honor of the tanned and pristinely dressed vacationers he joined one day, walking about a gentrified Colonial Williamsburg. (Although the unavoidable inference to static, cast statues is relevant as well.) The term "the bronze people" refers to a twisted worldview that exists to mask the reality of dying, in which even the most tame death is perceived as a mutilation of the ideal of unending life:

> People commit themselves to the realm of nice appearances and do not fear death, do not long for death. No, just the opposite: they long for life, life, and more life…. The artistic and fabricating impulse has triumphed over that terrible awareness that Americans have of dreadful reality and over their intense sensitivity to suffering. So Americans let themselves be fully absorbed in the appearances of life, in the clean air, in the nice lawn, in the streets without beggars, in the homes without the aged. In truth reality is intolerable. Fabricating this illusory world is a high and necessary calling. *The bronze people should not be denigrated.* They exist to veil the horror, and their obligation, therefore, is to be as purely bronzed as possible.[12]

If this language sounds religious—cultic if you prefer—it is. McGill's cultural analysis is that Americans unwittingly worship Death as Lord: the One who motivates all activity, all ethics, all worship. Not mincing words, McGill says Christians should find this activity nothing less than demonic. But they rarely do.

There is no question that there is a fear of death that spans time and seems natural. But Ariès, Callahan, and McGill argue that the fear of death exhibited in modern times seems to go beyond the natural disturbance of seeing the integrity of a person's bodily processes break down. Callahan, who does not write as a theologian, notes the obvious: "A dying that is accepted without overpowering fear and a death that has lost its power to terrorize" is at the core of a tame, or peaceful, death.[13] And for many people in our society—although not all—death involves an overpowering fear and terror. There is no other way to explain the treatment of death, even a relatively gentle death at an old age, as the enemy of public health. We are of a culture and generation that read, and apparently took to heart, Dylan Thomas's classic battle cry of a poem: "Do not go gentle into that good night…Rage, rage against the dying of the light."

If we can remove the crust of faked appearances that McGill describes as the life of the bronze people and look more closely at the reality of dying—while moving from McGill's continuous death to something approaching medical, or clinical, death—we can move beyond the desperate mode of resistance to a more calm and sober look at dying, and what the reality of dying as sign is.

Stages Of Death And Dying, And The Death Awareness Movement

Most people are familiar with Elisabeth Kübler-Ross's groundbreaking 1969 text *On Death and Dying*.[14] Her offered stages of the dying process were born out of her work as a hospital psychiatrist working with the dying, and are meant to be descriptive of the typical emotional reactions to one's impending death: denial, anger, bargaining, depression, and acceptance. Although she does not say that these emotional markers are necessarily experienced in this order, they are certainly presented as the plausible progression. The paradigm has its critics, but the overwhelming influence of the book indicates a chord has been struck. In addition, the stages model has been applied to all profound changes: losing a loved one, chronic illness, divorce, etc. It is the Western world's conventional text for treating dying as a process with psychological realities.

Kübler-Ross's work—and many psychologists' praise and criticism of it—has evolved into a 30-year-old "death awareness" movement. The name of it comes from the sense that death was culturally denied (at least in the United States) well into the 1960s, a view enshrined in Ernest Becker's classic 1973 text *The Denial of Death*.[15] Awareness of how death proceeds was regarded as a knowledge that could and should be gained, and that knowledge is power, the key to a "death with dignity." As Lucy Bregman summarizes: "Early in this movement, the cry seemed to be for a secular, psychological, even scientific approach to topics such as death that had previously been the domain of clergy and religions. The implication was that a realistic and empirical approach to death required a secular, not sacred environment and method of study.

Psychology could provide such a framework.... Today, there is a movement away from such a resolutely secular stance, a move to include spirituality as a dimension of the human encounter with dying, death, and loss."[16] Bregman's study focuses on the hidden and overt spirituality of the death awareness movement, and notes that, despite statements made by many in the movement to embrace spirituality:

> What may seem surprising—and it has shocked me repeatedly—is how little that is distinctively Christian seems to be said.... 'Where is Christ in all this talk of death and dying?' is not a rhetorical question. "Death is natural and we should accept it,' is one basic motto repeated endlessly...and pastoral care experts have, almost without exception, joined in with this chorus. Is there nothing else to say about death? Yes, but it is being said most eloquently by Buddhists. By contrast to a lively and creative American Buddhist literature within the death awareness movement, there is little that is identifiably Christian.[17]

Bregman is not saying that there is nothing to learn from Buddhist insights into the dying process. What she is saying is that the movement simply doesn't take Christian insights into account, for reasons that are complicated but not deliberately determined. Spirituality has become watered down beyond any recognition. Within Christian theology, spiritual theology is a significantly rigorous subdiscipline. In the death awareness movement, it usually translates into knowing your values and a higher power. Bregman argues that the death awareness movement needs to move away from "the nice" and into "the mess"—that is, away from platitudes and into "the mess" of religious traditions and doctrines and ethical challenges and devotions. She says this should be the way it is done simply because this is where most dying people are: they deserve people to be with them in their mess, to honor that part of the life while they still live.

One assumes that the reason the death awareness movement has moved in this direction is that most hospitals—where the counselors meet the patients for the first time—serve people from various religious backgrounds, and the assumption is that churches (and synagogues, and mosques, and temples) will walk with the dying person in a specifically religious manner befitting the patient. Sometimes that happens. Other times, perhaps most times, it does not. In my anecdotal experience—confirmed only by conversation with others—ministers of all ways seem much more comfortable, more trained, and more willing to work in bereavement ministry, even crisis counseling, than in the longer walk of helping people to die well. Being with those who are dying is challenging, takes time, and often, there isn't a detailed script.

The Prophetic Role Of The Hospice Movement

In the midst of this movement joined another: the creation of hospice, a caring (or hospitality) for the dying. Cicely Saunders was a medical doctor in Britain who established the first stand-alone hospice in the late 1960s, recognizing that people needed a safe place to die, and medical professionals needed a space to focus on treatment of pain and symptoms exclusively. Hospitals were not serving that need well, and she was convinced that hospices could honor the whole person better.

Sheila Cassidy, director of a hospice in England, speaks to the prophetic or "spokesperson's" role well:

> Perhaps, like the prophets of old, we are spokespersons for the oppressed. We listen to the cries of the people and try to speak out for them. We relate that they want to be treated as normal responsible people. They want to have their illness explained to them in words that they can understand and to be consulted about its treatment. They want to retain their dignity as individuals and keep some control over their lives. They want to participate in their care and share in our decision-making. They want us to be honest with them, warm and humble. More than anything, they want us to combine our competence with compassion and, when our hands are empty, to stay our ground and share the frightening darkness with them. More than anything, they need our *love*.[18]

Perhaps a shorter way to put much of the above, also by Cassidy: "Everything depends on the quality of my listening."[19] Hospice is rather different in Britain than in the United States. (Great Britain tends to embrace stand-alone hospices, and the United States runs a home-based hospice model.) And increasingly, there are palliative-care programs in hospital settings. But whatever hospices' pros and cons, they do seem to have a role in modeling an intention to treat the whole patient and honor dying as a natural process. One of the flaws of the hospice movement is not that it is not used, but perhaps that it is not used soon enough: ideally, hospice should be involved from the beginning of the diagnosis of a fatal disease. The way compensation is structured in America, hospice is offered at the end of all attempts to cure (through chemo, radiation, surgeries, etc.): with Callahan's "technological brinkmanship" in play, that means hospice could be employed only in the last days, even hours, of life.

So, if we try to "strip down" dying, and get to the ensouled body and its base relationships, what do we see? What happens? Often, there is fear: at least at the beginning of a diagnosis if not the end. People are often afraid of pain, of handling their body's failure (dementia, breathing, eating) in any given way. People are often grieving the ideal life they cannot live any longer, the loss of that control. People usually carry with them a constellation of troubled relationships that want resolution. People want to be sure other dependents are taken care of. People are afraid of hurting their spouses, causing them grief and pain by their death, and are dealing with their own loss. These are all incredibly important realities to face and address. Many may not be "new" realities, but they are highlighted and condensed when the limit of one's life is known. Many hospice programs actively try to provide space for addressing these realities.

Overlapping with those concerns are spiritual realities, suddenly under glass. How is my relationship with God? When handed the cross of dying, how do I respond? People like Bregman question how good a job we are doing in addressing those concerns. In centuries past, there was a whole literature devoted to *ars moriendi*, or the art of dying well. Erasmus's *Preparing for Death* and St. Robert Bellarmine's *The Art of Dying Well* are prominent Catholic examples. There is nothing of the like written in the past few decades.[20] It is true that Bellarmine said that the key to dying well is to live well. It remains wise advice, especially in a time when the process of dying is often not sudden, but extended for years and complicated by multiple impairments: revisiting the *ars moriendi* tradition seems prudent. It is not as though the quest for the good death goes away. We are all amateurs when it comes to dying. And the conversation on how to die has not disappeared, but is held in the ethical and legal arenas of euthanasia and physician-assisted suicide. I would stand with the Christian tradition that deliberately causing one's own death is deeply wrong. But I am focusing on another issue here: if we do not sit with the dying, if we avoid our own received death, do we miss the dying process as a natural sign? Is dying, shorn of its sinful weeds (extreme pain, and the sundering of relationships), a sign that points toward union with God? And if it is, what does it mean that we tend to do all we can to avoid that sign?

Death As Evil vs. Death As Gift: The Medicinal Value Of Dying

Obviously, there is a great deal of felt ambiguity (at best) around the experience of dying. Before going any further, we need to examine theologically how Christianity understands the experience and process of dying: specifically, the tension between the gift of limit as a form of protection, and the tragic phenomenon of suffering.

On Protection

The end of God's sentencing after the Fall (Gn 3:21-24) gives us our first clue:

> And the Lord God made garments of skins for the man and for his wife, and clothed them. Then the Lord God said, "See, the man has become like one of us, knowing good and evil; and now, he might reach out his hand and take also from the tree of life, and eat, and live forever"— therefore the Lord God sent him forth from the garden of Eden, to till the ground from which he was taken. He drove out the man; and at the east of the garden of Eden he placed the cherubim, and a sword flaming and turning to guard the way to the tree of life.

First, this passage—which immediately follows the "judgment" we considered in chapter two—tells us what the human being's relationship to God is. Verse 21—where God tailored "garments of skins" to clothe Adam and Eve after their realization of nakedness—could be seen as a gracious act of protection, assuring continuing divine presence in the midst of the fallout of the Fall. (See Ez 16:8-14 for a similar sense of God clothing humanity out of love and protection).[21] It is a touching reminder of the providence of God, but even more important in interpreting what follows. God expels Adam and Eve from Eden to keep them from eating the fruit of the tree of life, and living forever. This divine act preventing humanity from eating of the tree of life, following the protective care of the clothing, should not be seen as vindictive. Preventing humanity from eating of the tree of life is a *protective gift*. The question is *how* this can be perceived as a gift.

The entire Jahwist passage can be read as an etiology of our current experience of death as loss and pain,[22] but it never defines exactly what death is. On one hand, death *as we know it* is a consequence of eating from the tree of knowledge of good and evil. ("The wages of sin is death," as Paul says.) On the other hand, there is no direct statement that human beings were created immortal, and Terence Fretheim (in the Methodist-sponsored *New Interpreter's Bible* series) interprets from that perspective:

> Death *per se* belongs as a natural part of God's created world....It would be a mistake to think of death in these chapters as defined solely in terms of the cessation of heartbeat; death becomes a pervasive reality within life before the exclusion. Yet, these intrusions of death into life would not have led to physical death if the human beings had discovered the tree of life.[23]

As a consequence, says Fretheim,

> Preventing humans from living forever might seem to be a defensive move by the deity, yet if death (in the comprehensive sense) has already become a significant part of life, then never-ending life offers no blessing. God continues to protect human beings.[24]

However, if there is no statement that human beings were created immortal, there is no statement in Genesis that they were created mortal, either. The lack of specificity reflects ancient Judaism's general lack of focus on immortality and afterlife—concepts simply not as pronounced in the ancient Jewish tradition as they are in the Christian tradition.[25]

The Catholic magisterial interpretation of this Scripture is nuanced. Bodily death is "in a sense natural" and "in faith" a consequence of sin.

> 'It is in regard to death that man's condition is most shrouded in doubt.' (*Gaudium et Spes* 18) In a sense bodily death is natural, but for faith it is in fact 'the wages of sin…. Even though man's nature is mortal God had destined him not to die. Death was therefore contrary to the plans of God the Creator and entered the world as a consequence of sin.'[26]

This nuance is appropriate: human beings were clearly created as limited, physically boundaried through our incarnation. In this sense, death as a boundary in time is natural. Since God did not destine humanity to die, that boundary could have been felt before the Fall differently than the way we experience the boundary of death today: before the Fall, it was perhaps felt as natural movement to greater life in God; after the Fall, death feels like an unnatural break. But the classic "sting" of death as a destructive invasion into natural life is indeed a consequence of sin, and we see original sin's scorched earth in the devastation of the human body.[27]

What is held in common in Fretheim's interpretation and the Catholic interpretation is that God is presented as *protecting* the human race by preventing access to immortality "as is"—while in a state of unredeemed original sin. A life of endless alienation from God, twisted relationships with others, and pointless toil and scarcity is not a life one desires eternally; even when one does desire it, God's wisdom sees that such a life is no blessing. In the expulsion from the garden, God shapes physical death to be not just a consequence of original sin (the result of illness and injury), but also a call to God. *A natural death*, without the overgrowth of the consequences of original sin such as pain and suffering, *is a sign*: limitation points to our needed relationship with God, and death as limitation is the door to union with God. It is the closure of the dying with Christ that was sacramentally completed in baptism and leads through the revolving flaming sword[28] to full union with God. Ignatius of Antioch's approach to death serves as a sign when he writes just before his martyrdom, but don't be distracted by the fact that his death was a martyr's death—there is a universal sense where his words serve for many Christians who see death as doorway to full union with God.

> It is better for me to die in behalf of Jesus Christ, than to reign over all the ends of the earth. "For what shall a man be profited, if he gain the whole world, but lose his own soul?" Him I seek, who died for us: Him I desire, who rose again for our sake. This is the gain which is laid up for me. Pardon me, brethren: do not hinder me from living, do not wish to keep me in a state of death; and while I desire to belong to God, do not ye give me over to the world. Suffer me to obtain pure light: when I have gone thither, I shall indeed be a man of God.[29]

So there is a theme that death is a protection from evil in these treatments. We don't need to be protected from our limits—in fact, we may be able to see physical limit as a grace. But we do desire to be protected from evil: a desire that God shares in his act of clothing Adam and Eve, a desire that is prayed in the last breath of every Our Father, a desire that is awakened when an encounter with evil causes us to undergo suffering. Our impulse is to recoil and fight. The sign of dying, of reaching that limitation, should encourage us to trust God to fight for us. In fact, He has already fought for us:

> Death has been swallowed up in victory. Where, O death, is your victory? Where, O death, is your sting? The sting of death is sin, and the power of sin is the law. But thanks be to God, who gives us the victory through our Lord Jesus Christ (1 Cor 15:54b-57).

If the suffering of death is referred to as our opponent in battle, a battle where God has won the victory for us, then the death of Jesus Christ ("...through death he might destroy the one who has the power of death, that is, the devil...." in Heb 2:14) is logically seen as a protective act. The suffering of death is not eliminated, but it is not the last word.

We can sense the natural sign of death as a gift: shaped by God as an end that draws people to his redemption. The medicinal value of dying lies in the *approach* toward that limitation, which usually involves suffering.

On Suffering[30]

There is a way the human person is "clothed in protection" from the beginning, and especially in the redemptive death of Christ. Suffering is not prevented. But its worst consequence—that is, the destruction of the very self—is removed for those who turn to God. Suffering will happen, and at minimum suffering is tragedy. It is not what God created human beings for in the beginning. But as Alasdair MacIntyre says, the morally interesting question is not whether we are asked to suffer—because we inevitably are—but how and for what.[31]

To suffer literally means to undergo. (Pain, technically, does not need to be a part of undergoing, but is assumed in our common usage.) To undergo gives us a sense of the "how." There is a loss of control in any form of it—whether the suffering comes in the form of pain, frustration, or despair.[32] And the process of dying can involve all three forms. The holistic character of suffering can spread the experience of pain to frustration with one's increasing limitedness, and despair in the seemingly random reality of it. Suffering, as an encompassing reality, can overwhelm to the point where a person cannot communicate. People involved in hospice care often argue that the best reason for good pain management is not simply dampening physical pain, but enabling the dying person to communicate to family and friends—to be able to spend quality time, forgive, to say goodbye. Most people want accompaniment, and many argue that physical pain relief serves the quality of that accompaniment. Suffering can be, and usually is, more than physical pain.

The difficulty and the power behind suffering is that suffering is almost inevitably perceived as personal. People can feel insulted by suffering—even when the suffering is caused by nothing personal (you walk along, a decaying tree falls on your leg, and the leg breaks), it *feels* like a personal attack. As Reimers notes, suffering "touches the core of one's personhood." Because suffering is holistic and feels personal, suffering demands a response—and it is a response of protecting oneself from evil. There are better and worse responses, and that is where we encounter dying (undergoing suffering unto death) as an art of dying well.

Here is the problem: if we look at the suffering body, in and of itself, we see little but the consequence of original sin. This is appropriate, since suffering is not a good in itself. We are compelled to relieve it, if at all possible; suffering, in a world spiritually bound by the solidarity of brotherhood and sisterhood, serves as a cry for help. But when we cannot relieve it, if we see suffering as a reality of life that is undergone—resisting its evil, and giving it to God—suffering can be understood as part of the path God has shaped for you. And while suffering is not good, God is Goodness Itself, and the path He shapes is meant for your good. Always, you treat the person who is suffering (whether that is yourself or your companion) as one seeking healing: not trying to be a super-Christian and suffer heroically because suffering is an achievement. We are called to address suffering by relieving it through physical healing or comfort, or if inevitable, recognizing it as a way to give one's body in dying to God. The passage of dying is created to bring you to God's door. The journey unto death is meant to be a journey of healing; after all, it is a journey home to God.

This giving of one's life to God by a willingness to let go of control, and suffer death with trust in God the Father's nourishment, is the heart of the passion of Christ itself. And this particular giving extends the Theology of the Body's insights into the reality of death and dying by asking one primary question: *how is the dying body given in love?*[33] If the body was created with a spousal meaning, then it is intended for love, and intended to be given in love, created for fruitfulness. Jesus Christ's body was given in love through the passion, and the fruitfulness was the redemption of the world. We are called to give our ensouled bodies in love to God. We may not know the fruitfulness borne in that, which is likely a matter of deep trust. But we let go. The Theology of the Body teaches us how to die, and for whom. It provides sight into what it actually means to join our suffering with the passion of Christ. "Life finds its center, its meaning, and its fulfillment when it is given up."[34] Or to move to John of the Cross (through Iain Matthew): John's image of a mountain climb in *The Ascent of Mount Carmel* "speaks of communion, where the goal is not to sink a solitary flagpole into the summit, but to 'make an altar of oneself' there for 'a sacrifice of love.'"[35]

So to say suffering is "medicinal" is not to say that undergoing suffering is like taking a magic pill, and suddenly you're all better. It is also not to say that suffering is easy, or valued entirely in and of itself. But suffering seems to be a part of most people's dying processes: even with the very best palliative care, death causes the often aching leave-taking of relationships. For people who love others, death can be painful. To say the relationships continue is an article of faith, but there is no denying the relationships are changed. Death will signal an end to earthly plans, hopes, and dreams. But a person can accept the unpreventable suffering that comes with the dying process and through that learn to cling to the One who can accompany us and heal us. For most who die, if they do not die immediately, that healing process begins before their physical death, and people can see it. This is one reason that Cassidy can say:

> I believe that an important part of the vocation of the carer is to support people during a period of trial so that they may indeed grow and transcend the bonds of their captivity. When I write about spiritual growth of this sort, I sometimes take a sideways look at myself and wonder if I am imagining it: talking pious language to comfort myself and others. I was fascinated therefore when a nurse with whom I work commented: "It's really such a privilege to do this work, to be with these people. The way they grow—it's fantastic." This sort of language in fact is quite common in the hospice world.[36]

If it is difficult for medical doctors to discern the line between life and death, it is difficult for Christians to discern the line between accepting the dying process as a natural sign pointing to union with God and the dying process as the bed of painful consequences of sin. It is for this reason—especially in a culture that deeply fears and hides death—we should speak clearly to the sign of death, and reclaim the *ars moriendi* not as a rule book, but *as a way of seeing the natural sign of dying*. If one sees rightly, one will be better able to offer one's dying body in love to God. We need people willing to offer that sight, to help others die well. Some may be called to it as their life's work, but everyone is called to it when a family member is dying. And each person, of course, yearns to find that sight as he or she undergoes the dying process.

Theology Of The Dying Body: In Weakness, Ecstatic Strength

How Is The Dying Body Given In Love?

Many of the themes of the Theology of the Body we have worked with are relevant here: attending to the present moment, *disponibilité*, self-abjection, hospitality, love and tenderness are all part of seeing rightly the given sign of dying, of receiving our true identity from God. This section will employ a "spiritual seeing," or better yet, a contemplative attitude throughout. Perhaps more than any other time in a person's life, the spiritual aspect is visible (or perhaps we attend death so much more closely we are able to perceive the spiritual more clearly). The "ecstatic" reality of dying, of giving one's life to God in love, is abundantly witnessed when we know how to perceive God's presence.

It is important to note that a reading of the spiritual sign of dying—a Theology of the Body *ars moriendi* if you will—is not prescriptive. Although I do think there are patterns and common themes within the dying process, every spiritual director knows that the Holy Spirit leads the person in a manner most befitting that person's particular relationship with God. If you are dying, you need not be troubled by a mocking scrupulosity that some "stage" has happened or not happened.[37] For one accompanying the dying, it may be impossible to "plan out" where the person is at: attention to the Holy Spirit in your conversation (or quiet sitting together) is key. But as Iain Matthew says on John of the Cross: "He gives us the schemas, not to help us predict, but to encourage us to surrender,"[38] as evidence that God is indeed working—and likewise, there are signs to read in the dying process, and the process itself is not meaningless. The *ars moriendi* witnesses the movement of one's healing in God through dying, and while there are moves to encourage and provide space for, we always must remember that healing cannot be plotted. Healing is its own mystery, coming from the heart of God. And it always feels, in some real sense, like a surprise, an explosion of grace into time. It is sensed as the mercy that it is.

But although we cannot predict how the process of dying unfolds, there is enough common experience of approaching that limit called death that we can discern and perceive it as natural sign, pointing to union with God. Since the late medieval *ars moriendi* tradition assumes dying is a public event, bearing an element of instruction, the reality of death as sign is no new argument. But in modern realities of dying, the sign is often smothered by all the details enumerated in a modern experience of death in the Western world. Rob Moll, in his contemporary *ars moriendi*, agrees much with the classic tradition: that a good death requires preparation, that the process is a deeply spiritual event, it is to be actively undertaken, that death is public and instructive, and that death injures the community.[39] The Theology of the Body wraps those insights under its question—how is the dying body given in love? And how is that a sign to us of God's desired union with humanity? No irony intended, death is intended to be more than something to "survive." As Moll says, "Rather than merely awaiting or dreading the terror of the grim reaper, death can be—in fact it is when we let it be—a spiritual journey as real as our salvation."[40] To perceive the fullness of this sign, let's attend some of the themes embedded in the Theology of the Body literature, applying them to the process of dying.

The Present Moment

One of the real challenges of life is attending to "the sacrament of the present moment," as Jean-Pierre de Caussade said. It gets no easier in the dying process. But to dismiss the present moment, no matter how difficult it is, can be a real disaster.

One of the insights of the hospice movement is an obvious one, but often ignored nonetheless: the dying are still living, and should be treated as such. To be alive means to be in (sometimes messy) relationships, to have specific likes and dislikes, to live with a history and a future. And frankly, history and future play a huge role in the dying process, more than at any point in a person's life. Dying is a privileged point where history, future, and the present meet.

But to gain entry to the history and the future rightly means to be attentive to the present moment. And at minimum, it means accepting where you are in the dying process, accepting where you are in your journey to God.

Many examples could serve here. Fr. Stephen Rossetti remarks on working with a man dying of AIDS who couldn't pray and hadn't in a long time.[41] When Rossetti asked him how he prayed, he responded that he goes to the hospital chapel, and tries to praise God, "that sort of thing." Rossetti pointed out he seemed angry, and why didn't he pray that? After all, he continued "I know you're angry, and if I know, certainly God knows. Get angry with God!" So he went to the chapel, "prayed angry" with God, and his spiritual life opened up and became honest. Rossetti remarked that he went on to die a holy death. But his good death required attending to the present moment, and that moment was anger at God. Moving back to a mode of praising God (his history?) was not going to work; it was an escape, not true praise. Moving forward to the joy of the Resurrection was not possible either. He had to accept the present moment to move through it to a future of joy.

Another example of a common "present moment" is an awakened desire for reconciliation with friends and family.[42] Most hospice programs make a concerted effort to see if there is reconciliation between family members that the dying person wants. While nurses and chaplains would not force a meeting or reconciliation, it seems that most people want a reconciliation, and respond positively, often tearfully, to offers to find an estranged son or daughter or sibling.[43] Indeed, those who are dying often want this more than the nearby loved ones, who in the spirit of protection (at best) remember too well the falling out and want to preserve the one dying from reopening old wounds. The overprotective loved ones are the ones living in the past.

Requests for reconciliation should be honored, and may be built in to the process of a Christian death. The dying body may lead us in this regard, as we know it is time to make a gift of our body through love: "... when you are offering your gift at the altar, if you remember that your brother or sister has something against you, leave your gift there before the altar and go; first be reconciled to your brother or sister, and then come and offer your gift" (Mt 5:23-24). Henri Nouwen had a brush with death a few years before he died of a heart attack, when he was hit by a car and sustained massive internal bleeding. The medical professionals had not thought he was dying, but were preparing to remove his spleen, recognizing it was the source of some internal bleeding. Nouwen felt strongly that he was dying and questioned the doctor about it, but the doctor said there was no evidence of that. Nonetheless, Nouwen had experiences that he described as "entering the portal of death."[44] One of the things he felt strongly compelled to do was to make a friend at the hospital promise to tell everyone he knew that if they had ever wronged him, he forgave them from the heart, and he begged their forgiveness as well. She agreed, mostly humoring him since no one else thought death was imminent. When Nouwen went into surgery, the surgical team realized the internal bleeding was much greater than they expected and admitted he very nearly died. Perhaps there is something about the natural sign of the limit of death that impels one to reconciliation. Perhaps the sense of God coming close inspires the reconciliation. In any case, it is a noted desire, often repressed until the last moment because the dying person thinks the situation is hopeless. It is telling that people often "wait" to die until the reconciliation is accomplished...or at least attempted.[45]

Some of attending to the present moment means to step out in faith and say "God is here, right here." In modern venues of dying, this can be a delicate issue. Most hospital chaplains and hospice workers tend to be very sensitive to the religious belief and nonbelief of their patients, and "let the patient lead"—and there is some sense to this. In hospice, one of the core values is that everyone, regardless of belief or background, deserves every effort that can be made to die peacefully, so there is often an attempt to honor specific religious beliefs or lack of belief. However, when the person is Christian, or when the person was raised Christian and is asking religious questions, or when the dying person agrees to see a Christian counselor, that strikes me as full permission to be open about your shared beliefs. This is not imposing your beliefs on another; in all these cases, you have been given consent to speak freely. Moll mentions that nearing death awareness literature is rife with experiences of seeing Jesus, Mary, loved ones, and angels—but many Christians are so uneasy with this we yield that ground to New Age interpretations, and do the dying Christian a massive disservice.[46] But as this section is focusing more on the one dying than the helpers, let's say this: staying with the present moment means being willing to see God and witness to God within the dying process you are undergoing.

Whether or not to accept various kinds of pain medication really ought to be seen in the light of what keeps the patient most fully in the present moment. There is nothing wrong with accepting pain medication. Studies indicate that nearly all physical pain can be managed without getting into issues of shortening a person's life, or overdosing the patient and causing his death. But the pain medication may cause side effects the patient may not want. I would argue that a patient's decision in the medication process ought to be one that helps the person be attuned to the present moment. A morphine-enabled sleep may be better for being spiritually attuned to the present moment than the gasping breathing that is often part of lung cancer, and the fear of it. Some pain may be considered a worthwhile exchange for being fully awake for others. God can work with you wherever you are, awake, asleep, in pain or not. But pain management is ultimately a discernment issue, made in collaboration with a doctor.

Finally, Catholics cannot talk about the process of dying without mentioning the sacramental anointing of the sick. The sacrament deliberately attunes one to the present moment, and places that moment in its fullness before God. One of the remarkable aspects of sacramental anointing, consistently mentioned by people who receive it (and observed by others) is the felt sense of profound peace, often visible through quiet and relaxation. It is, in fact, one of the defined effects of the sacrament[47]: the Holy Spirit's gift of "strengthening, peace and courage" that "renews trust and faith in God and strengthens against the temptations," especially temptations to discouragement and despair. The dying body is given in love in the acceptance of this gift, in the act of consenting by saying "Lord, I need your help, and I need it now." To live in this present moment is to embrace vulnerability by stepping into the sacrament.

The acceptance of the grace of this sacrament may be part of the natural sign. As we reach the limit of our earthly span, we know in our mind and in our bones that we need help. Sacraments are understood to be valid depending only on whether they are done correctly and by the valid minister of the sacrament (*ex opere operato*). The work is God's, and God fulfills His promises embedded in the institution of the sacraments. But the sacraments are efficacious in correspondence to the openness of the person receiving the sacrament. The dying process may bring you (although not force you) to that place of willingness to receive grace, and to that recognition that we are called to God. Receiving this sacrament is a tangible response to the call to union with God.[48]

This language of the sacrament of the present moment joined to the fullness of the past, present, and future in the dying process is met in a somewhat loaded phrase: abandonment to God. (Indeed, de Caussade's book is alternatively titled *Abandonment to Divine Providence*.) But abandonment is simply another word for giving the dying body in love to God. It is an act of trust that the God of Life is present, actively nourishing you in your dying into new life, and that love is stronger than death. God will nourish you, the fullness of you, into life everlasting with God. But it does call you to die. And that brings up the reality of God's will.

> This whole universe cannot fill the human heart, for its capacity is greater than anything other than God. It is on a higher plane than material creation, and for this reason nothing material can satisfy it. The divine will is a deep sea, the surface of which is the present moment. If you plunge into the sea you will immediately find it more vast than your own desires.[49]

The "surface of the present moment" is the dying process, and the will of God can look as murky as the ocean depths. But when Moll says we must actively engage the dying process, he is saying that we are called to respond to the will of God that is calling us to Himself, and that involves our death. There is a giving in that ought to be acknowledged. Margaret Guenther, an Episcopal minister, recalls working in a nursing home on Ash Wednesday, distributing ashes by making an ashy sign of the cross on these frail foreheads, murmuring "Remember you are dust, and to dust you shall return." She wondered if that phrase bore a little too much reality for people who had the pallor of ashes themselves. But she noted that they all responded calmly, and said thank you.

When you are losing your natural abilities to think well, eat, walk, etc., you are called to abandon the ways you knew and place yourself in the Way to come. Acknowledging that this is what it means to be called to God, this is what it means for a dying body to be given in love, makes clear the meaning of the natural sign of death. It requires perseverance. But to die in friendship with God is safe, and even amid the sadness of leave-taking, abandonment to God can be a joy. Dying is the most public moment of *disponibilité*, of being available in sometimes difficult circumstances for God's beckoning.

Self-Abjection

When we encountered this phrase last, we were in the childbirth chapter, noting that the period of transition in a woman's labor is a prime example of the reality of self-abjection: you are not making yourself abject, instead, you are *realizing* your utter poverty. The body leads you in this and does not lie. It steers you in giving *everything* to God.[50]

This, I think, is where the fear of death is rooted: not so much in pain (although that can be real), but in the reality that the call to union with God, through the process of dying, involves loss. There is no escaping that. We resist those terms. As mentioned in chapter two, a fear of God's call is seen in shrinking away from the call, redefining the call's terms, or attempting to "get ahead of God" and take control of the situation. It may require change and less being "in charge." Kübler-Ross's descriptive stages of dying speak to this common resistance well: denial (of the call), anger (about the timing or shape of the call), bargaining (to change the terms of the call), depression (that efforts to resist the call aren't working, and feeling the inescapable loss), and acceptance (of the call). Dying in this way—that is, responding to God's call to yield your ensouled body to God—starts far before the physical dying process begins. But the call is nearly unavoidable once the dying process starts.

John of the Cross speaks of the night of the spirit and the night of the soul as a kind of dying process. Dying to "putting the world first" is the response to a call from God for more intimate relationship. Night is the reality of loss: that all the good things God has graciously given us are less than God Himself. There is nothing we can do, no quick route to absorbing this reality, other than stay with the present moment. As Iain Matthew says, "what I have to 'do' is not run away....For John, the very act of not running away is an exciting event."[51] You may say that the person who is actively dying obviously cannot run away, but running isn't a physical move. It is a spiritual one. I recall my Divinity School professor talking about meeting with a clearly dying elderly woman in the hospital, and praying with her over Paul's classic Scripture, 2 Cor 4:16: "So we do not lose heart. Even though our outer nature is wasting away, our inner nature is being renewed day by day." Her response was stony silence, and then livid: "But I am not wasting away!" Others can ignore the spiritual promptings by endless channel surfing, diversion, etc. Spiritually "running away" is indeed possible, and acceptance of the fullness of the call to God through dying is a free choice in the most important ways.[52] But there is no question the body leads us to a place where we can embrace union with God, if we choose.

The key in negotiating self-abjection is to recognize that there is no map in the dying process, but there is a guide. And there are practices to "stay on the path" to a good death. The guide is Christ Himself, and the practices involve the virtues of patience, compassion, and hope.

First, Christ as guide. In addition to the effect of strength and comfort, the anointing of the sick has another effect: to unite one's suffering with Christ's passion.

> The sick who receive this sacrament, "by freely uniting themselves to the passion and death of Christ," "contribute to the good of the People of God." By celebrating this sacrament the Church, in the communion of saints, intercedes for the benefit of the sick person, and he, for his part, through the grace of this sacrament, contributes to the sanctification of the Church and to the good of all men for whom the Church suffers and offers herself through Christ to God the Father.[53]

The suffering is not meaningless, nor is it necessary. But when the emotional, physical, and spiritual pain is offered to the Father through uniting to the passion of His Son, God wraps that gift in the dynamic of the Trinity's self-gift. Christ's suffering and death are fully efficacious in themselves for salvation. But we are privileged to enter into that dynamic of giving and receiving when we are open to uniting our suffering with Christ's. The giving is endless, and the dynamic secure.

The Catholic phrase "offer it up" (often muttered by mothers tired of their children's complaints) has a bad reputation in many circles, and not without reason. The why and how and what for are rarely sensed or explained. And I question whether it should be suggested for minor afflictions—those may be opportunities to grow in large-heartedness, for example. But to unite one's dying process with Christ's is to allow Christ to show each of us, individually, the way to the Father. It is self-emptying, as we explored in the last chapter, a radical trust that we will be filled. It is to take Christ as brother and guide in this part of the path of life.

If there were a map, there would be little relationship. But Jesus Christ, in the loving acceptance of the Father's will and His active trust, is our guide. And He gives us the Holy Spirit as our advocate, to give us the words and knowledge in time of trial. The brotherhood of Christ is rarely more apparent than in the relationship of the dying person to God.

Second, the key to negotiating self-abjection in dying is embracing the virtues of patience, compassion, and hope. Christopher Vogt has written a helpful book examining these virtues in relationship to dying. He states that the *ars moriendi* tradition expects the development of virtues through an entire lifetime. To live well yields to dying well. But given the *length* of the dying process in the modern day, he says there is a new need for focusing on these three interdependent virtues: patience, compassion, and hope.[54] Patience is the virtue wherein we persevere in sadness and resist despair.[55] Compassion is the virtue to suffer with: the one who is dying, the ones you are leaving behind, suffering with Christ Himself. Hope is living with a love of God as the last word, an act of faith in God's providence. These virtues, encouraged for all working through the dying process, change our focus in necessary ways: "…what is to be imitated must properly shift from self-sacrifice to the sacrifice of absolute autonomy and independence."[56] We move through the practice of these virtues to depending on the Other (God), and others.

Arguably Vogt's virtues are well-characterized in many people, but one of the best known is the absolutely abject dying of St. Thérèse de Lisieux. Thérèse's death is in one way, very modern: she died of tuberculosis, and her death was very lengthy and expected. She died young, at age 24. What is striking about Thérèse's death is that Thérèse had lived a joyful life, brimming with security in her vocation as a Carmelite nun and in God. Indeed, people cannot read her posthumously published autobiography, *Story of a Soul*, without being struck by the absolute joy of the book. But in the months before her death, she felt plunged within a spiritual darkness that she admitted to a couple of other nuns felt absolute. Additionally, her death was difficult: she died literally coughing up bits of her lungs. Dying of tuberculosis, with no palliative care other than milk and the company of sisters, is a physically painful death. As her sisters watched for the beginning of "the agony," Thérèse responded (nine days before her death) "Ah! What is the agony? It seems I am always in it."[57]

Thérèse's dying was a remarkable witness of patience, compassion, and hope, in very difficult circumstances. Her *patience* was seen in her embrace of her humanity, admitting her weakness and constantly depending on the God she could not "sense":

> What would become of me if God did not give me courage? A person does not know what this is unless he experiences it. No, it has to be experienced![58]

> Earth's air is leaving me…When will God give me the air of heaven? Ah! My breathing has never been so short! …I am afraid I have feared death. I am not afraid of what happens after death; that is certain! I don't regret giving up my life; but I ask myself: What is this mysterious separation for the soul from the body? It is the first time that I experienced this, but I abandoned myself immediately to God….[59]

The virtue of *compassion* in dying is clear in the next passage:

> Do not be troubled, little sisters, if I suffer very much and if you see in me, as I have already said to you, no sign of joy at the moment of death. Our Lord really died a Victim of Love, and see what His agony was![60]

Thérèse, recognizing that her suffering would be joined by her sisters', tried to prepare her community for a difficult death, a death unlike the remarkably peaceful one died by their spiritual father, John of the Cross.[61] This was a sensitive move of love, in that it prepared them for being at the foot of this smaller cross, the cross of her very painful death. She reminded them that a painful death of much suffering had the most profound precedent.

Finally, the dying of Thérèse was a dying in *hope*: in that last year and a half of spiritual and physical suffering, she wrote some her lightest, most joy-filled poetry, stubbornly saying, "I will write what I believe." Her constant reliance on God and offering of her ensouled body despite the darkness was a courageous act of faith, an act that seemed to receive no reciprocation until moments before her death, when she was told she probably still had hours to live (and suffer):

> Her head fell back on the pillow and was turned to the right. The Prioress had the infirmary bell rung, and the sisters quickly returned....Hardly had the community knelt at her bedside when Therese pronounced very distinctly, while gazing at her crucifix: "Oh! I love Him!" And a moment later: "My God, I love you!"

> Suddenly her eyes came to life and were fixed on a spot just a little above the statue of the Blessed Virgin. Her face took on the appearance it had when Therese enjoyed good health. She seemed to be in ecstasy. This look lasted for the space of a "Credo." Then she closed her eyes and expired. It was 7:20 in the evening....A mysterious smile was on her lips. She appeared very beautiful.[62]

Thérèse's death is arguably not typical in its degree of desolation and suffering. Most people have gentler deaths. And her life, where she says God carried her through multiple hardships to abiding joy in the love of God, did not give many a clue as to what darkness was coming for Thérèse. But she embraced abjection in a thoroughly heroic manner. The virtues she had cultivated for love of God—patience, compassion, and hope—were on full display to her sisters, and through them, to the world.

Hospitality

The natural sign of dying is embedded within the call to hospitality, in that dying and death create a privileged space for hospitality to be lived. You may assume that hospitality is a luxury one cannot extend in the face of death. Ariès would disagree, arguing that offering hospitality—visiting the ill, and the ill being in the family front room and receiving visitors—was the norm for dying people until the hours just before their death. But it is true that I am going to shift gears for a moment, and focus on those who attend the dying person. It matters less whether we start with the caregiver or the dying person, because it is the relationship that makes clear we each have gifts to offer in the process of dying, that hospitality is always mutual. And hospitality opens space for the strange fruitfulness of dying.

There is a way in which a time of dying, as sad as it is, is always a time of new life. We need look no further than the parable of the sower and seed to recognize this in Scripture. Henri Nouwen, who wrote extensively on "befriending" death, sees an example of this life from death in the death of L'Arche community member and friend Maurice:

> Maurice has made his home in the L'Arche Daybreak community in Toronto for fourteen years. He was known for his joyfulness, gentleness, and love of home.... Somehow his condition—Down's syndrome—seemed only the other side of his great gift: to give and receive love....
>
> The days that followed were full of sorrow and joy. Moe was dead, but it seemed new life became immediately visible....[P]eople came to pray, to eat, to tell stories, to look at pictures—to remember with smiles and tears. Of all the days that I have lived at Daybreak, those after Moe's death belong to the most intimate, the most uniting, and, in a strange way, the most sacred. A man who, through his fragility and weakness, had helped us create community during his life did so even more through his death....[W]e shared a deep sense that not only does life lead to death, but death leads to new life. The spirit of gentleness and kindness that surrounded and pervaded our conversation, the spirit of forgiveness and healing that touched each one of us, and most of all the spirit of

unity and communion that bound us together in a new way—that spirit was gratefully received as a gift of Moe who was dead and yet very much alive.[63]

The sense of the inbreaking of new life, of God's life, is the fruitfulness that is part of the dying process. Although Nouwen mentions seeing this in a powerful way after Moe's death (and his descriptions are mirrored by many after-death gathering experiences), this may also be seen in the dying process itself, on this side of the mirror. To die is inevitably to change. Dying well is to *grow*. And Nouwen points out, "Your own growth cannot take place without growth in others. You are part of a body. When you change, the whole body changes."[64] To die well means to offer growth for the enrichment of the body of Christ. And mutual hospitality requires *disponibilité*, that vulnerability, which is the seedbed of growth.

In the chapter on childbirth, we examined the crucible of otherness as the core of hospitality. Sheila Cassidy, the director of a hospice in Britain, has a powerful reflection on otherness in the hospice ritual (and scriptural ritual) of washing feet, beginning with a poem by Sydney Carter:

No revolution will come in time
to alter this man's life
except the one surprise
of being loved.
He has no interest in Civil Rights
neo-Marxism
psychiatry
or any kind of sex.
He has only twelve more hours to live so never mind
about
a cure for cancer, smoking, leprosy
or osteoarthritis.
Over this dead loss to society
you pour your precious ointment,
call the bluff
and laugh at the

fat and clock-faced gravity
of our economy.
You wash the feet that
will not walk tomorrow.
Come levity of love,
show him, show me
in this last step of time
Eternity, leaping and capering.[65]

"You wash the feet that will not walk tomorrow" is a powerful recognition that hospitality can be wonderfully frivolous, and usually is. There is little utilitarian about washing a dying person's feet or anything else. But it has everything to do with offering dignity and love, and honoring the ensouled body. It is offering hospitality—even to one who may be unconscious.

The ritual of washing is sometimes one of the last gifts of hospitality one can offer a dying person. Much of our hospitality centers on conversation and food. A dying person may not be able to talk much or at all. And usually people dying of a lengthy illness begin to refuse drink and food as part of the process, a move that is often hard for families to accept: they know the person is dying, but it is hard to not be able to offer the care of sharing food and drink. Usually doctors and nurses need to explain carefully that forcing an actively dying person to drink or eat causes discomfort and does not help. But a gentle washing is usually welcomed, as is simply being present, holding a hand, praying. These tender and hospitable acts make space to see the inbreaking of God.

But I said this hospitality is mutual. How can a dying person offer hospitality? This is part of the genius of the Theology of the Body. To give one's dying in love doesn't require a deliberate Emily Post-scripted welcoming of visitors. The meaning of the dying body seems to offer its own hospitality. Maggie Callanan and Patricia Kelley's *Final Gifts: Understanding the Special Awareness, Needs, and Communications of the Dying* is an excellent resource on how the natural death of a human being bears its own fruitful gifts. The dying persons often will try to do what they can in love for those around them.[66] But in the dying process, there are often big and little gifts offered. We've already mentioned that dying as a natural sign does seem to produce a desire for reconciliation, which can be the greatest of gifts. But some unusual little things occur when the dying person is often semi-conscious: for example, people seem to "time" their own natural deaths.[67] There are numerous examples of people "hanging on" until a loved one arrives from far away. There are also numerous examples, especially in the case of dying children (adult or younger) of surviving parents, where the dying person dies as soon as the parents leave their bedside. Parents often feel very badly about this (even if they left just to use the restroom), feeling that despite best efforts, their son or daughter died alone. Callanan and Kelley suggest that it may be that the child wanted to spare the parents of the moment of death (especially if the dying patient mentions concern about how hard the dying will be for the parents). Or it may be easier for the dying person to "let go" when the grieving parents were out of the room. In any case, Callanan and Kelley suggest that people consider thinking this last act as intended gift.

However, one of the greatest gifts in an extended death could be the gift of sensing the presence of God and heavenly hosts. In hospice work, it is common for people to slip into a period of hours or days when the dying person has some sense of a spiritual reality within the dying process. For example, people not uncommonly mention deceased family members being present at their bedside, even family members the dying person does not know have died. Others mention a bright, beckoning light, sensing it as God. Others, like Nouwen, specifically mention the presence of Jesus and Mary. Most cannot say much at all, and do not, even when asked, often saying, "I can't describe it, it's beautiful," etc. But they also report this with a remarkable sense of peace, smiling. One of many lovely witnesses in *Final Gifts* talks about Clare, a hospice patient who had asked the hospice nurse about her own dying experience. (The nurse had survived a near drowning and remembers a fearless state of God's presence and light). Clare was intrigued.

Two months later, Clare died. In her final week, drained of energy, she often seemed to be looking through people. Sam [her brother] asked Clare if she might be seeing something or someone. He'd asked her and received no reply, just a slight smile.

"Clare, what are you seeing?" I asked.
"It's that place, you know, you were there," she said.
"Clare, what's it like?" Sam said, putting a hand on her cheek. "You have to tell me."
Clare snuggled against her brother's hand and smiled.
"I can't," she said. "You'll have to wait your turn."[68]

I do not look at these incidences, many though they are, as *prima facie* evidence of an afterlife. I do not need to, because revelation gives us this gift. If you look at them through the lens of hospitality and final gifts, they are graces: to know "the one surprise of being loved," and to see yourself that your loved one is loved by God, and at peace. As such, these experiences contribute to the sense of wonder that is built into the destiny of every human being. They are part of beholding death with a contemplative attitude. We do not always see effects of the drawing back of the veil (when a person is in a coma, or dies suddenly, or even in the prolonged darkness of Thérèse de Lisieux's dying); but as Christians, I think we must say they always occur: in the dying process, seen or unseen, or in the passing into death. Sometimes, more often than we may expect, we are privileged to see beyond the veil. And in seeing, in that consolation, we bear God's fruit to others.

The intensity of the grieving of the loved ones can make these "gifts" hard to see and accept. The sundering of death can overcome sensing the fruitfulness, at least at first. But this is all the more reason to attempt to create a space of hospitality: to honor the crucible of the dying process, and to honor the presence of the Other, God Himself. Hospitality clears a space for Jesus Christ, who teaches us how to die, as example and guide.

It is only fair to note that not all experiences of dying seem to be as warm. *Final Gifts* focuses entirely on positive spiritual experiences. (There are tragic stories in that book as well, but they mostly focus on estrangement and unforgiveness.) It is worth mentioning that, at least in the realm of Near Death Experiences (which is slightly different from what *Final Gifts* focuses upon—the days and hours before death—but there is overlap), there are experiences that seem much more centered on a sense of being in hell. One is written in detail by Howard Storm,[69] and he describes in some harrowing detail a state of being attacked by faceless evil spirits after his "death," calling to God in desperation, and being "rushed" toward the light. He was revived and went from being an ardent atheist to a Christian minister. When asked why people never hear of stories like his, he suggests that *he* hears these stories—people tell him after reading his book, but say they have been too ashamed to admit to anyone what happened, and too frightened by it to openly relive it. Once again, I don't think we need NDEs as evidence for a heavenly or damned afterlife, and it's true that the experiences seem to be culturally translated. But theologian Terry Nichols argues they do make strong supporting evidence for the revelation of the Christian tradition, and the scientific explanations simply do not explain the events away. We also know that dying can be difficult, and while I don't want to assume that a person wrestling with his or her dying (it does happen) is in a spiritual battle, praying for their perseverance and the power of God to help the dying is always a wise move. Such prayer and companionship is an act of love and tenderness. So from the perspective of a harder death, let's look at the last theme from the Theology of the Body literature we have used to extend the spousal meaning of the body: love and tenderness.

Love And Tenderness

What makes a death hard? We've already mentioned the reality of loss, being forced to give up everything but God. Uncertainty also can be hard. Long-held estrangements can suddenly loom in the foreground. The physical suffering can be hard, no question. Anger, depression, and anxiety—not abnormal reactions in the journey—can be hard to bear (both personally and in someone you love). Frankly, I don't want to ignore that the Evil One has a rich field to exploit: and the late medieval *ars moriendi* tradition does focus upon Satan's last attempt to disturb a soul's rest in Christ.

As we've said, Ignatius of Loyola absolutely assumed the reality of spiritual warfare, that the biblical witness of a conflict between good and evil spirits was absolutely true. Tertullian has said that Satan attempts to counter God's plan of salvation by diabolical mimicry.[70] If marriage—this call to union with God—is the primordial sacrament, as John Paul

II claimed, then it makes sense that the Evil One would attempt to undermine that sacrament by sabotaging it or creating "false marriages" (that is, lived out signs where you give your life to something else other than God's will). It follows that all natural signs are likely targets to be usurped and twisted. If the dying process was shaped to be a natural sign that points to union with God, then perhaps something like this occurs here as well, at the deathbed. Satan has no need of exposing his evil to the light of day—after all, someone may recognize him and expose him—if he can do his damage "underground." And taking the natural sign of the limit that is our physical death and twisting it, and making it a playground of doubt, fear, excessive grief, and more seems like demonic work.[71] Perhaps there is an effort by evil spirits to pull all the strings that make us avoid seeing the welcome of God at the dying person's door.

Perhaps most people dying are not in a space where active discernment is reasonable. This is where those accompanying come in, and where an insight widely attributed to St. John Bosco comes in:

> When someone is critically ill, I don't tell him to prepare for death, for such an approach would hardly allay his fears. Rather, I insist that we are all in God's Hands, that God is the best Father we could possibly wish for; ever watching over us, ever knowing what is best for us. I urge the patient to abandon himself to Him, just as a child does with his father, and to be tranquil. This allays the patient's fear of death. He is delighted by the thought that his fate is in God's hands and he peacefully waits for God to do as He wills in His infinite goodness.

I am grateful for the sacramental assistance provided to the dying within Catholicism—in reconciliation, anointing, and viaticum—which often vanquishes some of the physical difficulties of death, and regardless makes a spiritual impact. If difficulties remain, they are transformed for the spiritual good of the person and others. But whether the one accompanying the dying person is a priest or not, the call here is to pray: often silently, so as not to tax the energy of the dying person, but sometimes aloud too, because there is evidence that hearing is the last sense to be lost in dying—even those who are comatose. The call is to remind the dying person of the loving call to God through prayer, direction, and presence. Love and tenderness, offered through the sacraments and prayer, through the hospitality of standing your ground at the foot of this cross—strengthens perseverance in the dying. "Over this dead loss to society/you pour your precious ointment,/call the bluff/and laugh at the/fat and clock-faced gravity/of our economy"—such seemingly frivolous love and tenderness is a sign of faith and hope. It makes visible the loving care and providence of God. We are called to express this love and tenderness to the dying, and the dying ensouled body, rightly seen, impels us to it.

How do we best engage the sign of dying in others? How do we express the love and tenderness the sign evokes? Encountering the dying process as a privileged space where God can shape one's healing, leading one through to the call to union, may be engaged best through the act of presence and prayer. To pray is to talk with God, but more important, it is recognize your dependence on God. It is to clear a space in your life for God's work to take place, to open oneself to the vulnerability of receptivity.

In a simple book written by Barbara Shlemon,[72] her introduction into the power of healing prayer came when a patient she cared for pleaded for her to pray to God to control his pain, which was intense at that point. Spontaneously, she replied she could "pray to the God who loved you enough to die for you," and held his hand while she said an Our Father. The man's pain ceased, and in a comfortable peace, he died a few days later. This response to prayer was unexpected and striking to Shlemon, and she began a prayer group for fellow nurses, who would gather a few minutes before shifts to pray in the staff lounge for the patients' health and well-being. Shlemon focuses on the power to heal how God wills, rather than how we will: but she also believes that God has the power to confront and change the evil that flocks to death. One of her most helpful suggestions, I find, is that when the caregiver does not know what to pray for—physical healing, pain relief, a good death, or all of the above?—one could always pray that Christ *pour His life* into the patient. This simple prayer recognizes many of the truths held in the Theology of the Body:

1. the dying person is created to receive God,

2. Jesus Christ empties Himself on the cross and similarly into our lives, and

3. we are created for dynamic union with God.

The prayer also underlines many solid pastoral points: it encourages the dying person to trust in God's providential work in this particular situation, to seek God in the present moment, and to open oneself spiritually to receive God.

Tenderness, according to John Paul, is something we feel for another when we are conscious of the ties that unite us, the tendency to "make one's own the feelings and mental states of another," and is bodily expressed through accompaniment.[73] When we accompany the person who is dying, we may often be a friend or relative. But we are bound in solidarity as adopted sons and daughters of the Father, brothers and sisters to Christ. And we are bound by the reality that we are ensouled bodies, called to die, called to union with God. All these points together should yield to the fact that a companion, present in a contemplative attitude, may have an ability to "make one's own" the dying person's feeling and mental state. But even if that is difficult—the companion may be wrapped in his or her own grief, for example—the act of spiritual presence is powerful. Dallas Willard, an evangelical Christian, states this well when he says, "What we want to do is to carry with us at all times a consciousness that we are spiritual beings with an eternal destiny in God's universe."[74] This does not mean crafting speeches on the immortality of the soul. What Willard is talking about—this solidarity that points to God—is communicated via a companion's presence. People often don't know what to say, and that may be just fine—the reality of the situation may be beyond words. But the right words, prayerfully offered, may amplify that spiritual presence. Prayers of love and tenderness, through presence or words, when we accompany the dying are ways of standing at the ground of the cross. This reality reminds the one praying and the one prayed for of something important: we are, together, people destined to die and rise, adopted children of the same Father. We are companions on the journey, waiting for the promised help of our Guide. And it is a fiery gift.

The Challenge Of Alzheimer's Disease

Although this topic deserves a book in itself, I do need to comment what many consider to be the most challenging of deaths, at least from a caregiver's perspective: Alzheimer's disease. When a popular writer (Roger Rosenblatt of *Newsweek*) opens a memoir for his mother by stating "My mother died 17 years too late," a chasm opens between the understanding of death as natural sign that we have tried to present and the reality perceived by Rosenblatt. Alzheimer's touches upon many of the fears that are most prevalent in our society around death: an extended dying process (although 17 years is much longer than the average seven for Alzheimer's), increasing dementia, possible uncontrolled mood swings, and complete dependence. While there isn't a simple one-to-one correspondence, it is worth pondering that the rise in Alzheimer's disease has roughly corresponded with the rise of the "death with dignity" movement, which advocates for euthanasia and physician-assisted suicide. Every age has had its "terror disease": the bubonic plague, tuberculosis, polio, AIDS. In the past, much of the terror came from not understanding how the illnesses were spread. The terror in Alzheimer's is more rooted in the excruciatingly slow and near total decline, both physically and mentally.

A primary caregiver for her husband, who suffered from Alzheimer's for years, Beverley Bigtree Murphy notes wryly that despite the palpable fear around Alzheimer's, "it's just another way to die."[75] She notes that ALS creates the same slow decline and dependence, without the dementia, and ALS does not quite have the fearful stereotype. Alzheimer's bears a bias as a disease because it is solely identified with the loss of memory. There is more to Alzheimer's than that fact, but it is often the only symptom people know, and the one that is mentioned with the fear: "I won't know who my spouse is, who my children are." Murphy argues that even this fact tends to be misunderstood—some long-term memory is there, and how memory is affected can be spotty. What should become important for the caregivers, and communicated throughout the disease to the ones suffering it, is that sufferers can trust that they are loved. As Murphy adds autobiographically: "So when asked if Tom knew who I was when he died, I respond…Tom died knowing he was loved. And that is all that ever mattered to me."[76]

Murphy's argument that people abnormally fear the loss of memory (and therefore control) was also argued by Stanley Hauerwas. I remember an academic meeting where Hauerwas was speaking to a jam-packed room, probably of 300 academics in theology and religious studies, speaking on "a theology of Alzheimer's disease." I suspect that Alzheimer's strikes fear in academics more than many other people—we are people accustomed to being defined by our good memory and ability to think well. Hauerwas's main point, as I recall, was that we fear a loss of control in the face of God more than anything else. We fear coming to God without personality, memory, achievement—all the ways we define ourselves—stripped bare. Perhaps Alzheimer's teaches us, if we let it, just that: God is in control, not us, and we are by definition dependent on the grace of God. After the paper was delivered, I looked around as the hearty applause died away, noting that more than a few had given him a standing ovation; I even saw people trying not to weep. Trust me that this is rare in academic circles. We often go to meetings ready to argue, not give standing O's in tears.

While there is no doubt that Alzheimer's is a hard path, for both those who die of it and their caregivers, to say that God *cannot* act within this dying process makes God very small indeed, and to say God *does not* act in this process dismisses the love of God. We need to care for the caregivers, absolutely, but we also have to train ourselves to perceive God's work despite this disease.

One of the final prayers in the Catholic sacrament of anointing—the prayer specifically denoted for extreme or terminal illness—refers matter-of-factly to the gift of participation in the passion of Christ:

> Look with compassion on your servant N., whom we have anointed in your name with this holy oil for the healing of his/her body and spirit. Support her with your power, comfort her with your protection, and give her the strength to fight against evil. Since you have given her a share in your own passion, help her to find hope in suffering, for you are Lord forever and ever.[77]

Theology Of The Dying Body: In Weakness, Ecstatic Strength • 231

If we take *kenosis* seriously, the idea of participating in the Passion (Paul's "I make up what is lacking in my body") is not about suffering, but about giving one's identity to God the Father. There are ways in which Alzheimer's may be the clearest example of giving up one's known identity, and entrusting it to God.

Alzheimer's—or any other mortal disease—may impel one to work toward a response well-embodied in an Ignatian insight that has hovered in the background of this entire book: indifference. The term is misleading, because colloquial English uses indifference to suggest lack of necessary care. Ignatius uses indifference to suggest a disposition of wanting no other way but God's, to put God's will before our preferences. We are called to be "indifferent" as to how God calls us to Himself as a measure of trust in God's love. Obviously, this is difficult. We all have our pet projects, real interests and loves, and opinions as to how to serve God. Ignatius's insight is simply that God knows best, loves us more than we love ourselves, and we should spiritually compose ourselves to be open to God's path. Proper sight, perceiving our call to union through the natural sign of death, calls to response: and the response is to trust in God's love, power, and providence within the details of this call. One important response to dying is trusting that God's call to union is real, bigger than our pain, and can scatter all our fears.[78]

***

How does the Theology of the Body, extended, lead to the natural sign of dying as a sign that points us to God? The body has meaning, a spousal meaning, and the process of dying simply cannot be seen as meaningless. As Michael Waldstein summarizes, "God's plan and its renewal by Christ, the redeemer, is imprinted deeply within the bodily nature of the person as a pre-given language of self-giving and fruitfulness." An *ars moriendi* for our time should attend to the natural sign of limit as a pointer to union: we are called to self-giving by offering our dying in love to God. This requires spiritual scouring, honesty, and radical detachment. But it is met, embraced, and lifted up by the lavish love of God. Dying is part of the path to union with God: we see it, and so we step onto it. We are shaped to offer our lives in death as part of the path to union with God, and at a deep level, we know how to do this. As

Christ says through the evangelist John: "And if I go and prepare a place for you, I will come again and will take you to myself, so that where I am, there you may be also. *And you know the way to the place where I am going*" (14:3-4). (Italics added.) But as the natural sign of childbirth points to the calls to spiritual motherhood (and, indirectly, fatherhood), and impairment points to the calls to brotherhood and sisterhood, the sign of a natural death points to another call within the Family of God: the call to elderhood.

The Call To Elderhood

It says something about the English language when one has to create a word. "Elderhood" is a well-known concept in many other world cultures. The respect one accords elders is often a cultural absolute. Americans, particularly new immigrants and those who serve new immigrants, have a ringside seat at this struggle: recognizing that elderhood is a cultural construct unfamiliar to most European Americans. Likewise, many other languages do not have the term "caregiver" because the concept of elderhood and the primacy of family is entrenched, and there is no need for a word that specifies who is providing care to those in a late stage of life.[79]

Although there are many studies on this phenomenon, I will simply share three examples from different cultures to make the point. I live in a region of the United States with a significant Native American population, with numerous reservations and tribes with sovereign nation status. My small town hosts the annual Great Dakota Gathering to promote understanding and reconciliation between Natives and other Americans. A woman from the Pine Ridge Dakota came to speak at our church and mentioned she was in her 60s, but still uncomfortable in speaking without given permission when our own community elders were present (that is, older women and men from the parish who came to listen to her). Respect for elders as sources of wisdom is very strong. Especially now: both Dakota and Ojibwe tribes find themselves in a race against time to save their native languages and traditions, after many native children were forced to attend boarding schools to "become white" and others moved off the often-ravaged reservations. The elders are embraced as necessary teachers, embodied resources of an identity that is close to slipping from their grasp. When these elders become seriously ill, the overwhelming preference is to care for elders at home, although this is a preference difficult to manage without palliative care on most reservations.[80] But difficulties or not, elders have been traditionally honored across Native cultures, and caring for the elder at home is part of that respect.

In Hispanic (or Latino) cultures, we have a similar phenomenon. *Abuelos* (grandparents) are in most ways the rock of a family, and the deep attachment to family is one thing most Anglos do not understand or appreciate about Hispanic culture. Indeed, although the immigration debates in the United States are deeply divisive, one point consistently lost on all sides is what a cultural sacrifice it is for individuals from Mexico and much of Latin America to immigrate (legally or illegally) to the United States: to separate oneself from family is only done for the most serious of reasons, primarily, earning enough money to survive. I have seen with my own eyes long lines at small town Mexican Western Unions, filled with people expecting to receive wired money from a relative working in the United States. The money sent makes the difference in many families between a relatively comfortable survival or a short, brutal life.

Finally, I worked for a time with a professional woman from South Korea, who immigrated to the United States with her husband, children, and her aging mother. She was genuinely floored when she realized that her medical insurance would not identify her mother as part of her immediate family. The issue was not the extra money needed to cover her mother's medical needs: the issue was the very idea that her mother was not immediate family, and that our medical practices devalue her mother's essential role and importance in their family.

European-Americans have a great deal to learn from these cultures in terms of fulfilling the commandment to "Honor your father and mother"—and to honor those people of greater years as well. But I do want to continue to focus on those who are in the process of dying, old and young. We may be called to give our life in love through the dying process. We may live in a culture that needs a revived *ars moriendi*, more attention in teaching people how to die well. Given that, does it make sense to honor those who are dying as our elders in faith? As the ones who teach us, who show us the way?

If we honored those who are dying as our elders, we would treat them with respect rather than expediency. We would take the time to stop, to listen. We would learn to see spiritually what is happening in the dying process, as well as provide physical comfort care. We would learn the language that the dying tend to speak.[81] We are not asking them to stand up and teach a class how to die,[82] or write a book. Given the nature of the experience of dying, this teaching is almost always in the form of witness. The late medieval *ars moriendi* tradition states that people should attend the deaths of others so as to learn how to die. But the point here is not to gain experience. The point is to seek wisdom. *And wisdom, as a gift of the Holy Spirit, is only found in places where God's mystery is held.*

Story after story of those close to a person dying recall the small and large graces of that time. It is a period of intense attention. That deliberate effort to perceive will inevitably teach. When a loved one has died, the focus is often turned to the family and friends, and bereavement ministries. This is appropriate and right. But it also may be appropriate to follow up with families and friends beyond the funeral, to sit and ask them gently where God was present in the dying process of their loved one. Indeed, so many people find it so striking, they bring it up immediately after the person's death. It may help them in their grieving, but it also teaches the person how to die when his or her time comes. There are real and painful losses with death. But God is present, so there is wisdom to be gained, and for some, a sense of lightness as well.

We had mentioned that anyone dying may be considered as our elder *in faith*, which means that the person honored as an elder may not be elderly at all. Any person, young or old, who dies in friendship with God is our elder, because as we still live, they move ahead of us on the road to the Father. Christ is our elder brother in this regard. And your dying child can be your elder in faith as well. This is not an uncommon sense at all: many parents of dying children remark with awe at the wisdom and patience of their children in their last days. Indeed, the dying children are usually more accepting of their coming death than their parents are. The experience of dying as limit is embedded in the body: seen easily when a person is withering with age, but still sensed with the inescapable fragility of human life at any age. To see that limit as a protection given by God, a door shaped to open to union, is hard medicine to swallow. But it is a medicine that yields wisdom, and it is a gift given to a person of any age open to receiving God.

We need elders in the family of God, and the natural sign of death provides those elders, over and over again. To resist and avoid death, as McGill suggests we tend to do, means we dismiss an essential part of the family. It also means to dismiss an essential part of who we are and are called to be. Another cultural insight of African Christianity—the source of the family of God language—is a twist on a Western philosophical stalwart. Descartes's "I think, therefore I am" has been taken by many Westerners as the way to define humanity by placing first emphasis on the rational.[83] By contrast, many Africans say "I am because you are."[84] When we devalue and ignore the vocation of any member of the family of God, we do not know who we are. All are necessary and all help us define others and ourselves. We are family, and we are enriched by embracing our relationships to those who are mothers, fathers, spiritual mothers and fathers, spiritual brothers and sisters, and our elders in faith. In knowing them, we know who we are in God. And in knowing God, we celebrate the gift of seeing Him at work in others.

To honor our elders does not diminish that dying is a struggle in many ways. It is a physical struggle, since the body naturally bends toward life. It is an emotional struggle in its inevitable leave-taking. And it is a spiritual struggle for all the reasons that make up a person's spiritual life, condensed. But dying is a call: it is (in the most spiritual sense) safe, and amazingly, it is fruitful. It is one of the paradoxes of the faith, but we are a Church of the Resurrection, and to approach death without shouldering that it is—by God—a language of fruitfulness is simply wrong.

ENDNOTES

1. These numbers are from a well-executed study from Britain—and while numbers vary across the Western world, the contrast between a majority of people wanting to die at home versus the reality of most dying in hospitals does not change. Graham Thorpe, "Enabling More Dying People to Remain at Home," *British Medical Journal*, October 9, 1993, 307(6909):915-918 http://www.pubmedcentral.nih.gov/articlerender.fcgi?artid=1679030 (accessed July 24 2013).
2. Daniel Callahan, *The Troubled Dream of Life: In Search of Peaceful Death* (New York: Simon & Schuster, 1993), 26.
3. Ibid.
4. Christopher Vogt, *Patience, Compassion, Hope, and the Christian Art of Dying Well* (Lanham, MD: Rowman & Littlefield Publishers, 2004), 53-6.
5. Daniel R. Tobin and Karen Lindsey, *Peaceful Dying: The Step-by-Step Guide to Preserving Your Dignity, Your Choice, and Your Inner Peace at the End of Life* (Reading, MA: Perseus Books, 1999), 4-6.
6. Callahan, 48.
7. Callahan, 37.
8. This entire discussion and the quotation are found in Callahan, 64. Quoting Jessica Muller and Barbara Koenig, "On the Boundary of Life and Death: The Definition of Dying by Medical Residents" in *Biomedicine Examined*, ed. Margaret Lock and Deborah Gordon (Dordrecht: Kluwer Academic Publishers, 1988), 369.
9. Callahan, 47.
10. Callahan, 73-4.
11. McGill, *Death and Life*, chap. 1, esp. 18-19.
12. McGill, 16. The italics are McGill's.
13. Callahan, 53.
14. Elisabeth Kübler-Ross, *On Death and Dying* (New York: Macmillan, 1969).
15. Ernest Becker, *The Denial of Death* (New York: Free Press, 1973). There was also an influential article written in the 1950s, "The Pornography of Death," that argued that death was treated like porn in that it was often present but rarely acknowledged. Geoffrey Gorer, "The Pornography of Death," *Encounter*, October 1955, 49-52.
16. Lucy Bregman, *Death and Dying, Spirituality and Religions: A Study of the Death Awareness Movement* (New York: Peter Lang Publishing, 2003), 3.
17. Ibid., 5-6.
18. Sheila Cassidy, *Sharing the Darkness: The Spirituality of Caring* (Maryknoll, NY: Orbis Books, 1991), 21.
19. Ibid., 29.
20. The two exceptions are Christopher Vogt's *Patience, Compassion, Hope, and the Christian Art of Dying Well* (Lanham, MD: Rowman & Littlefield Publishers, 2004), and Rob Moll's *The Art of Dying: Living Fully Into the Life to Come* (Downers Grove, IL: IVP Books, 2010). Although there are other autobiographical books that may fill the gap—the popularity of Joseph Cardinal Bernandin's *The Gift of Peace* (Chicago: Loyola Press, 1997) is a good example—there is nothing close to a how-to book written from a theological perspective available.
21. Walter Brueggemann, Terence Fretheim, Walter Keiser, and Leander Keck, *The New Interpreter's Bible*, Vol. 1, (Nashville: Abingdon Press, 1994), 364. This understanding of clothing is important in light of the Letter to the Romans' call to

"Clothe yourselves with the Lord Jesus Christ" (Rom 13:14, NIV), and Letter to the Ephesians' admonition to "Put on the whole armor of God, so that you may be able to stand against the wiles of the devil" (6:11).

22. See Rom 5:12-21.

23. Fretheim, 369.

24. Ibid., 364.

25. The extremely brief version of the Christian tradition on death is that human beings originally appear destined to live with God forever, through God's gracious providence. The language of "immortal soul" is Greek and really introduced in the New Testament (and the wisdom literature of the Old Testament) as an way of describing this everlasting life. The subtle difference is that the Hebrews understood the immortality of humanity as an extension of God's continual sustenance of the human being, whereas the Greek influence allowed the Christians to describe the sustenance as designed at the beginning in the gift of the immortal soul, which remains immortal no matter what. See Terence Nichols's *Death and Afterlife: A Theological Introduction* for an excellent and thorough introduction to the Jewish and Christian doctrines regarding death and afterlife. See chapter 1 for a treatment of the limited (but important) language used throughout the Hebrew Scriptures. Terence L. Nichols, *Death and Afterlife: A Theological Introduction* (Grand Rapids, MI: Brazos Press, 2010).

26. *Catechism of the Catholic Church*, #1006, 1008.

27. My focus here is on how sin damages the clarity of the sign of the body, and how we may experience this in the sign of death. But of course sin does more than twist the language of the body; it harms the soul. This damage to the soul is expressed through the body (although it may be subtle). But the damage sin does to the soul is real, regardless of the body's expression of it and our interpretation of it.

28. Making way through the flaming sword was a somewhat popular image in patristic literature: Origen wrote about martyrdom as a way through the sword in Exhortation to Martyrdom 36 (OSW 67-68), Bede writes of Christ extinguishing the flame (*Homilies on the Gospels*, HOG 1:116-17), and Ephrem the Syrian also speaks of Christ removing the sword through being pierced by it (*Hymns on Paradise* 2.1, HOP 85). See the *Ancient Christian Commentary on Scripture*, Vol. I, Genesis 1-11, ed. Andrew Louth and Marco Conti (Downers Grove, IL: InterVarsity Press, 2001), 101-2.

29. St. Ignatius of Antioch, *Letter to the Romans*, 6, in *Christian Classics Ethereal Library*, http://www.ccel.org/ccel/richardson/fathers/Page_74.html, (accessed February 15, 2013).

30. Suffering is a difficult topic to address in abstract: on the one hand, it seems suffering is not in and of itself a thing to be embraced. In so far as suffering is destructive, it is healthy to resist it and to seek healing. On the other hand, it cannot be avoided; human beings after the Fall do suffer. Depending on how one responds, suffering can be turned to good. For example, Cassidy's work as a director of hospice is to assure pain management for the dying, but she admits that suffering can purify a person; she sees the suffering as a place where people grow (Cassidy, 80). One of the things that makes Cassidy's insight so compelling in her book is that in addition to her found vocation as a person who helps others die, she herself had dealt with enormous suffering when she was a medical doctor volunteering in Pinochet's Chile, and was jailed and tortured in solitary confine-

ment for medically treating an injured revolutionary. When she says suffering can purify, she does not do so without recognizing the evil behind the suffering. I think, in the end, she is closer to Hauerwas's position that physical suffering is not a school for character, but a test of character. Hauerwas, *Suffering Presence*, 26.

31. *Suffering Presence*, 25.
32. See Adrian Reimers, "Human Suffering and John Paul II's Theology of the Body," *Nova et Vetera*, 2, no. 2 (2004). He covers a brief and helpful phenomenology of suffering in this paper: found "in the feelings and perceptions, the engagement of the will within the world, and in the meaningfulness of one's life."
33. Ibid.
34. *Evangelium Vitae*, #51.
35. Matthew, 87, quoting 1 Ascent 5.7.
36. Cassidy, 80.
37. This is one of the prominent criticisms of Kübler-Ross's stages, that people may be expected to follow a standardized emotional schema and rushed to move through that, contrary to God's desire for that person. Any person helping anyone to die should remember that at some level, the person dying knows more about dying than you do. This admonition to not control your understanding of the process is spoken to well in Margaret Guenther's chapter on the spiritual direction of the dying. Norvene Vest, ed. *Still Listening: New Horizons in Spiritual Direction*. (Harrisburg, PA: Morehouse Pub, 2000), chap. 8.
38. Matthew, *The Impact of God*, 88.
39. Moll, 56.
40. Moll, 77.
41. Stephen Rossetti, *When the Lion Roars: A Primer for the Unsuspecting Mystic* (Notre Dame, IN: Ave Maria Press, 2003), 27.
42. Of course, there is reconciliation with God as well, concretized in the Catholic tradition through the grace of the sacrament of reconciliation. That experience will be explored more in discussion with the sacrament of anointing of the sick.
43. This perspective is amply recorded in the hospice literature. See chapter 11, "Needing Reconciliation," of *Final Gifts* for a good presentation. Maggie Callanan and Patricia Kelley, *Final Gifts: Understanding the Special Awareness, Needs, and Communications of the Dying* (New York: Bantam, 1997), chap. 11.
44. Henri Nouwen, *Beyond the Mirror* (New York: Crossroad, 1990), 34ff.
45. I do not mean to gloss over how difficult reconciliation can be. Also, not everyone who dies reaches for reconciliation with estranged friends and loved ones, and those contacted for reconciliation do not always agree to meet. Other times, the person they are in conflict with is dead, which creates its own challenges. Other people are in such a condition that they cannot ask for reconciliation (in a coma, suffering dementia, etc.). People can and do die with fractured relationships. However, it is striking how often people want to be reconciled. Family members and chaplains ought to do as much as they can help the person in this regard... even if it is to pray with the person and help him or her offer love and forgiveness (if needed) to that person through Christ, who will continue the work of reconciliation as the other person is open to it.
46. Moll, 44.
47. From *Catechism of the Catholic Church*, #1520: "*A particular gift of the Holy Spirit*. The first grace of this sacrament is one of strengthening, peace and courage to overcome the difficulties that go with the condition of serious illness or the frailty

of old age. This grace is a gift of the Holy Spirit, who renews trust and faith in God and strengthens against the temptations of the evil one, the temptation to discouragement and anguish in the face of death. This assistance from the Lord by the power of his Spirit is meant to lead the sick person to healing of the soul, but also of the body if such is God's will. Furthermore, 'if he has committed sins, he will be forgiven.'" The internal citation is from James 5.

48. Thomas Aquinas argued that extreme unction (as the sacrament was called in his time) had the effect of removing temporal effects, or punishments, of sin. That is, the suffering that is the result of venial and mortal sin is removed. These sufferings can be felt in numerous ways, and many would say there is a natural cause and effect in action here: living a sinful life has its own consequences. Could the felt peace be an expression of the spiritual reality of the removal of temporal punishments? Could the path to courage and living through the dying process be cleared through that effect? I thank Fr. (now Bp.) Andrew Cozzens for bringing this up in conversation. The sufferings may also be joined consciously with the suffering of Christ, which will be explored more in the next section on self-abjection. See CCC #1522, on page .

49. Jean-Pierre de Caussade, *The Joy of Full Surrender*, ed. Hal M. Helms (Brewster, MA: Paraclete Press, 1986), 42.

50. One is reminded of Greene-McCreight's insight during her severe depression: her body and mind were ravaged, but her soul was held safe in God. Greene-McCreight, 111.

51. Matthew, 89.

52. Many people I have known who were dying have said they just wanted to be treated normally, for people to remember that he or she was still the same person, and not just a diagnosis. This point is well taken. Not every moment or conversation needs to be about dying, union with God, and prayer. The problem is when the person never has a chance to have that conversation on how to die, or is offered the chance and rejects it for unhelpful reasons.

53. *Catechism of the Catholic Church*, #1522.

54. Vogt, 2.

55. Vogt quoting Hauerwas, 5.

56. Ibid., 107.

57. Thérèse de Lisieux, *Story of a Soul: The Autobiography of Saint Thérèse of Lisieux* (Washington, DC: ICS Publications, 1996), 268.

58. Ibid., 264.

59. Ibid., 268.

60. Ibid., 267.

61. John of the Cross did die by accounts of those present a peaceful death, and earlier in his life John spoke of those dying in love with God: "The death of such persons is very gentle and very sweet, sweeter and more gentle than was their whole spiritual life on earth....The soul's riches gather together here, and its rivers of love move on to enter the sea, for these rivers, because they are blocked, become so vast that they themselves resemble seas...." John of the Cross, *St. John of the Cross: Selected Writings*, ed. Kieran Kavanaugh (New York: Paulist Press, 1987). See *Living Flame of Love*, stanza 1, no. 30.2.

62. Ibid., 271.

63. Henri Nouwen quoted in *Angels Over the Net*, videocassette, prod. Isabelle Steyart and dir. Bart Gavigan, 30 min. (Spark Productions, 1995) in Michelle O'Rourke,

Befriending Death: Henri Nouwen and a Spirituality of Dying (Maryknoll, NY: Orbis Books, 2009), 60-1.

64. Ibid., 33, quoting from Henri Nouwen, *The Inner Voice of Love: A Journey Through Anguish To Freedom* (New York: Doubleday, 1996), 57.

65. Cassidy, 25-6. This was handed to Cassidy on a scrap of paper as she worked in her hospice. The poem is very similar to Sydney Carter's published poem, "Mother Teresa," in *The Two-Way Clock: Poems* (London: Stainer & Bell, 1974).

66. Some of these gifts may be well-intentioned but not at all good, unfortunately. One of the most common, when the dying person says, "I don't want to be a burden," is a sad example of this. The intention—to save their loved ones pain—is good, but misplaced. They should be assured with words like these: "We will reach out for help when we need it, but making sure you are cared for is not a burden. Human beings are not burdens." And churches and extended family should actively make sure caregivers receive the help they need. Another example of a well-intentioned but problematic gift: when the dying person refuses to offer his or her challenges. It's true that people often do not know what they need, but do know "where it hurts." If that is not shared in the hope of not bothering the caregiver, the challenge cannot be met. Finally, it is clear that some of the impulse for legalizing euthanasia uses this language: when the dying person does not want to be a burden, become needful of others, and essentially change, a chosen and self-induced death is preferable. The "death with dignity" argument needs to be reclaimed by people working in spiritual theology and theological anthropology, to persuade people that the dignity of the human being can be seen in all stages of life, and to intentionally end a life before its time is not only a moral evil and a public menace, it destroys a window to the work of God.

67. This would be the case in an extended illness, not a traumatic accident. See Maggie Callanan and Patricia Kelley, *Final Gifts: Understanding the Special Awareness, Needs, and Communications of the Dying* (New York: Bantam, 1997), chap. 15.

68. Callanan and Kelley, 111.

69. Howard Storm, *My Descent into Death: A Second Chance at Life* (New York: Doubleday, 2005).

70. See Tertullian's *The Prescription Against Heretics* XL, and *On Baptism* V. Thanks to my friend Mary Gibson for pointing to these texts.

71. For example, when talking to a very holy friend about an acquaintance from my parish who died young, he smiled gently and responded, "ah...some people are just lucky!" From the wrong person, this could seem misanthropic, but he is a person who truly loves life. The key is he loves God more than he loves life. Most people would not respond to a person dying young in this way—instead of seeing the opportunity to move into the embrace of God more immediately, they focus on the (real) tragedy of dying out of the seasons of life.

72. Barbara Leahy Shlemon, *Healing Prayer* (Notre Dame, IN: Ave Maria Press, 1976).

73. See chapter 2, pg 81ff.

74. Moll, 104.

75. See Beverley Bigtree Murphy's *He Used To Be Somebody: A Journey Into Alzheimer's Disease Through The Eyes Of A Caregiver* (Boulder, CO: Gibbs Associates, 1995). The book title is ironic; she argues that he was and is "somebody" throughout the progression of the disease. See also her site dedicated to caregiv-

ers of loved ones with Alzheimer's, http://bigtreemurphy.com. The "Alzheimer's is just another way to die" is the title of a lecture by Murphy, and her notes from the lecture are extremely provocative, questioning why Alzheimer's, difficult though it is, has the designation of the "terror disease." See Beverley Bigtree Murphy, "Alzheimer's Is Just Another Way To Die," http://www.bigtreemurphy.com/Death%20home.htm, click on title in left navigation bar (accessed October 3, 2013).

76. Ibid.

77. Lizette Larson-Miller, *The Sacrament of Anointing of the Sick* (Collegeville, MN: Liturgical Press, 2005), 14. The actual rite says him/her; I chose one option for readability's sake.

78. *Man and Woman*, Introduction, 105.

79. Justin Buchbinder's short essay "Cultural Traditions and Respect for Elders" at *Strength for Caring: A Place for Caregivers* website, points out the lack of "caregiving" language in three case studies, involving women described as Chinese-American, Latina, and African-American: "Neither Kia, Hellen, nor Esmeralda knew what the term 'Caregiver' or 'Family Caregiver' meant, and with good reason. To them, 'caregiving' is simply a natural part of life, and respecting the family unit. It's not something that needs a special name...it simply is what it is." See http://www.strengthforcaring.com/manual/about-you-celebrating-cultures/cultural-traditions-and-respect-for-elders/, (accessed Feb 1, 2013).

80. Some of these issues particular to Native American populations are addressed in *Palliative Care Nursing: Quality Care to the End of Life*, ed. Marianne Matzo and Deborah Witt Sherman (New York: Springer Pub, 2001), chap. 1.

81. See *Final Gifts*, chaps. 5-6. Realizing that the dying sometimes speak in symbol or code (especially around issues of travel, or impending death: when those who are days from death begin saying phrases like "I need to catch the bus, we need to get gas in the car," etc.) is part of what Callanan and Kelley call "Nearing Death Awareness" (NDA), and they encourage more people to be familiar with it as part of the dying process, resisting the urge to immediately call it delusional behavior that needs to be medicated. They even suggest nurses "chart" events that seem to indicate NDA (229).

82. Although it is interesting how "The Last Lecture" has caught on as a series on many college campuses, and the "last lecture" of the late Carnegie-Mellon computer science professor and pancreatic cancer patient Randy Pausch, captured on video, became a viral phenomenon. The full video lecture may be found at http://www.cmu.edu/randyslecture/.

83. This is admittedly not what Descartes was arguing; he was simply attempting to find a way of philosophically proving his own existence.

84. For example, see Baffour Ankomah's article "I Am Because You Are," *Odewire*, http://odewire.com/48941/i-am-because-you-are.html, (accessed November 7, 2013).

Afterword
The Gift of the Praying Body

> *This underscores the extraordinary dignity of the human body as a sacred place of worship, although it may be desecrated from within and without. For those united to Christ in the Holy Spirit, the body is a living, mobile location of prayer, a living monstrance for Christ.* —Sr. Mary Timothy Prokes, *Toward A Theology of the Body*

One of the elements that attracts many to the Theology of the Body literature is that it counters the very heart of the prevailing attitude toward prayer: that prayer is the uttering of words, a single bodily act, then done. But if the ensouled body serves as sign, prayer is never "done." Prayer is the ongoing initiative of the Holy Spirit to draw one's entire life, seen in the ensouled body, into the fullness of God. And the Theology of the Body literature is John Paul's attempt to bring the life of prayer out of its domesticated box (that is, something I initiate and do, right here, and finish) and into the daily lives of all believers. Prayer, when received, absorbs all of life. There is nothing tame about prayer. There is not only a wideness, there is a wildness to God's mercy.[1]

Prayer is where we learn to receive. It is the reverse of the Fall—that act of sin that made each of us tempted to be our own sources of goodness, virtue, and life. It is an act of humbling oneself, an act of trust, an act of love. It is, essentially, a primer in *kenosis*, and a first step in imitating the life of Christ, and thereby be drawn into the life of God. The Theology of the Body is through and through a praying theology. It opens our sight to God through the posture of *disponibilité*, and helps us to become, as the desert fathers encouraged, "all eye."[2] This spiritual posture helps us to receive God's presence and help us see God's constant loving work in our world.

As ensouled bodies, the posture of *disponibilité* never remains just on the spiritual level. The body, as "sign," expresses and indicates the reality of its relationship to God.[3] In the experience of prayer, this manifests itself in different ways. People in prayer often close eyes, clasp hands, kneel.

Others may manifest the attitude of prayer simply by getting themselves into a church, and despite preoccupation or anger or confusion, doggedly stay there. For others, it may be physically standing up and stating publicly: "I believe in one God, the Father, the Almighty...." Actions have meaning: they usually express what is spiritually present. To kneel, bow, genuflect, stand, stay, cross oneself, sing, speak, be silent, put on a head covering or take one off—all these actions are, when deliberately done with a proper will, gifts of self to God the Father. They are not done as witnesses to others, although they may serve as witness. They are not done as adherence to rules of worship, although those rules may have value. And for those who cannot physically do any of these acts, the comportment of the will and the spiritual posture of *disponibilité* are what is essential. Bodily expression may look different, more subtle, but when it is possible, wills naturally express through the body.

The body does not lie. As a sign, its actions point to God, or it points to what is not God. We are always—not once, but always—responding to two connected calls: the call of the Holy Spirit to "pray in the Spirit at all times,"[4] and the call of our individual vocations within the family of God. Our constant response (or lack of response) is what we return to God. We return to God a gift of self or continue to live in our sin, taking what is gift in selfishness.

The "pray in the Spirit at all times" admonition in Ephesians 6:18 is often a challenge to people—dismissed as overstated impossibility, or the distinctive call of the cloistered. It's true that the statement doesn't have to mean pray discursively every minute of the day, but it does mean that our life and actions should be wrapped in prayer.[5] I would say it also means we need to put aside time for dedicated prayer, time consecrated to God alone. I recall reading advice given to a young woman who had just given birth not being able to find time to pray alone. Given that new mothers barely have time to eat, sleep, and shower, this is not surprising. And that time of life is temporary. God values any attempt to pray under such circumstances; indeed, the desire to pray is itself a prayer. But the advice given to this young mother intrigued and disturbed me: the priest suggested she think of the work of motherhood as her monastery, making the work of caring for her child her offering and prayer. While it is good he reminded her that her work is holy work, there is a big difference between life at home with an infant and the monastery: monks have dedicated prayer time, and this young mother would benefit from it as well. It may, for a couple of weeks or perhaps more, be impossible. But her family and her church should be encouraged to make it a priority and possibility for her—for example, provide babysitting for half an hour while she prays. To equate holy work with prayer without the dedicated time making oneself available to God can easily fall into multi-tasking. The danger is that we can *lose sight* of why we work, and for Whom. If we put time aside to perceive and receive God in prayer, then we can more easily see the sign of the ensouled body in our daily work. We can live out more easily "praying always."

So we return to the person cited at the very beginning of the book, who urgently called the spiritual director, pressing that she needed to talk to someone desperately: then showed up, embarrassed, admitting "I don't know what I want." The Theology of the Body literature has a first suggested response to that statement, one uttered by so many approaching Jesus in the Gospels: Lord, I want to *see*. Not just physically see, although that is a legitimate request. I want to perceive where God is acting in my life. I want to see myself, and others, rightly. I want to see with more transparency my relationship to God. I long to see your face, O Lord, in your holy temple. Because only then may I respond in fullness, only then may I give my ensouled body in love. *Sight always calls for response.*

We may be entering a new age where the visual (and by extension, all the senses) has become the new rhetoric. But whether that is true or not, perception has *always* been an act more primordial than reading and writing, *always* part of the way of the life of faith. To recognize that God has embedded in human nature a way of perception—and that this perception, dimmed in the Fall, has been redeemed in Jesus Christ—is to recognize that from the beginning of time, God has wanted us to see His face. An open response makes clear the ongoing, active grace of God in our everyday lives. But risking that sight comes at an immediate cost: our manufactured security and control.

Sr. Mary Timothy Prokes is especially pointed on this:

> While divine revelation is an effective word, it is offered, not imposed. There is no certainty it will be received *as* revelation…. More than a conveying of information, Revelation is Self-manifestation of a divine communion of Persons, inviting response from those who receive it. [Those recipients of divine revelation]…*found that in receiving divine Self-manifestation, they, too, were disclosed, known to the depths of their being….* From Abraham, through Isaiah and Peter, there was an instinctual dread before the immediacy of the divine which required *everything* of them and affected all humanity.[6]

The recipients of primordial divine Revelation were able to recognize and receive it because they lived in *disponibilité*. How many prophetic books begin with the core statement of availability: "Here I am, Lord"?

John Paul's insights within the Theology of the Body literature are important because they remind us that the cultural issue of our time is not unbelief, or logical doubt (despite the popularity of the "new atheists"). The cultural challenge of our time is dimness of sight and confusion. Somewhere, in the crossed lines of 20th century horrors, information revolutions, and the rise of relativism, individualism, and consumerism, we lost some of our clarity of sight. Many Christians today are like the partially healed man in Mark 8:22-26—we see, but our interpretation of what we see needs clarity. The clarity makes clear the call and the response. And this is our healing.

When we pray in *disponibilité*—which is when we say "Lord, I want to see," directly or not—we more fully enter the mystery of call and response, of giving and receiving. We sense a pattern played for our attention, imprinted upon our lives and our universe. The world: given. The Crucified: given. The Holy Spirit: given. Our lives: given. Grace: given. The body and blood of Christ: given. Vocation: given. In the sea of all this divine givenness, this revealed pattern of love, how do we respond? Does perceiving all this givenness help reveal our greatest, hidden desire: to give our lives to God, in gratitude for God's goodness and mercy?

We are created to receive no less than the Master of the universe. The act of receiving binds us into God's pattern of love, and the evoked response is to offer one's ensouled body to God. Then, we may see more as God sees: not omnipotently, but we see God's love and our response to it. That is beauty enough for small creatures as ourselves.

The ensouled body, gift of God, given to God. This is my body, He said, given for you. Do this.

ENDNOTES

1. I received that turn of phrase years ago from Roc O'Connor, S.J., who composes liturgical music. He rearranged the classic hymn "There's a Wideness in God's Mercy" to the score for "Will The Circle Be Unbroken," and ended the hymn by repeating the first verse, substituting wildness for wideness: "there's a *wildness* in God's mercy, like the *wildness* of the sea...." As far as I know, his rendition has not been published.
2. "The monk should be like the cherubim and seraphim: all eye," Abba Macarius. See Thomas Merton's *A Search for Solitude: Pursuing The Monk's True Life, The Journals of Thomas Merton Volume 3* (New York: HarperCollins, 2009), xiii.
3. To quote John Paul II: "The visibility of the Invisible belongs thus to the order of signs, and the "sign" merely indicates the reality of the mystery, but does not 'unveil' it." *Man and Woman*, 5.
4. This is the NRSV translation of Eph 6:18; it is more famously translated "pray always."
5. The statement in Ephesians comes directly after the long extended metaphor on putting on the full armor of God—the breastplate of righteousness, the helmet of salvation, etc. "Wrapping" one's life and actions in prayer makes much more sense following this metaphor.
6. Sr. Mary Timothy Prokes, *Toward A Theology of the Body* (Grand Rapids: Eerdmans, 1996), 77.

Index

compassion as virtue, 3, 84, 112, 120, 130-1, 159, 201, 217-220, 231
"composition of place," 9
contemplation, 8, 16
contemplative attitude, 15-17, 43, 139, 210, 225, 229
continuous death, 197, 199
Creamer, Deborah, 109, 11, 163
crucible of otherness, 77-9, 222
Crysdale, Cynthia, 147-8
Cullen, Christopher, 30, 40
Cullinan, Colleen Carpenter, 106
"cult of normalcy," 115-7, 120-1, 126, 130-2, 137, 145, 147-9, 154

Darwin, Charles, 113
Davis, Lennard, 112
de Caussade, Jean Pierre, 32, 68-9, 146, 211, 215
Deaf culture, 110, 165
deafness, 110, 122, 152, 163-7
death, medical, 197
death awareness movement, the, 199-200, 213
"death with dignity," xi, 119, 230, 241
dementia, 152, 157, 160-4, 197, 202, 230, 239
demonic, the, 198, 227
depression, 135, 152, 157-63, 165
desert fathers, the, 77, 79, 243
detachment, 19-21, 24, 77, 125, 232
"deviant," 113, 122
Dick-Read, Grantly, 49, 58, 60
disability, 105-6, 108-17, 121-3, 125, 128-9, 137-8, 142, 150-154, 157, 163, 168, 172-3;
  definition of, 109;
  medical vs. social model, 109-11;
  disability studies, 109, 163, 168
discernment, 8, 139, 155, 214, 227
disponibilité, 14, 16, 24, 44, 57, 59, 68, 70-3, 124, 130-1, 134, 137, 139, 149, 168, 173, 210, 216, 222, 243-4, 246

doula, 49, 54, 59, 67, 73
Down Syndrome, 76-9, 112, 152-6, 159

ecce homo, 117-8
Ecclesia in Africa, 94, 170
ecstatic identity, 139-145, 150, 161, 171
Eiesland, Nancy, 176, 179, 183
elderhood, 95, 189, 233-6
Ellis Island, 114
emotional markers (stages of birth), 53
ensouled body, x-xi, 4, 25, 28-9, 31, 33-4, 44, 52, 57, 71, 108, 124, 189, 192-3, 196, 202, 216, 220, 223, 228, 243, 245, 247
Ephrem the Syrian, 238
epidural anesthesia, 46, 38, 50-1, 78
epilepsy, 108, 115
episiotomy, 48, 50
Erasmus, 202
eugenics, 113-5
euthanasia, 203, 230,
Evangelium Vitae, 14, 31
evolution, 113

Family of God, see Church as God's Family
Fatherhood of God, 83, 94, 145, 174
fear, 6, 26, 44-5, 49, 56-9, 63-7, 69-72, 75, 78, 85-87, 94, 111, 119, 121, 127, 130, 131-134, 136-7, 139, 142, 165, 168, 171-2, 190, 193, 198, 209, 214, 216, 227, 230-32;
  fear of death and dying, 171-2, 198, 216, 227;
  fear of vocation, 66;
  Fear-Tension-Pain syndrome, 58-9;
  fear vs. shame as border experience, 64-66
  See also resistance
fetal alcohol syndrome, 112

CPSIA information can be obtained at www.ICGtesting.com
Printed in the USA
BVOW01s1013220414

351018BV00001B/4/P